D1164126

How to Make Money in Real Estate

THIRD EDITION

By

Stanley L. McMichael

Realtor-Appraiser

Author of

How to Operate a Real Estate Business
McMichael's Appraising Manual
Selling Real Estate

Revised by

LESLIE E. MOSER

Real Estate Developer
Author of
How to Build a Fortune in Real Estate
How to Find, Qualify and Induce Real
Estate Prospects to Buy

Prentice-Hall, Inc., Englewood Cliffs, N.J.

PRENTICE-HALL INTERNATIONAL, INC., *London*
PRENTICE-HALL OF AUSTRALIA, PTY. LTD., *Sydney*
PRENTICE-HALL OF CANADA, LTD., *Toronto*
PRENTICE-HALL OF INDIA PRIVATE LTD., *New Delhi*
PRENTICE-HALL OF JAPAN, INC., *Tokyo*

© 1924, 1945, 1969 BY

ELIZABETH MAINS McMICHAEL

ALL RIGHTS RESERVED. NO PART OF THIS
BOOK MAY BE REPRODUCED IN ANY FORM OR
BY ANY MEANS, WITHOUT PERMISSION IN
WRITING FROM THE PUBLISHER

LIBRARY OF CONGRESS
CATALOG CARD NUMBER: 69–11140

Sixth Printing . . . . . October, 1975

PRINTED IN THE UNITED STATES OF AMERICA
B&P

A Word About the Revision

Stanley McMichael possessed an uncanny foresight concerning the real estate business. If ever a man could have written a book that would be relevant to the future of real estate, it would have been Stanley McMichael. But McMichael knew that he couldn't do that; as a matter of fact, he spells this out for us in his second chapter "Real Estate in a Changing World." Issues do change, and especially in real estate; that is, all except the one expressed as the title of Chapter One of this book: "Real Estate is the Basis of All Activity and Wealth."

Because real estate continues to be the basis of wealth, and because of constant change in all spheres of modern living, it has become necessary to revise McMichael's *How to Make Money in Real Estate*.

My first step in undertaking this revision was to examine closely the last edition of the book (1945) in order to single out the basic McMichael tenets. I was pleasantly surprised to discover that these tenets stood up exceedingly well in the light of today's market. As a result of that finding, I then concentrated my efforts on preserving the sound, basic techniques of the late author and devoted my time to updating the information to meet the needs of today.

Current opportunities in income properties have been stressed. These include high-rise apartment buildings, shopping centers, commercial buildings, and many others. Information on many types of FHA and bank loans has been carefully updated. Financing generally, as well as the lending of money with real property as security, has been treated. You will find the latest practices in modernizing property, as well as a discussion of one of the newest forms of real estate investment—the condominium. For your convenience, a modern condominium form has been included. A section has also been devoted to population growth and shift and how it insures promising money-making opportunities now and in the future.

Page by page, it has been my pleasure to give currency to this classic Stanley McMichael book, and I have continued to keep the book easy and practical to use.

It is my hope that you will find this new revised edition just as valuable a tool as the earlier book.

LESLIE E. MOSER

Contents

ONE

Real Estate: The Basis of All Activity and Wealth

Every person uses land in some form or other and makes payment to the possessor. Whether he is a guest at a hotel or a lakeside resort; whether he rents a cottage or a mansion; whether he runs a small store, a great business enterprise, or a manufacturing establishment, he directly compensates an owner of land. If he possesses the land himself, he considers the use of the property an offset for rent he otherwise would pay an owner. If he is a tenant, he pays an investment return to the owner, plus a suitable amount for taxes and general maintenance. Whether it be a farm, a home, a commercial enterprise such as a department store, an industrial activity such as a great manufacturing plant, or an apartment in a condominium, a very large part of the investment involved is always real estate.

Constant demand for land

Land is imperishable. With the development of villages and towns into cities comes an insistent demand for strategic sites. As tenants follow one another, they frequently demonstrate their ability to pay ever-increasing toll in the form of rent.

1

Unlike any other commodity, real estate cannot be manufactured a⁺ will. All the usable land in the world is for sale, and everyone is considered a potential purchaser. Even in new, undeveloped sections of the world where land may be secured by mere settlement, a heavy price is paid in breaking up and developing a wilderness into a state where it becomes habitable for human beings, the raising of crops, the building of freeways, and the creation of necessary business centers.

The trading instinct of humanity has been exercised to perhaps its greatest degree in connection with the buying and selling of real estate; greater, in fact with real estate than with any other commodity. From the beginning of time men have been acquiring land, renting, and selling it to their fellow men. Countless fortunes have been amassed through the bartering of real estate, or in the revenues derived from it. More profit in the aggregate has been realized from this form of trading than from any other branch of business activity.

Kings and rulers waged bitter wars and grew rich from new territories they forcibly annexed. Men for centuries have succumbed to the lure of accumulating lands, have fought, bled, and died for the privilege of leaving to their dependents real estate in some form or other. Who can point to any other thing which man has coveted, has fought for so savagely, or worked for so zealously as the possession of land?

Ownership and investment

Possession of land offers a satisfaction which cannot be equaled. It fulfills the purposes of the tenant who wants a place in which to reside while he employs himself elsewhere. A man has a strong drive to provide a home for his family, to establish a place of his own. To the investor who has surplus funds, the ownership of land, carefully and intelligently acquired, and properly managed, offers the finest investment that has yet been devised.

Many stock and bonds, as well as other forms of securities which are traded on an investment basis, have their chief values represented in the real estate owned and controlled by issuing companies. Where would the securities of the thousands of manufacturing enterprises be without their plans? Where would oil wells be drilled, minerals mined, crops raised, and food produced if land could not be bought or rented?

Why from prehistoric times has money been realized through real estate? Linked with real estate, its development and utilization, is the world's finest story of human progress. Next to man's instinct for the perpetuation of the race, there rests deep-rooted in the breast of almost every man a strong desire to own a piece of land. It is not a selfish instinct, nor can it be suppressed. With such an urge, is it surprising that dealing in land and its improvements has always been one of the world's chief sources of gain?

As man rose in the scale of human intelligence, the instinct became stronger, for he realized the inherent value of land and what could be done with it. He struggled to possess locations where he could conduct the most profitable business or rent the land to the persons qualified to pay the highest rental.

In ancient days man forcibly took possession of land. With his club he went out and slew a neighbor to gain control of a particularly favored spot. Gradually, law and order prevailed, more decorous methods were adopted, and land was transferred by legal means. Even then kings and emperors cast greedy eyes upon great areas owned or controlled by their neighbors, and barbarous wars resulted.

Today, in America at least, ownership of land is not associated with loot and pillage. The buying, operating, and selling of real estate for profit has become a respected, well-organized, and scientific business, engaged in by men who are governed by rigidly-enforced ethical codes. Thousands of men in America devote their entire time to the business of real estate. Many of them are Realtors, members of the National Association of Real Estate Boards.

Scores of legal tomes have been written about the development of laws governing the ownership and use of real property. Battles for individual ownership and the free use of land were waged for generations in Britain and were brought to this country where the fight was continued until now ownership and use of land in the United States is probably less restricted than in any place in the world. The right to hold and use it is held sacred, as is the right to freely convey it. This is in strange contrast to some of the practices in countries of Europe and Asia.

Take away man's right to buy, own, and manage land, and immediately freedom ceases to exist. Only through free and untrammeled ownership and use of real estate can progress be sustained in the world. And in such ownership arises the opportunity for profit.

TWO

Real Estate in a Changing World

Since 1945 the United States has experienced a vast and spectacular growth in business, manufacturing, agricultural, and investment life. New and important inventions have altered the manner in which people live. Business today is conducted in a manner totally different from the way it was managed before the depression years. Industry has groped its way up from a few hundred small, isolated manufacturing plants and reorganized its activities into vast factories operated on a mass production basis, mechanized and automated to an amazing degree, turning out tremendous quantities of goods at great savings over old-fashioned operations. Farms have been converted to modern crop raising. The one, two, or three hired men on the average farm of several decades ago have been replaced with tractors and other machinery with which an owner can singlehandedly produce bigger and better crops than were formerly obtained from the same land.

So, too, have investment practices changed There was a time when one type of real estate investor insisted on buying only farm land. Then there was the realty speculator who acquired nothing but corners—just corners! The Astors kept turning their dollars back into real estate in

5

early Nev York, buying miscellaneous property that an investor today
would shudder at purchasing or owning. Yet the Astor fortune blossomed
into one of the largest. The Van Sweringens in Cleveland started on
a shoestring. With a selling contract on land owned by the Shakers, a
religious sect, .he original small investment was built up to fantastic
figures. This was crowned by the acquisition of a railroad empire only
to have tremendous realty holdings come tumbling down. The Book
brothers amassed a vast fortune in Detroit's Washington Square district,
but later had their ambitious plans blocked and much of their pyramidal
values washed away.

Vast fortunes amassed by oil magnates such as H. L. Hunt have
been directly related to real estate. Many of the fortunes in oil were
amassed because the lands from which the oil was drawn were accumulated not as oil investments per se, but as timberlands and farming
properties.

Booms and recessions

*It is significant that many fortunes in real estate that disintegrated
in the depression years would have been largely saved had it not been
for burdensome bond and mortgage debts!*

In most instances where large holdings of real estate were free of
debt and of *an income-bearing character,* they survived the depression
despite lowered income.

Rowdy, exuberant boom years of the 1920's were followed by the
hungry, gloomy years of the 1930's. Fortunes in real estate that had
been built up from shoestrings, with many types of unusual financing,
came crashing down, leaving values equal only to encumbrances, or less.
Incomes on properties were halved. Owner equities which were sound
in the fat years of higher prices were wiped out in the years of adversity.
Had such properties been free of debt, or nearly so, owners would have
carried on, as they did in many instances where burdensome debt did
not exist. Stocks and bonds, however, that came tumbling down in value
to 10 to 20 per cent of their former prices, fared much worse than
improved real estate which, on an average, shrunk about 50 per cent
during the lean years. Vacant property with no income sometimes fared
much worse.

Real estate would probably have suffered a distinct decline even
had no business depression occurred. Unhealthy boom practices caused

the realty market to sag and decline years before the actual low point of the depression.

One of the movements that always takes place in a depression period is the return to the farm of many city dwellers who feel they will be more secure, and at least be able to eat regularly if they are close to the soil. Such a movement further sapped the population of towns and cities and lowered buying power, which was reflected in lower rents and lesser values for real estate.

The effect of technology

The introduction of the automobile in the first decade of this century created a chain of circumstances that changed the entire real estate picture. Prior to the use of the automobile, cities were compact population centers, containing many buildings closely packed together. Horse and trolley cars provided for a distance of about five miles. Beyond that radius few persons cared to live and endure the long tiresome rides into town. This condition was revolutionized by the appearance of automobiles. *Distance became measured in minutes and not in miles!* It became possible to live up to thirty miles from one's place of business and drive to work each day.

Real estate developers leaped the barriers of high-priced land on the borders of the older cities and promoted new subdivisions beyond, reached by automobiles. Owners who had been holding large tracts of land in the pathway of development found themselves left high and dry while owners farther out reaped fortunes. Many cities show conspicuous examples of these "passed-over" areas even today.

The automobile created another factor seriously affecting values of business properties—decentralization. This would probably have occurred anyway as cities continued to expand; however, it was accelerated when it became possible for many people to live far beyond what were formerly considered the borders of cities. Little business centers started to develop at outlying crossroads and soon blossomed forth as important subcenters of retail business. Chain stores, and even merchants, began to feel the necessity for establishing retail outlets in these centers which were adjacent to large populations. Naturally this offered new business competition with the already established business sections, particularly of the larger cities. "Downtown," as these sections were known, ceased to hold their own commercially and complained loudly. In some cities vast sums were expended for street opening and widening on the assumption that the bulk of the outlying buyers could be persuaded to continue to come downtown to make their purchases—which in most cases they did not do.

As automobile makers perfected their product, increased production, and reduced the prices of cars, it became increasingly possible for the poorest workman to own an auto of some kind. Gradually another change came about in transportation practices. The interurbans began to disappear, and even the street cars were driven out of business in many cities by the ever-increasing fleets of buses operating in all directions.

Another condition which has affected the demand for, and use of, real estate is the vast increase in the use of machinery in various lines of endeavor. Events have progressed to a point where today, men manning machines can manufacture many times the output of fifty years ago. The factory, despite its increase in production, may still occupy the same floor space. Of course, it must be recognized that another plant with a crew of men is engaged in manufacturing and servicing the factory's machines. It is doubtful whether, in the long run, fewer men are given employment. The point is that they are distributed over more territory than formerly, and the utilization of real estate has been changed.

Prospective investors in real estate must be constantly aware of changing conditions, since they will continue to present problems in the years to come. Nevertheless there will be many opportunities for buying and selling real estate that will result in substantial profits.

The coming of World War II presented new and perplexing problems. A vast preparedness program was launched by the United Nations to be ready for any eventuality. Many billions of dollars were spent for this task, and these funds filtering into business, industry, and agriculture stimulated the real estate market and resulted in many completed deals which would not have come about otherwise.

The second World War brought about the gigantic defense program and it definitely helped real estate because:

1. It stimulated buying power by the spreading of vast sums in wages and profits throughout the nation, allowing many persons to retain their real estate, clear it of debt and even improve it.
2. It removed many persons from relief, furnished them with employment and placed them in positions where they were self-sustaining families.

3. Many families earning good wages or salaries were in a position to buy homes, aided by government-guaranteed financing plans.
4. Business concerns bought their own quarters or enlarged existing ones.
5. Vast sums of money that in peacetime went abroad for the purchase of goods were spent in this country for products made here.
6. Business activity quieted depression fears, and many investors entered the market seeking real estate investments.
7. Many who had idle funds, fearing possible inflation, decided to place some of their money in real estate.

Among the closest observers and students of economic trends are the men who manage the country's large insurance companies. The depression brought many troubles to these executives who noted decreasing returns from their stock and bond investments and who cast about for means to hold the return on their idle funds at the highest interest level possible. Many of the insurance companies eagerly sought new real estate loans. They also manifested a new trend in that they invested large sums in important multiple dwelling developments in New York, Los Angeles, and other large American cities. When holders of vast funds of this type deliberately select real estate as the best available investment, it has much to say for its dependability.

Reasons for the present boom

Since the second World War, business has been in a constantly booming spiral with only minor recessions such as that in 1958. Population trends have turned upward with the war babies, and there seems to be no end in sight for the spiraling population, members of which will in the foreseeable future continue to need homes and consumer goods.

The space age has provided a "shot in the arm" for industries, thus increasing the demand for industrial sites and homes for the workers. The fast expanding educational opportunities of the last part of the twentieth century promise to provide the technicians and professionals necessary to project the country into an era of unheralded prosperity and business increases.

Current tendencies in real estate in the changing world are:

1. Families are demanding larger dwellings. No longer is the element of need dictating the pretentiousness of family dwellings. Homes are the prestige labels of this period of prosperity, and

it is not uncommon for a family of four in the middle income bracket to have a four bedroom house and own three automobiles.

2. Home buyers seek larger lots, or at least wider frontages, than formerly.

3. Most home buyers demand new houses. Old dwellings sell easily only when remodeled.

4. Many home buyers now demand a bathroom with every bedroom.

5. Apartment houses are becoming more plentiful and much more luxurious. More and more people are trying to escape the rigors of home ownership represented by the keeping of yards, etc., by moving into luxurious apartments. The transient nature of a large number of people is in part responsible for this.

6. The movement is away from the farm and back to the city, with over 70 per cent of the population now living in urban centers. Farming is being done more and more on a large scale in which hundreds of acres are managed by a city-dwelling investor-manager. Modern machinery makes it possible for hundreds of acres to be cultivated by a small labor force, and many of these workers commute out to the farm from city dwellings.

7. The automobile, as well as modern homes and the availability of many types of labor-saving machinery, have revolutionized farm life, causing many city-reared residents to acquire rural homes although the strong population flow is to the cities.

8. Although the downtown situation appears uncertain in many American cities, high-rise office buildings under construction continue to dot the skylines of many American cities.

9. Manufacturing plants are moving to the smaller cities with many of the giants of industry having multiple plants scattered over the country.

10. Vast amounts of remodeling and rehabilitation will have to be done to thousands of old houses built twenty, thirty, and forty years ago. Buyers and renters now demand modernly equipped and modern-appearing premises.

11. Most home owners now demand two-car garages.

12. New construction methods and new materials are holding home production costs pretty much in line with increasing incomes. There is growing ¬esistance to "row" houses and "standard plans." Home owners are demanding originality and individuality even in low cost homes. Thus, mass production of homes has not developed to a large extent as was earlier predicted.

13. Most commercial buildings are being built in suburban shopping

centers where stores of similar nature (shoe stores, etc.) are being grouped to attract the shoppers. Stores seldom are more than two stories in height with a common arrangement consisting of a main floor, a mezzanine available by escalator and a basement also available by escalator. Most stores, however, are on a single level.

14. Movie theaters are moving to the suburbs along with the shopping facilities. Such theaters typically are movie houses exclusively, with no facilities for stage productions.

15. Hundreds of new inventions, unusual materials, decorations, etc., in the next few years will be adopted for use, causing great obsolescence in all similar structures not possessing them. Periodic remodeling and installation of new equipment will overcome this.

16. Many types of wallboards, plyboards and siding made from straw, sugar cane refuse, sawdust and vegetable substances, chemically treated and subjected to intense pressure, have taken the place of ordinary lumber for many years.

17. Taxation practices are gradually being revamped so that taxes are collected on a property's ability to earn a reasonable rental return on its assessed value, and not on an arbitrary value fixed by a political appointee.

18. Percentage leases will become more widely used in business property rentals. Under this method a tenant pays a reasonable percentage rental return to his landlord on the volume of gross sales made on the premises.

19. Vast fortunes, including those made on real estate, will be definitely fewer in the future because of governmental activities in taxing large accumulations of wealth and profits of any kind.

20. Tourism is a growing business for many if not most sections oi the country. California and Florida continue to be winter playgrounds, but the ski lodges of the Northeast and the Rockies are attracting a great number of winter vacationers also Easy air travel by jet has brought distant sections of the country only hours away, and this has greatly increased travel by tourists who bring valuable dollars into local economies. Many cities are capitalizing on conventions.

21. Export trade in America continues strong from West Coast ports as well as Eastern and Gulf Coast port cities. Air freight has also come into its own making diversified industry possible for the inland cities as well.

22. Contrary to what many had thought, the entry of the federal

government into business at several points, including FHA insured real estate loans, has not seriously depressed the earning power of the individual who desires to make investments in real estate.

Americans are living in an amazing age. Remarkable changes in modes of living and the places in which people live and work are due during the next generation and every change will, in some degree, affect real estate, its value and sale.

THREE

Why and How Cities Grow

An investor, to operate successfully and profitably in times of swiftly moving economic events that promptly reflect their influence upon real estate and its ownership, should have some knowledge of the reasons why cities come into being and how they grow thereafter.

Most real estate operations take place in urban centers and the outlying suburbs. Great profits are made in real estate by those who buy and sell business and income properties in towns and cities. Some communities offer rich opportunities for real estate investment and speculation while others present little or none. To select a live town and then to spot the best locations for real estate development in that town require knowledge and keen observation. Without diligent study on the part of either the investor himself or some real estate broker or appraiser to whom he may go for advice, the investor will proceed more or less blindly and his efforts will prove profitless and vain.

Cities are subject to constant change. Even if a community is not manifesting much growth there is, nevertheless, a constant shifting about of business activity. Lusty growth, of course, creates new demands for business locations, for income properties of different kinds, and for new home sites.

Origins of cities

Cities are among man's most ancient handiwork. Earliest family life began in caves or in sheltered nests in trees. Later hamlets grew into villages, towns, and small cities. Many of the earliest towns were walled. Some grew up on piles in lakes, far from the shore, so that invaders might be repelled. Walls, however, were favored to hold back tribal enemies, and ancient history is replete with stories of fierce battles waged about and in these walled cities.

Sites of the earliest cities were picked primarily for defense. Venice was on a group of islands. Paris itself began on an island in the Seine River. London was originally a walled city. Even New York in its earliest days was walled, and the name Wall Street came from the time the original walled fort occupied that section of lower Manhattan island.

Many of America's important cities are located on harbors, rivers or waterways of some kind. Most of these points mark the beginning or the end of major trade routes which existed prior to the time the cities came into existence. Other cities were created at the crossings of such trade routes, either an overland route crossing, a water route or terminals of these two.

Railroads succeeded the old caravan, water, and stagecoach routes, and new cities sprang up where these railroads crossed important rivers or where they reached tidewater harbors.

Religious movements were the basis for the founding of some cities, for example, Salt Lake, Utah, was settled by the Mormons. Note also the long string of cities extending along the Pacific Coast from San Diego northward to San Francisco and including Los Angeles and Santa Barbara. These were established at river crossings, for the most part, by the early mission fathers. Zion City near Chicago and Benton Harbor, Michigan, are two other towns created by religious movements.

Washington would scarcely have become important had it not been selected as the capital of the United States. Likewise, Ottawa in Canada. Many state capitals have little importance other than that attached to them as legislative centers.

Climatic conditions and the presence of mineral springs created towns and cities in Florida and California as well as in other states.

It is significant that trade routes seek the line of least resistance between the source of raw materials and the markets for them. Wherever transshipping takes place, there a city grows.

Location of cities

The following, therefore, may be considered primary factors influencing the location of cities:

1. The defense factor—(originally very important).
2. Availability of food, fuel, and water supply, without which no settlement can exist.
3. Favorable topographical features. Rough, rugged mountain ranges and barren desert wastes seldom give birth to important settlements.
4. Religious motive influencing people to settle near a temple, shrine or monastery.
5. Centers of government—(political capitals).
6. Special climatic conditions and medicinal springs.
7. Locations favored for recreational reasons.
8. Geographical superiority of locations where commercial activities develop at focal points of trade and travel.
9. Proximity to manufacturing enterprises large enough to establish and maintain entire cities, like Dearborn, Michigan.
10. Space exploration centers often originally located away from population centers.
11. New mineral discoveries, especially oil and uranium.

No one factor can be said to be the sole cause for the origin and growth of a city. It is rather the combination of several favorable influences which have attracted settlers and created settlement.

Factors affecting growth

The story of the growth of an individual city is the tale of the activities of its inhabitants. The site may be a crossroad of travel, a river crossing, or a harbor. A handful of pioneers arrive and erect a few buildings. More come later, adding to the demand for houses at the fringe of the first settlement. Meanwhile business is expanding in the center of the village or town. Buildings originally meant for dwellings are removed or converted to business uses. Commercial areas steadily expand as new arrivals appear. Always on the border of a business district there are buildings which are being subjected to changing utility. These constitute the "blighted districts" of the larger cities and are to be found, in some degree, in almost all types of communities. It seems likely that every city will continue to have such a district as long as it continues to grow, although there are means of regulating blighted areas and minimizing their ill effects.

Most cities originated parallel to or at the intersection of some highway of travel or traffic. Only in recent years have attempts been made to actually plan the manner in which a community should grow. Crossroads were ever favored as sites for the beginning of a city. Fresh water in abundance and fuel of some kind must always be available. Likewise, there must be ample natural drainage.

Barriers such as steep hills, gullies, and watercourses, until they are tunnelled or bridged, frequently direct the growth of a community away from such obstacles of growth. Normally towns expand along highways leading to the nearest community of neighbors.

There are four types of cities, broadly speaking, insofar as topography alone is considered. These are the flat city, built upon a level plain or plateau; the rolling type, where slight undulations mingle with depressions and ravines; hill cities, where steep grades are encountered; and valley cities, flat in part, but surrounded with high hills and mountains. Chicago, Detroit, and Houston are examples of flat cities. Birmingham, Minneapolis, St. Louis, Washington, Columbus, Buffalo, and Cleveland are of the rolling type; San Francisco, Seattle, and Quebec are of the hilly type; while Pittsburgh, Salt Lake City, and Cincinnati are valley towns. The growth of a city is always governed and controlled by its general topography.

Cities on a north bank of a bay or river grow north as in the cases of Detroit, Toronto, and Montreal. Cities on a south bank usually grow south as in the cases of Buffalo, Erie, and Louisville. Such cities are typically fan-shaped. San Francisco, on the other hand, sprawls out over a peninsula. Los Angeles is both a flat and hilly city. The growth of the average city is away from its point of origin. Few cities grow "all around." Whatever the type of city, its best development will come from the logical utilization of the advantages it naturally offers for expansion, and from the aggressiveness of its residents.

Consider the subject of streets and highways and their effect on city growth. Streets are the arteries of a city, connecting the lands lying within to those beyond its borders. Without adequate streets, cities simply could not exist. Most cities, like Topsy, "just grew," so that few of the larger cities have adequate or desirable street plans. The freeways in the Los Angeles area are known around the world as an example of engineering genius.

Washington, D. C. is an outstanding example of a well-planned city, and New York can thank an early planning commission for its rectangular layout, with its fourteen great avenues extending north and south. Those only came after the lower end of Manhattan had been developed with a maze of narrow, crooked pathways.

It is now recognized that city streets should have various widths. Main thoroughfares which extend out and beyond a city's limits should be at least 100 feet in width. Secondary streets, leading to minor business and residential sections, should be from 60 to 85 feet wide, while purely residential streets may be as narrow as 40 feet, with suitable restrictions for the setting back of dwellings from lot lines.

Highways constitute the main structural framework about which a modern city is built. More important than railroads today are the vehicular highways leading to nearby growing communities. These sometimes develop later into the business thoroughfares on which substantial realty values develop. In the heart of a growing city there soon becomes evident a trend that makes one favored street the highest in value in the city. This is the "gold strip," with its "100 per cent locations."

Extremely wide streets are as detrimental as narrow ones. Pedestrian traffic often hesitates to cross very wide streets, as in the case of Canal Street, New Orleans. On the other hand, many cities are now spending huge sums to widen narrow streets, something that should be done early in a city's existence.

If streets are the arteries of a city, transportation is the very lifeblood which courses through its system. Moving people and goods from one place to another constitutes one of the primary economic functions in modern urban life. Cities would never have become the great wealthy centers of business and industry they are today had they not had adequate transit facilities.

With the coming of railroads a new force appeared to create and develop urban communities. Water transportation became a secondary consideration. Canals became obsolete. Impetus was given to commerce and industry, which became the prime influence in building manufacturing and commercial cities. New territories were opened, and concurrently new cities were born.

Growth from a railway station is usually outwards on one side of the tracks. Land adjacent to stations and railroad tracks is often undesirable for anything but industrial and railroad purposes. Cities grow away from railroad tracks. Land near terminals does not increase in value nearly as fast as it is thought to do.

As stated before, distance now is measured in minutes and not in miles. A generation or two ago a horsecar took one hour to carry a passenger four miles. Electric cars increased the radius to eight or ten miles. Interurban lines, now almost entirely nonexistent, had even better records. Then came the automobile, an element which has done more to upset, disrupt, and change customs, habits and real estate promotional work and values than any other single thing that has appeared in the history of cities.

Perhaps most important of all, automobiles have been the cause of the decentralizing influence which has created untold millions in wealth in outlying residential and business districts. This means of individual transportation has permitted the subdividing of land five, ten and even thirty miles out from the center of cities, which naturally resulted in the building up of outlying business districts of great importance that will become greater in the future. Northern New Jersey is an example.

The automobile has consolidated the downtown business area, but on the fringe of many cities, there has been created a "twilight zone," where realty values have steadily shrunk. A blight seems to have settled upon these sections. These "twilight zones" may improve, but improvement will come slowly.

The automobile as a means of rapid transit, assisted by the motor bus, has taken people out into newer districts, opening up vast territories far from central business sections. It has definitely widened the areas for present and potential growth in cities. Where main outgoing thoroughfares cross important crosstown highways, there secondary business districts grow up. There you will find real estate activity, with values firm and transfers frequent.

There has been witnessed during the past few years a striking phenomenon in city growth, the extensive decentralization of downtown residential and business districts, in large cities in particular. With the developing of great numbers of new subdivisions and the inevitable business districts which accompany them, there has been a moving out from downtown districts of many small merchants who have found it more profitable to establish themselves in outlying business centers. This had a tendency to check the rising flood of values in downtown areas and instead created new values in suburban business sections. Important chain store organizations continue to bid for stores in downtown areas, but there seems to be a definite limit to which values can go in any central business district.

Despite the fact that outlying business sections are steadily being created in larger cities, vehicular traffic congestion appears as a menace to orderly development. Not only subways, but also double-deck streets and super-arterial highways and "freeways" are being built to overcome this condition.

Is it possible to tell, in even a small city, what will ultimately become the best business street? There is a fundamental rule governing this which applies as truly to the small city as to the larger one. The best business thoroughfare usually develops along the shortest route, from the high-grade downtown retail business district to the city's highest grade residential district. Unless a very unusual and radical shift in the business district takes place, the street which performs this function will develop into the city's best business thoroughfare.

Foot traffic is the weather vane of values in main business districts. Where most pedestrians pass ordinarily are found highest land values. There is, however, a buying versus a nonbuying class of traffic. Foot travel is susceptible to many influences. The shady side of a business street is most favored, and women's stores, particularly, nearly always seek the shady side.

The last few years have seen a revolution in the building of shopping centers featuring weather-proof malls, some completely air-conditioned. This arrangement definitely attracts the shopper, especially women.

Obstructions always affect trade. Store fronts under construction, boxes stacked on walks, stairways to upper stories, fruit and newsstands, all detract from values for retail trade.

Foot traffic can be too dense. People go from one place to another for definite purposes, seeking the quickest and most direct route. Arcades are useful in diverting traffic and reclaiming inside land for retail use.

Here are several points that, if they are not adhered to, will detract from values in business districts:

1. Schools should not be placed on main thoroughfares. Noise and traffic is dangerous to children.
2. Churches should likewise be placed back from main arteries, so they will not have to move in later years as they have had to do in most large cities.
3. Public buildings should not pre-empt valuable main street business frontage. American cities are segregating their public buildings in group plans and civic centers. Conveniently placed, they offer advantages to those who must visit such structures.
4. Bus barns should not be located on main arteries where business

is later likely to develop. They have been moved constantly in large cities.

5. Lodge buildings, libraries, club houses, and so forth should not be built on main thoroughfares.

6. Large hotels and banks, if on main streets, should provide for stores on street frontages. Hotels of the old type where large lobbies were provided for lounging, as well as some banks, were the most wasteful users of high-priced street frontage.

Stabilization comes in the center of the city first and works out towards its circumference. It will first be manifested by an inclination of property owners to make long-term leases on their downtown land, once they realize that values are not likely to go higher. When land reaches a certain value, and rentals soar, tenants begin to move elsewhere, and that makes a city expand. Once a district is filled with skyscrapers, land values usually cease to advance, for the district has been developed to its ultimate use. All of the foregoing factors should be known and considered by investors in selecting investment properties.

The future of cities

One hesitates, in surveying the field of modern invention and in observing the rapid changes which are taking place in American life, to speculate on what the future has in store for American cities.

Will great urban centers continue to grow in the future as they have done in the past? It seems likely that when many cities reach the million mark in population growth, downtown values may begin to slow down perceptibly due to decentralizing influences. Problems encountered in great cities like New York, Chicago, and Los Angeles, in the matter of transportation, law enforcement, and the construction and maintenance of public service facilities of all kinds, are manifestly greater than in smaller communities. There are so many changes which are likely to take place in building construction that one wonders whether life in smaller communities will not be more attractive than in the larger ones.

What is air travel going to do in regard to the future growth of cities? It seems certain that it will vastly widen the potential limits of cities. A city which now extends five or ten miles in different directions may a few years hence claim a metropolitan area extending fifty, seventy-five, or one hundred miles. A businessman may hop into his helicopter each mo.ning, and his pilot will deposit him on the roof of his own office building or factory, sweeping through the air for possibly fifty miles in fifteen or twenty minutes. At night the air chauffeur will call and take him home again.

Why do cities grow?

1. There is an incessant drift of population to urban centers where life can be lived more fully than in rural centers and in the country. More than half of the people of the United States live in urban communities.
2. Man has had his social senses developed and desires to live in communities where he can meet and mingle with others.
3. He can be entertained. This is being offset to some extent by the return to rural areas due in part to the availability of radio, television, and the automobile. The stronger trend is toward the cities, however.
4. There are greater opportunities for business and cultural advancement.
5. The birth rate is several times the death rate. The latter will probably decline in the future.
6. Formerly many immigrants gathered in cities. Immigration laws now tend to control this type of growth.

How do cities grow?

1. They grow from center to circumference by the building up, one by one, of new subdivisions, automatically accompanied by business districts.
2. They grow by absorption, through annexation, of suburban towns and villages which originally grew up at some distance from the main center of the original city, intermediate spaces having finally been developed for city life.
3. They experience a constant shifting in business and residential districts, nearly always away from the point of origin.

FOUR

How Land Values Come into Existence

Value attaches to land because of the service it offers those who can acquire and use it profitably.

Where there are no human beings to occupy land, it has no value as the term is commonly understood. One definition of value is that it is a *measure of desirability*. There must be those who can use land before it will evidence any kind of worth.

The value of a corner lot of land in the center of a city of 1,000,000 persons in the middle of China would doubtless be different from the value attributed to a similar piece of real estate in the center of a city of 1,000,000 people in the United States. Mere presence of population presumably creates value, but greater value is created by the use to which the land is put, the nature of the improvement placed upon it, the volume of buyers attracted, and the services rendered by the owners or tenants.

Productivity

Productivity is the measure of value when agricultural lands are considered A tract of 1,000 acres of barren grazing land in Utah or

Montana would have but the fraction of the value of a 1,000 acre rich-soiled farm in Iowa that produces great crops of corn. Likewise the corn land has much less value than a 1,000 acre ranch in California on which oranges or lemons are produced.

As soon as land becomes useful primarily for human habitation and is pre-empted for laying out villages, towns, and cities, a new type of value becomes attached to it. The village of 100 acres in area, over a period of years, develops into a townsite of 1,000 acres or several square miles. Originally, let us assume, the land was perfectly flat, alongside a stream of water, served with a roadway which later was paralleled by a railroad. The original 100 acre site sold, probably, for $100 an acre as farm land. Then a trail towards a neighboring town was developed into a highway crossing the original one. Two corners of these crossroads became the sites for a few stores, a mill placed on the third and, later, a small inn or the fourth. Every once in a while a new house or two was built until there was quite a cluster of them. As more were built, there seemed to be a greater demand for houses, and they were erected faster. In a period of some years the village expanded into a town. It became a natural trading place for farmers and others living for miles around. Also, there were mines or oil wells not far away whose workers patronized the stores.

Enterprising businessmen discovered the town, wondered why the product of the mines and oil wells was shipped to distant points, and proceeded to erect a big oil refinery and a mill for processing ore. This brought many more workmen to the area. A river was dammed in the neighborhood to give more power to the mill, and its excess power was sold cheaply, attracting more industries. So the village that had grown into a town developed into a city by a process of expanding business and industry, together with servicing other human needs.

Meanwhile, the corners where the two original frame stores were located were purchased, one by a bank, another by a department store, and new and imposing buildings were erected. The little inn was torn down on the third corner and an imposing hotel erected. Likewise the fourth corner was improved. Along the main street in both directions new business enterprises sprang into existence. Lots which originally sold for $500 developed a demand value of $1,000, $2,000, $5,000, and upwards. Main street land frontage grew steadily in value as new stores were erected and became the homes of successful merchants who became able to pay increasingly higher rents. Carried on over a period of years, from the time of the town's inception until it grows into a sizable community, this is the story of the creation of land values in cities.

Furthermore, all those persons who were attracted to the city from time to time required housing accommodations. So, after the first few dwellings were built, there developed a demand for residential construction. Subdivisions were laid out from time to time and improved with homes. These were of various grades, catering to different types of wage earners and salaried workers. Finally there came an exclusive and expensive park-like development where the famalities of the principal businessmen of the city had their homes.

Values of suburban land areas develop in relation to their productivity either of crops, timber, or of minerals taken from the ground. Land in urban centers gains in value chiefly because of its availability for building sites, productivity of soil being a negligible element. It is much more important that a site shall offer a sound foundation for any building placed upon it, than for what it will grow.

Supply and demand

Because the supply of land within the borders of a town or city is limited and because the demand for sites in the most favored locations is always apparent, especially if the city is growing, there is created a series of spots where land values are pyramided. This is apparent in that section of the city commonly known as the "100 per cent" retail district where the principal shops, usually catering to women, are located. Here cluster the department stores and alongside of them the usual variety stores, as well as a miscellaneous representation of chain stores. These merchants enter into competition with each other in bidding up rentals for the choicest locations. Rentals capitalized are translated into land values and thereby the owner and the broker are enabled to establish a definite range of prices for land frontage in these and similar districts.

Price is the translation of a measure of value into units of money. The price paid for a property may be too high, or even too low, when the actual earning power of the site is considered. Price may be merely an interpretation of an owner's insistent demand for a parcel of land he seeks to sell, or the mistaken opinion of a buyer. The cost of a building does not necessarily represent its value. Perhaps too much has been spent for its construction, when its net earning power has been calculated.

Most retail purchasing is done by women. They patronize the

stores and handle much of the money that goes into the merchant's cash register. For this, as well as other reasons, stores catering to the sale of women's goods always monopolize the choicest business sites in a city's highest grade retail district. Rentals demanded and paid for small retail units by representative chain store concerns are surprisingly large in many cities. Such chain store units like to build near the larger department stores that conduct voluminous advertising campaigns, thus attracting large throngs of customers daily. Many of these small chain stores do little advertising, depending upon window displays and the shopping propensities of women to draw their customers.

Some of the highest rent payers, incidentally, are the stores which sell the commonest types of merchandise—variety stores. The nickels and dimes pour in, and high rents go to land owners lucky enough to be in the pathway of such retail development. If you want to find the highest priced land values of any city, discover where several of the most important variety chain stores are clustered about a department store and that, in all probability, is, or very near, the spot.

Central business property frontage is, essentially, one of the most satisfactory types of land in which to invest. It does not always furnish the largest profits, but it gives a good investment return with safety and as a city expands, it should increase in value and rent-producing capacity. It takes a considerable amount of money to handle it and investments in it are usually large, but it is substantial and satisfactory as a type of ownership. However, it should be noted that in recent years some central business centers have been fast depreciating and that determination of value must depend upon the individual case.

Many cities grow in a fanshape. From the center of such a city main arteries extend out in different directions like the ribs of a fan. Out some distance and towards the borders of the city a main thoroughfare will intersect one of these radiating arteries. Here is a natural location for a shopping center. Starting first with a gas station and a store or two, such a district will develop until it becomes a well-contained little town, with its own markets, theaters, sports pavilion, schools, churches, chain stores, and all the trimmings of a complete business community. Here land values steadily climb until the rent-paying capacity of tenants is reached. If a landlord is so unwise as to attempt to boost rentals higher than a tenant can reasonably pay he will probably lose his tenant Study your town and its outlying areas for prospective shopping centers due for development three, five, or ten years hence and quietly acquire some land, preferably with improvements that will carry the property until it is ripe for future business improvement.

Is there any means of determining just where a "100 per cent rental district" is likely to develop? This can be done, in a general way, after a town has grown sufficiently to establish what will probably be the center of the main business district for some years to come. After a few good-sized stores become well established and the national chain units have begun to move in, look the town over and locate what is, or seems likely to become, the town's highest grade residential district. The main street leading from the most active business district out to the high grade home section will, in all probability, become *the 100 per cent retail store district of a decade hence.* This has happened so often in the past that it has almost been established in a rule.

Depression years brought a slowing down of expansion on the part of many chain store concerns. At the same time it showed an amazing growth in companies such as Sears, Roebuck & Co., Montgomery Ward & Co., and several other large concerns that created new establishments in many cities. A fight went on for years against chain stores of all kinds, but unsuccessfully. Independent merchants fought the chains bitterly but without much success. Today, chain store merchandising is here to stay for various reasons, the principal one being that they often give better goods at lower competitive prices, through mass buying power and lower unit profits.

Land in residential districts seldom increases much in value beyond the original prices paid for it, unless there has developed a change in utility. If it is still suitable for a dwelling, whether improved or not, it is not likely to show much additional value. If, however, such land may be used for multiple dwelling construction or for minor types of business, it may show enhanced values *if there appears to be a demand for it.* Never buy residential lots for speculative purposes unless there are definite plans for their prompt use as building sites. Even in this kind of an operation the profit on the building construction must help out if the deal is to be a profitable one.

What the investor should watch for

Almost every large city has an active group of what are known as professional apartment house operative builders. These constitute shrewd speculators who buy a single site or a group of locations suitable for several buildings. They then proceed to erect apartment buildings of six, eight, sixteen or even twenty-four and thirty-six suites, for resale to investors as soon as completed. These builders incorporate all the very latest ideas in their structures and make profit by creating an enterprise at a certain figure, plus, a suitable profit, the combined sum representing a satisfactory return to a buyer of that class of property. This is a thoroughly businesslike proceeding and offers a satisfactory form of investment. A buyer however, should look carefully into any project he is asked to purchase to see that it is well constructed and that it is earning, and will continue to earn, the return represented. Depression and war years caused a suspension of this type of speculative building in many cities that later revived. Primary consideration in the acquiring of property of this type should be the very definite evidence of a need for the additional rental units. It may be fine to be the owner of a fancy new apartment house structure, but if it does not promise to continue to earn a satisfactory investment return for years to come it will scarcely be a wise purchase. However, if inspection shows that there is a need for such properties, if they are well built, in a neighborhood well-adapted to them, land values in such a district will be visibly enhanced through such operations.

An alert investor will watch continually for focal points of business demand—sites suitable for improvement because business can be transacted there. One fortune was made at the depth of a depression by an investor who selected corners on which to erect drive-in sandwich stands in the city of Los Angeles. Land values have a wav of rising in most unusual places, provided sites can be furnished with necessary accommodations to make them useful as rental quarters for businesses which are awaiting their creation.

Just outside of San Francisco is one of the most profitable gasoline stations in the country, placed at the vertex of an angle created by the coming together of two rural highways bearing heavy loads of automobile traffic. No one suspected that a fortune was awaiting a man who would purchase and improve that property. Opportunities of this kind are countless for the man of imagination who has money to back up his ideas.

Out at the borders of many a city can be seen strategic sites at what are now merely crossroads, with a store on one corner and a decrepit gas station on another. One of the roads may be a main highway extending directly out from business activity, while the other road passes on through what may be a future subdivision of fine dwellings or a grouping of suburban homes. Here a satellite business center may flourish a few years hence and land values of $500, $1,000 or $2,000 an acre today will be worth many times that in a few years to come.

Unlike other commodities land is unique and individual in character. No two parcels are exactly alike if for no other reason than that they are differently located. Land values are relative for each parcel is different, and judgment of value varies in almost every case.

Without population pyramiding in certain locations, which are commonly called cities, land would have relatively little use beyond its productivity of agricultural products. Urban land and land immediately adjacent thus becomes valuable primarily because of the services it is able to perform. These services are measured in the rental which some tenant is willing to pay for each tract, or the sum a buyer is willing to give for the ownership of a tract that meets his needs. Highest rents, it may be noted, arise from land used for high-powered retail sales. Then come types of land used for commercial, manufacturing, storage and residential uses, all of which attract their standards of values through sale and resale and the working of the laws of supply and demand in a community. If a certain type of land becomes scarce and the demand persists, the price naturally advances until more land of that character becomes available.

FIVE

Perils to Investors of Shifting Business Districts

Many a fortune has been made—and lost—through the shifting of business districts.

Seldom is real estate absolutely static. Certain business districts will have a tendency to rise slowly and steadily in value. Sometimes, because of depression influences which have been suddenly overcome, such as a long and protracted war or business backset, a commercial section may enjoy phenomenal growth. Then will come a term of some years when the area will seem thoroughly stabilized. Then, in many instances, the parades of fashion and demand march on and the district may decline. It may long remain substantial and satisfactory from an income-bearing standpoint, but never again, in all probability, will it reach its former peak of values.

Expansion and decentralization

New York, during the past century or more, has seen a number of different points when, during certain periods of time, highest rentals, and correspondingly highest values, have prevailed on Broadway and Fifth Avenue. From the Battery to Wall Street business jumped to

31

around Fourteenth Street, then to Twenty-Third Street, and later shifted to the vicinity of Forty-Second Street. It has since expanded on a broad scale in the Fifties.

Cleveland, Ohio, witnessed four distinct shifts in as many generations. High-grade business was originally established on lower Superior Avenue at West 9th Street. About 1850 it shifted to around Cleveland's Public Square. Around 1900 it swung off at an angle and moved into lower Euclid Avenue, extending as far as East 9th Street. About 1915 it left East 9th Street and worked its way eastward along Euclid Avenue as far as East 20th Street. Curiously enough it met with some difficulty in this new area due, probably, to overexpansion and the fact that depression caught up with it. After 1930 business had an inclination to re-establish itself more firmly on Euclid Avenue between the Public Square and East 12th Street.

Los Angeles has had five or six business sections which at one time or another have been regarded as the choicest commercial centers. From Main Street, around the Plaza, retail business shifted at an early date to lower Broadway. It then marched southward until it reached West 10th Street when an interesting thing happened. Business suddenly took a right hand turn and started to expand on a large scale westward along West 7th Street for some blocks. The reason for this was the age-old tendency for a retail business district to develop out toward the highest-grade residential section of a city. During the years business houses were prospering on Broadway, residential growth was to the south. Then vast new subdivisions to the west were placed on the market, and it became apparent that these were to attract the high-grade residents of the city. So business promptly took an abrupt right-hand turn and followed. A later tendency in Los Angeles had been for business to leave the downtown district to itself and develop several large outlying shopping centers, one in Hollywood and others along Wilshire Boulevard at intersections of Western, La Brea, and Fairfax Avenues.

Metropolitan Los Angeles today has become such a complex of neighborhood shopping centers within the municipality, satellite towns which have defied incorporation, and concentrations of residential subdivisions along the coastal highway and the individual valleys, that a tourist can hardly tell when he enters or leaves the city.

In several areas of the nation there are "strip cities" which appear to the traveler like one great city stretching for hundreds of miles. Actually, these are myriads of smaller municipalities abutting one upon the other, but many of these have common water and sewer systems, and for all practical purposes constitute one great city.

Every large city in America has seen this shifting in its main central business district. In eastern cities the cycle has taken from fifteen to twenty-five years to accomplish a rise and then be eclipsed. In Los Angeles changes took place even more rapidly.

The investor who can recognize a new and promising business center as it is about to blossom forth and who has the courage and funds with which to anchor himself in the territory and grow with it, is on the highroad to making money in a big way. He must recognize when a competitive district is developing elsewhere that may rob his particular center of some of its mercantile glory and prepare to dispose of his holdings and go elsewhere into newer fields of activity. Usually, however, a successful operator is willing to rise and fall with one section as it usually takes a generation for this to come to pass fully.

A factor which is accelerating the shifting of business to a measurable extent has appeared during the past few years in the distinct decrease in cost of real estate financing, particularly of small homes. The Federal Housing Administration has guaranteed hundreds of thousands of mortgages on small homes which have built up entire new districts in some American cities. Minor new business districts have been created which will become major tomorrow.

How this tendency has had its effect on the large department stores is related by an eastern economist, who has as his clients many large retail stores throughout the country:

> I have been advising my department store clients to prepare for a marked decentralization of business. It is a trend resulting directly from the factors behind the manifest increase in residential building. These larger stores will be forced, and some of them have already acted, to open branches in the smaller cities and outlying centers.
>
> As department stores move with this trend, the building boom will receive additional impetus from investments in new buildings and modernization of older quarters.

Rapid transportation and the lowered cost of building financing are accounting for a substantial drift of urban population to the outlying communities, according to this observer's summary. It is particularly true in the East, where streamlined trains cut commuting time in half. The desire to own and operate an automobile also explains the movement of many urbanities to smaller communities. Here they can own their own homes and enjoy weekened automobile travel without the worry of wrestling with traffic on the way back to the city.

Enjoyment of home life in this country is returning, according to his reasoning, purely as the result of these economic factors. And the import is unmistakable to department stores, furniture stores, and other businesses catering to the household.

Cities seem inclined to grow away from their point of origin. Examine the historical background of almost any city, observe where the pioneers erected their first buildings, and it will be noted that steadily but surely business and residential development has drifted away from that point. Right at the beginning are sown the seeds that later demonstrate themselves in the long series of movements towards the newer and better residential areas.

While a city is small the tendency to shift will not be so apparent as it is when it really begins to expand. Then it seems to suffer growing pains and evidences a desire to set itself up in new places and in better and more modern buildings. In the past the largest dry-goods concern in a city was usually a leader in leaping from one district which seems "slipping" to a new one where it became housed in a more modern retail outlet.

Doubtless the element of obsolescence has something to do with the tendency of a business district to stop growing and move backward after twenty or twenty-five years. That is about the period that elapses before a building begins to suffer keenly from such obsolescence. The proprietor of a big store does not feel like tearing down his old building, realizing that it still contains much physical and some economic value. He feels the need, however, for newer and often larger quarters, so he quietly slips up the main business street to the point where land frontage has not yet advanced to fancy figures and buys a big parcel of it, sufficient not only for his store site but automobile parking facilities as well. His new establishment soon becomes popular, attracts other merchants and smaller competitors, and a new shifting of business occurs.

New urban communities

In this later part of the twentieth century it is not uncommon for a city to be established by plan and purpose where no city existed at all before. This is a definite variation of the growth outward of cities. In many cases investors will select a point on the map which is equally removed (thirty miles or so) from three or four large metropolitan cities or about halfway between two strip cities which follow two highways that are separated by fifty or sixty miles. The investors go out to this open land and acquire large amounts of it in spite of the fact that no major highways, airports, or railroads serve it. They buy the land cheaply and confidently build a huge shopping center, knowing that because they acquired the land cheaply, they can merchandise consumer goods at prices which will induce the customers to drive the thirty or forty miles required to arrive at the shopping center.

The buyers *do come,* and a new city begins to develop around this merchandising center. The land the investors bought for $300 per acre quickly becomes worth ten times that much as the new city continues to propagate itself.

Business will sometimes expand from one focal point in opposite directions at once. This may occur at an "island" of business on a main outgoing business artery that has grown up at a crosstown intersection perhaps a mile out from the main business district. Consisting of a small group of establishments at first, business will spread, going farther out the avenue and also growing *towards* the main business district at the same time. Finally, business comes together midway, and the commercial development of the city is definitely strengthened.

In a town originally built around intersecting highways, it is sometimes difficult to guess where the better business development will come. It may be in any direction of the compass. As indicated, however, the location of the homes of the better class will definitely prove a magnet and good business will build up and out to meet rich and promising retail buying power. If this residential district later changes for any reason and it becomes necessary to leave the existing business districts by another main artery to reach it, then watch for business developments of importance on that outgoing highway.

The Great Depression caused an almost total cessation of new building activities. Downtown areas of larger cities contented themselves with extensive remodelling operations but comparatively few new commercial buildings were erected. There were constructed, however, a great many public structures, including post offices, city halls, supply depots, ports, military camps, armories, as well as a vast array of war factories.

Will future years see as much shifting of business districts as has taken place in the past? The most marked shiftings of business districts in the past have taken place in downtown areas of cities, where buildings have grown old and outmoded. Lacking the urge to erect newer and bigger retail establishments, the day may come when the average merchant will become more interested in rehabilitating and completely remodelling his existing establishment in preference to moving a few blocks into a new and more expensive building. He may still remain keenly interested, however, in establishing new branches in the suburbs.

Traffic congestion has, in recent years, had something to do with shifting of business to outlying areas. Many women who drive cars consider the downtown section of a large city a veritable "madhouse" insofar as traffic conditions are concerned. They will even drive a long way in another direction to patronize a desirable store with its own automobile parking yard. Parking is a problem which is becoming more acute every year, and many small and large cities are studying it anxiously. In some areas around Los Angeles, property owners will not even consider erecting retail business buildings unless they can provide adequate parking space for cars.

In newer communities special attention is being given to parking in the planning of business developments. One favored plan is to take a large city block and rim it with stores, reserving the entire central portion for automobile parking. Patrons may step from their cars and walk around a covered corridor at the back of the stores and enter from the rear. Some stores even have the same window display spaces on these corridor approaches that are to be found on the street frontages.

Shopping center developers have simply accepted the fact that a greater amount of space must be provided for parking than is utilized in retail floor space. Downtown merchants, trying to survive, have encouraged the development of relatively high-rise parking buildings where the autos are taken up by elevator, parked, and then returned to the owners when they finish their shopping or their day of work.

Decrease in importance of the main business districts of large cities is freely predicted. This usually occurs to some extent; however, they do retain their place in the scheme of things. It may be that they will not continue to expand much further but, if property owners are wise enough to provide parking facilities, they will continue to be important buying centers for many years to come.

Golden opportunities await alert promoters of new outlying business districts to supply shopping facilities for many housing projects which came into being as the result of war boom activities in large industrial cities. Hundreds of new houses have been grouped with little thought to furnishing shopping facilities. Here awaits work for promotional genius to supply definite needs. In some cases, vacant land was left for this purpose in the original survey of individual projects. In other cases, they will have to be newly designed and fitted into each picture.

Influences are at work in cities and in connection with merchandising that may have a tendency to change retailing conditions in the future. The coming of drive-in lunch stands, drive-in banks, drive-in laundry agencies, drive-in shoe repairing concerns, drive-in-this and drive-in-that may mark a departure in business that might spread to many other lines of business. Perhaps some day your dentist will be waiting at your car door with his drill to give you emergency relief on your way to work!

Retail business development is in a state of flux. No one really knows what will happen in the years to come because the conditions under which retail business is operating are changing from year to year. It is certain that there will continue to be vast volumes of retail buying, and large numbers of merchants will vie with each other to care for the demand. Consequently, there will continue to be great activity in real estate of a business and income character. Money will continue to be made in the future just as it has been made in the past. It behooves the man who is interested in business property development to keep close watch on what is taking place from year to year, to discover where, why, and how business shifts will continue to occur.

Modern merchandising methods would appear rather peculiar to the average merchant of a half century ago whose chief worry was competition. Cooperation is taking the place of competition in merchandising to some extent in that merchants who deal in a certain type of goods are prone to place their stores side by side in a large shopping center, thus attracting hordes of buyers, some of whom may be expected to buy at a given store. Actually there is some planned diversification of goods among the merchants and each is fully aware of the specialities of the other. For instance a group of stores catering to women might include one dress shop which specialized in apparel for tall women. This "Tall Girls' Shop" would be well known to all the dealers in the block, and when occasion demanded, the customer would be sent by a competitor to the shop which could fulfill the need. So, a combined competition and cooperation marks one aspect of modern merchandising.

By and large, downtown business districts may be expected to grow slowly, but there will be substantial expansion in many outlying business areas where there will doubtless appear many golden opportunities for buying and selling business properties.

SIX

Investment Problems in
"Blighted Areas"

A wise investor seeking profits from real estate should avoid with extreme care any "blighted" area in which property is submitted for his consideration.

He should know how to determine when an area *is* blighted or *about* to succumb. These "twilight zones" exist in almost every city of any size that is more than several generations old, especially where rapid progress has been made in physical growth and building development.

Where blight begins

How can an area that is becoming blighted or will succumb later be detected? One of the surest places to look for a blighted area is just at the edge of a main downtown business district. Often the entire downtown commercial section is surrounded by a wide belt of old dwellings and semi-business improvements created by the remodelling and adapting to commercial uses of old homes that were built a generation or two previously and had outlived their usefulness as dwellings. Blight will also be found on the edges of industrial districts, caused by the invasion of smoky or noisy factories that have driven out the original homeowners.

39

Decadence will likewise be caused by the infiltration into a normal district of undesirables, even when there is no proximity of low-grade or commercial activity.

Twilight zone conditions will sometimes arise through the mere running down of an old residence district to which no new construction has come because of the absence of vacant lots. It simply "wears out." Meanwhile, those who inhabit these old districts fail to pay enough rent to permit a landlord to expend more than the amount required to keep roofs watertight and the plumbing in good order. This is a wasting-away process, for houses wear out just as automobiles and personal apparel do. Finally, a neglected district will reach a state where it does not seem worthwhile to spend any more money on it, and there is no demand at the moment for the use of the land for other purposes. Even if there comes a call for the use of an industrial or business development, the land is held under so many ownerships that it often becomes almost impossible to negotiate purchases at anything like fair prices. This, then, becomes a slum and an economic sore on community life.

An investor sometimes comes in contact with a blighted territory by being offered a business property which, to all appearances, seems to be enjoying a big return for the price asked. People residing in these sections have to live, and they buy largely in their own neighborhoods. Consequently some merchants do a fine business and pay good rentals but these diminish as the neighborhood wears out. What may be a good return today may be greatly reduced in a few years. If an investor is not thoroughly familiar with all of the neighboring influences that exist in any given territory, he should move cautiously at this point, circling the district several times, studying the types of residents, their buying power, the condition of their dwellings and ascertain, if possible, whether the section is subjected to blight already or seems likely to succumb to it shortly.

Real estate blight, actual economic decay, is likely to infect other districts nearby if it is not controlled. It may never be entirely eliminated since real estate is not immune to conditions caused by age and the processes of physical depreciation. It behooves the investor, therefore, to know his town thoroughly and be aware of the places where blight is in progress. He should determine, if possible, the directions in which the blight is proceeding and the rate of progress it is making in those directions. The investor should dispose of property in its destructive pathway and avoid buying any that may be engulfed in the near future.

It is not always the large cities alone that suffer from blighted areas. Even the small town will have its district "across the tracks" where the lowest income groups live and where, sometimes, conditions are just as bad as in the slums of the big cities.

Curiously enough there are some real estate speculators who make a business of owning shack houses and business quarters in the slums of some cities. Here relatively higher rents prevail than in other sections, considering the accommodations offered. Hovels almost unfit to live in bring rentals as high as those charged for much better quarters in many workingmen's neighborhoods. Rentals obtained from some stores, saloons, and night clubs in slums show a high rate of return on the actual investment involved. This is not a desirable type of ownership, however, and relatively few investors are attracted.

For years municipal authorities and housing experts have been studying this subject of blighted areas and how to prevent them, as well as how to reclaim districts that have already succumbed. In a number of important cities, large districts have been wiped out through condemnation of land for use in connection with group plans of public buildings. In other cities, railroad terminals, erected through powers of land condemnation, have likewise resulted in the reclaiming of many acres of slums for higher and better use. Highway and street extension projects have improved some locations where decay has prevailed. There have been so many areas affected by blight however, that it has been impossible to eliminate any but a small portion of such sections.

It is somewhat remarkable that a nation of our means has been unable to deal with blight and slum areas successfully. It is estimated that over 22,000,000 people lived in slums in the late 60's.

In recent years the government has made serious efforts to deal effectively with slum clearance through many avenues of attack including the Poverty Program, Job Corps Training, Urban Renewal, and Model Cities programs. In 1965 the Department of Housing and Urban Development was given full cabinet status, and a myriad of programs has emanated from this department of the cabinet. Certainly much has been accomplished, but much remains to be done.

Causes of blight

John Hilder has suggested several causes of blighted areas and classifies them, in part, as follows:

Industrial. Due to changes in transportation, to intensive land use, to change in character of industries, to obsolescence, to plant expansion, to lack of employees' housing and recreational facilities, or to other causes that made new areas more efficient or more economical for industrial operation.

Commercial. Due to shifts in population or purchasing-public centers that made new areas more accessible, or to an overintensive development of land use that rendered the old areas less susceptible to improvement or less comfortably accessible or attractive to customers. Removal of a prominent store to, or erection of a large office building in, a new area is sometimes cited as a cause, but really is a result.

Residential. Due to new lines of transit and habits of travel, invasion by sporadic commercial or industrial establishments or apartment houses, land-overcrowding that made "modernization" impractical, and obsolete types of dwellings coincident with a higher standard of living and the attraction of great spaciousness and "modern" conveniences offered in new areas.

Causes, as given by Mr. Hilder, are both primary and secondary as follows:

PRIMARY CAUSES

1. Land overcrowding:
   A. District: inadequate public open spaces.
   B. Lot: buildings occupying too much of lot; lot sizes too small.
   C. Building: multifamily dwellings overshadowing old one-family dwellings, raising land values, and depreciating old building values.
2. Obsolete buildings.
3. Invasion by incompatible uses—usually a sign of weakness due to other causes, especially the two above. Where this has not been true, the old districts often have maintained themselves. (Washington Square, New York; the Battery section, Charleston; Louisburg Square, Boston).
   A. Social or racial changes.
   B. Boarding houses.
   C. Sporadic business or industry.
   D. Heavy traffic.
   E. Smoke or smells from nearby areas.
4. Inaccessibility due to transit facilities making new areas more accessible in terms of personal effort.

SECONDARY CAUSES

5. Natural handicaps, as swampy soil (mosquitoes), steep hillsides, a basin location, such as Cincinnati's old town.

6. Rising standard of living expressed in terms of:
   A. Greater spaciousness. For the district:
   Parks and playgrounds; more accessible open country.
   For the lot:
   Larger yard area.
   B. More light, air, and sun, due to spaciousness.
   C. Modern buildings—arrangements and equipment; architectural design.
7. Fashions, advertising, nostalgia for open spaces, snobbishness, craving for novelty.

Another authority, professor C. Louis Knight, has declared that causes for blighted areas may be classified in two categories:

1. Influences which make an area *absolutely* less desirable for usage for which it is devoted, and
2. Influences which make an area *relatively* less desirable.

To the first category are assigned such factors as:

1 Encroachment of industry or business upon a residental area
2. Presence of nuisances such as slaughter houses, swamps, marshes, penal institutions, noisy and smelly factories.
3. Elements of inaccessibility.
4. Overcrowding: buildings which are too high for the width of streets; excessive concentrations of population.
5. Destruction of neighborhood amenities.

To the second category are assigned influences which draw people away from old business or residential sections and contribute to the growth of new areas, including:

1. Development of new real estate subdivisions.
2. Improved transportation facilities—automobile, and bus and train service—permit people to live farther from their work and under less-crowded conditions.
3. Shifting of industrial plants from one part of a city to another, causing workers to follow them to be near their employment. This is a type of local industrial decentralization

Efforts to control blight

There are investors who have discovered too late that they own property in districts which have already become blighted or are about to be affected by blight. These people are naturally interested in means whereby their properties may be saved and made salable, or at least more productive of income. A definite remedial measure may include the creation of a neighborhood improvement association to cope with the situation. Through the instrumentality of the National Association of Real Estate Boards, there has been sponsored in recent years a movement for the reclaiming of blighted districts by the establishing of voluntary neighborhood associations that would proceed to get complete control of large areas and rejuvenate them by repairs, rebuilding, and rehabilitation. A whole section would be converted into a new and higher type of residential district than had existed theretofore. Most blighted districts are best adapted for residential purposes for those persons working in the business and mercantile districts nearby. Older sections could thus be reclaimed on a large scale. Instead of governmentally inspired slum clearance projects, it is felt that a reclaiming of such blighted districts would be much more useful for all concerned.

If blight has not extended to too great a degree, it is possible to form a voluntary association of property owners and encourage each owner to go about a systematic program of rehabilitation. Action on the part of a few soon spreads to action on the part of most of the owners in the neighborhood. This checks the tide and perhaps saves untold loss that might have followed.

Harland Bartholomew, planning expert of St. Louis, gives the following as the dominant influences, or combination of two or more influences, that cause blighted districts:

1. Obsolescence.
2. Lack of homogeneity.
3. Inaccessibility.
4. Decentralization.
5. Inadequate utility service.
6. Character of tenancy.

"The blighted urban area is the result of uncontrolled large scale urban growth," declares Mr. Bartholomew. "It can be corrected and prevented only by control of unsound speculation and the promotion of those forces which create permanent values."

Zoning laws, often bitterly complained about by owners and investors who want to use their real estate for unauthorized purposes, are definitely a deterrent against blight in urban sections. Districts in cities should be used for those purposes for which they are best adapted, and zoning laws, when adopted, usually take these uses into consideration. Had it not been for the existence of zoning laws for the past half century, American cities unquestionably would be in a much worse condition than they are now. The strict observance of these laws in days to come will do much to control and prevent blight, though they will not cure that which has already made itself apparent.

Planning department records show that one-third of the privately owned land in central cities in the United States is vacant and unused. To the degree that decaying districts of cities can be checked, the rapid ballooning of urban areas which has continued for the past forty years can be controlled with a consequent cutting down of the enormously increasing tax cost entailed in carrying sidewalks, sewers, power lines and municipal services in general out over a wider circumference. If adequate living quarters for large numbers of persons can be created in these rehabilitated blighted districts, a great economic saving can be effected, and many adjoining areas kept from degenerating into a similar condition.

It is recognized by all students of real estate that some significant factors will surround the purchase and sale of real estate in the next few years:

1. There will be a great need for reclaiming blighted areas by replanning, rezoning, and rebuilding such sections, largely for residential use by those employed in nearby business and industrial establishments.
2. This will inspire co-operative ventures by private capital, probably backed by governmental guarantees of mortgages or bonds to be issued for rehabilitation purposes.
3. This should re-create valuable real estate equities which will bear their fair share of tax burden, thus relieving other real estate now too heavily taxed.
4. Transportation lines will find their burdens lighter by reason of the fact that many persons will move to such rehabilitated districts to be in close proximity to their work.
5. This task of reconstruction must be carried on by property owners who have control of the real estate, assisted by real estate men who will sell and manage it.

A properly planned city, subject to adequate regulatory laws and strictly enforced zoning practices, might continue indefinitely without experiencing decay or blight. Slums would never develop because the influences which create slums would not be present. In such a community an investor would never be at a loss to know how to spend his money, for the sign posts of control would be apparent to everyone.

Few such ideal cities exist, however, so an investor, to protect himself from the dangers of becoming entangled in a district where blight has or is about to lay its heavy hand, must make close and frequent inquiry into the conditions prevailing in any neighborhood where he plans to assume an ownership of property.

Cities which have progressive leadership definitely can do something about their plights. The Department of Housing and Urban Development stands ready to assist, although it is hampered somewhat by lack of funds in some of its phases, especially the Model Cities program.

There are prevalent a number of planning specialists whose services come high, but whose intelligent analyses are necessary in order for the modern floundering city to get moving again. For a fee, these planning experts will come to a city, study its history and its possibilities extensively, and offer a detailed plan for progress. Sometimes the plan may involve the revamping of the downtown section, closing certain streets to automobile traffic and creating malls for pedestrians. Sometimes the plan will include the construction of a convention center. Almost always the plan calls for spending money, but that is the only way a city can constantly improve itself. Without proper planning, the money would be spent unwisely and unprofitably.

SEVEN

Why Real Estate Is the Best Investment

Two points should be considered in any deal involving an investment of funds: (1) Is it safe? (2) Does it pay a satisfactory rate of return?

Frequently, where one factor predominates, the other is lacking. United States bonds are absolutely safe, and they return 4.15 per cent to 4.75 per cent interest. Investments that show abnormally high returns, on the other hand, are sometimes found to be hazardous.

Safety and rate of return

Real estate, if carefully selected and managed, will present every element of safety one desires and at the same time can be bought at a price which will net a satisfactory investment return. Real estate may also increase materially in value over the years.

Many a man has retired from active business life with a modest fortune and, seeking to invest it safely, his attention has naturally been attracted to real estate. Frequently these investments have grown tremendously in value. Even when overtaken by years of depression they weathered the storm safely, furnishing a good income return.

Real estate is a good investment for the following reasons:

1. It is surrounded with substantial elements of safety, if wisely chosen and skillfully managed.
2. It cannot be easily dissipated.
3. If properly selected, it continues to reap income year after year, despite changing business conditions.
4. Its owner is not subject to questionable management by others, as in the case of industrial or business enterprises and stocks issued by them.
5. Real estate does not have to pay expensive underwriting and other promotional charges. Income from properly chosen real estate will begin at once and continue unabated, paying a steady return in addition to any increase in value.
6. That real estate is not always a liquid asset is, perhaps, one of its most commendable features. This characteristic has saved many a person from losing money by investing in "get-rich-quick" schemes that later proved to be failures. Likewise, an owner is not easily "rushed off his feet," in an unwise effort to dispose of it.
7. When you invest in real estate, you may go and look at it, and see that it is there. There is a sense of personal possession implied that is attached to no other form of investment.
8. Real estate, since it is limited in amount, attaches to itself monopolistic features, which, capitalized into business use, bring profits to its owner.

The safe and profitable investment of surplus funds always has been one of the puzzling problems of the businessmen of this country. Because of the ease with which stocks and bonds may be purchased in any denomination, much investing has taken this form. Businessmen have from year to year poured money into such securities, receiving a nominal rate of interest from enterprises that sometimes had but questionable merit.

Lack of knowledge of how to select and manage real estate has kept great masses of investment funds out of the real estate market, where the largest profits have always been made. With the organizing and standardizing of the real estate business through the medium of real estate boards and operating companies, there have come into existence new conditions. Trained broker managers now stand ready to render service in assisting those who are attracted to realty investments. Basic principles have been established, and fundamental methods of acquiring safe and profitable investments have been developed.

John Jacob Astor, when he went to New York in 1782, found a little city of 25,000 inhabitants. He cautiously began setting aside his surplus income for investments in real estate. He died, leaving an estate worth $20,000,000. His son, William B. Astor, added tract after tract of real estate to the family credit, increasing it until it was worth $45,000,000. John Jacob Astor III continued the family policy and died leaving $75,000,000. The Astor estate, and those who built it up, believed in buying property *and never selling it*.

Alva Bradley, a lake captain living in Cleveland, amassed a shipping fortune, leaving $450,000 when he passed away. He stipulated that the estate should be held intact for twenty years. When it was divided among his heirs, it had grown to $4,070,000. The heirs continued their realty investment, and the estate increased tremendously in value through additions, successful management, and the natural increase which came with the years.

United States government bonds, regarded as one of the most secure forms of investment, pay from 4.15 to 4.75 per cent in interest return, but with small possibility of increasing in value. Bonds of large corporations such as railroads, illumination, power, telephone and telegraph companies, oil refining concerns, and similar large enterprises, pay 4 to 8 per cent, but fluctuate with the markets to such a degree that one is never certain what the next dividend report will be. Stocks issued by industrial and commercial enterprises are considerably less stable than bonds, and are subject to all the sins of commission and omission of management, so that they are constantly falling and rising, or disappearing altogether as the stock ticker tape unwinds its story.

Real estate, it must be remembered, has two definite elements of gain. It not only pays an income, if the property is improved, but it also benefits by the steady increment in value which usually comes with growth in population and clever utilization.

Mortgages on real estate, the best investment next to actual possession of real estate itself, pay from 6 to 8 per cent consistently. Real estate, in most cases, should pay a 6 to 10 per cent net investment return not counting the possible increase in value.

The choicest form of real estate investment usually is to be found in improved business property and properties subject to long-term leases. Central business property makes money for the real estate investor if he has the necessary amount of capital to enter that field. Rental receipts totaling into the hundreds of millions are flowing into the pockets of central property owners throughout the country. No other source of revenue can compare in volume with this great inflow of wealth.

What is a good investment?

What constitutes a good investment? Any piece of real estate which has a proven net investment return of at least 8 per cent and is situated in a locality where growth seems reasonably certain, will, in the course of years, return more real income to its owner than any other form of investment, considering its safety.

It is often difficult to buy property in an active downtown business district of any live city except at a price which is in advance of market value. This is due to the confidence and satisfaction of owners who will not consent to part with it, except for a marked premium. In any instance, such real estate cannot be bought at any price, so well satisfied are owners to hold it for future use and increase in value. There is a constant effort by investors to get possession of such property, which nearly always furnishes a splendid return, especially when one considers the original price paid for it by the owner.

The trend of population towards the urban centers of the country makes cities profitable investment centers. In 1800, less than 4 per cent of the people in the United States lived in cities. In 1890, 33 per cent had gravitated to cities, while the census of 1940 showed that the pendulum was still swinging cityward, and for the third decade in American history, a greater portion of the population lived in cities and towns than in the open country. Census figures in the late 60's show 70 per cent of the population residing in urban centers. The furnishing of housing accommodations and the attendant commercial and industrial activities in cities create a tremendous volume of manufacturing, wholesale, and retail trade, conducted by businessmen and merchants who demand adequate accommodations for which they are willing to pay substantial rentals.

It is certainly true that all real estate is not always advancing in value, but it is equally true that real estate is probably less subject to backward movements than other forms of investment The secret of profitable real estate investment lies in the application of knowledge of conditions to the buying of specific properties. This knowledge can be acquired only through intensive study, and to those investors and operators who are willing to apply themselves come golden awards.

In no other country in the world does real estate offer as attractive an investment as in the United States. In European and other foreign countries, cities do not grow as rapidly as in America. Cities there develop more slowly. A much larger proportion of the people live in the country, where they are less dependent upon the cities than here. Modern inventions have transformed American cities into havens which constantly attract people from the country. Moving picture shows, theaters, parks, amusement resorts, brightly lighted thoroughfares, comfortable homes and apartment houses, attractive workshops and offices, draw the country's inhabitants cityward, creating new markets and requiring new property accommodations. With labor deserting the farms, machinery is slowly but certainly taking its place, and it is probable that the time will not come again when more people will live on the farms than reside in the towns and cities of the United States.

Uncle Sam has always been a consistent believer in investing in real estate. In all probability he has been the world's biggest buyer, for it was learned at an early stage of this country's history that it is far cheaper and much more satisfactory for everyone concerned to buy land rather than to wage costly wars to take it away by force from someone else. Following the firm establishment in their own right of the thirteen original colonies, the Louisiana Purchase added more territory in 1803 than the whole thirteen colonies occupied, at a cost of approximately $16,000,000, a small fraction of its actual value.

Monroe and Livingston, the negotiators selected by the colonies, hurried the sale through because Napoleon realized how unpopular the transfer might be in France and because Jefferson did not dare to subject the purchase to a constitutional test. Monroe and his associate had been directed to buy only New Orleans but discovered that they could get much more land at about the same price and so extended their operations.

Having made a good bargain, the young country started out somewhat later to buy Florida from Spain. This territory cost $6,500,000 in 1819, the value of an average small village in that state today. For good measure Spain threw in a quitclaim to Texas which it was not able to deliver, however, as that future state was still claimed by Mexico. Later, the United States acquired Texas by annexation.

In 1867 the United States acquired Alaska from Russia for $7,200,000 a small fraction of the wealth it has produced since that time. Today it is worth many times that sum. Then came the purchase of the

Virgin Islands from Denmark, the leasing of the Canal Zone from Panama and the annexing of the Hawaiian Islands. In the late 50's Hawaii and Alaska were granted statehood.

Real estate, then, is the best investment for very practical reasons:

1. It affords the soundest security.
2. It furnishes an ample income if properly improved and managed.
3. It increases steadily in value, if properly selected.
4. It meets human needs.
5. It satisfies a democratic urge to own the land on which one lives or conducts his business.

EIGHT

How You Can Profit from
Real Estate

It took man thousands of years to develop to his present intellectual and physical status.

Slowly, through the centuries, the evolution occurred. With it came development of the mental powers of human beings. History descended by legends passed from generation to generation by word of mouth. Writing on tablets of stone was superseded by the use of crude pens and parchments. Then came one of man's greatest boons—printing. By means of modern educational methods, and through the medium of books, one is now able to learn more in a month than a man living in the tenth century could ordinarily have absorbed in a lifetime.

Experience, of course, is the great teacher, however, it is often a slow and harsh instructor. Today the seeker of information endeavors to learn by the experience of others which he adapts to his particular needs and environment. That there is an unlimited fund of experience from which to draw concerning the problem of profiting from real estate is undeniable.

Ten rules of thumb

In almost every community there is someone who has been a conspicuous success in the field of real estate, and if it is possible to consult with such a person, many valuable lessons will be learned. He will tell of the careful analysis which is made of every property purchased. Such a successful operator will point out, for instance, some of the following rules:

1. That land increases in value with age and use, while buildings decrease in value.
2. That the presence of population has a direct relation to the demand for land, and that as population centers in a town or city the value of all land there increases.
3. That the more accessible land becomes through the presence of highways, railways, and avenues of transportation, the greater the price that may be demanded and received.
4. That in towns and cities, the more public service facilities that are afforded, the more readily a profit on land and building can be secured.
5. That neighborhoods have character, whether used for residential or business purposes, and that the higher the grade of use to which land is put, the higher the price obtainable for it.
6. That land unlimited in quantity is distinctly limited as to its worth.
7. That land with monopolistic peculiarities commands a greater price and is more readily sold at a profit.
8. That the greatest increment is enjoyed by land which is adequately improved for use by its owners.
9. That there is a constant and steady shifting in the use of real estate, particularly in growing cities. A fine home district sometimes degenerates into a neighborhood of boarding houses, then into a cheap business or manufacturing section. On main arteries extending out to the circumference of a community, there develops a constantly growing line of business establishments, where land finds its most profitable use.
10. That the successful operator learns when to sell as well as when to buy real estate.

These and many other fundamentals, to be touched on hereafter, will be learned from the experienced real estate investor, if he chooses to reveal the methods whereby he operates. Learning these lessons, which have been assimilated through years of actual contact with realty problems, will save the student of real estate many costly experiences.

Perhaps in no business in the world is there more need of careful and painstaking study than in the buying and selling of real estate. Pitfalls exist for the unwary, and discouragement comes with the realization that the business embraces such a wide field and needs constant and unremitting investigation.

Printed matter on every subject relating to land and its development should be carefully read, so that a foundation may be laid for future operations. Contents of books, magazine articles, lectures, and addresses may well be absorbed by the man who would make a success in this profitable field of investment.

Having learned a few of the fundamentals, others will be revealed by experience and observation. Mistakes will be made and lessons learned. The man who fails or refuses to benefit from the mistakes of his own experience, or of others, seldom evidences enough genius to continue long as a successful real estate operator and investor.

Seek the advice of experts

The best way for the inexperienced to buy and sell real estate is through the acceptance of the services and counsel of one who makes such a business his life's work. When you are ill, you consult a physician. When in business trouble, you consult a lawyer in whom you have confidence. When spiritual matters disturb you, you seek the solace and peace to be found in counseling with a spiritual advisor. When you desire to engage in a business transaction involving the acquiring or disposing of real estate, what could be more sensible than to seek the guidance of a Realtor?

A Realtor is a member of a real estate board that is associated with the National Association of Real Estate Boards. His membership in that body vouchsafes for him a standing in his community. He is to the real estate business what the ordained minister is to the church, or the qualified lawyer is to a bar association.

Successful operators in cities all over America make a practice of dealing through Realtors when acquiring or selling their holdings. It stands to reason that a man who has properly qualified himself through years of study and experience can assist in many ways that will more than repay the usual commissions involved for service.

What is of greater importance, however, is that the operator identifies himself with a man who assumes the relationship of agent or broker between contracting parties. In most instances this is of definite value, for when the buyer and seller come together directly there are many opportunities for disagreement that an agent in his negotiations may skillfully avoid. The broker can act as a referee and peacemaker in many controversies that arise in even the simplest transactions.

No deal is good unless it is fair to both parties. This element of fairness the agent is able to inject into the transaction, smoothing over the difficulties which sometimes threaten negotiations.

Seasoned judgment on the part of an operator will do more to avoid difficulties in real estate operations than any other element, but this comes only after years of studious effort. By taking another into partnership to direct the course of negotiations, the element of risk will be greatly reduced.

It is significant that many men who have had long experience as brokers invariably operate through other brokers when buying or selling on their own account. An entirely different status is given the transaction, and a relationship is established between buyer and seller which is impossible when the contracting parties come together.

It is interesting to note, furthermore, that the most careful and skillful agents usually try to keep their parties apart until the main conditions of a transfer are decided upon. In many deals, contracting parties do not even see each other when they sign, at different times, escrow letters that outline the obligations of the respective sides.

With regard to the element of profit, the buying of real estate is often more important than the act of selling it. A property rightly bought is half sold, if one desires to part with it. It then doubtless contains the elements of speculation which will induce a buyer to pay a profit, feeling satisfied that he is acting wisely. If the property is not acquired with this in mind and has been taken over without study, the new owner may find that he has an unsalable property on his hands, and that he has defeated the purpose of his investment, that is, of selling it at a fair profit.

Never forget that the element of time must enter into most real estate transactions. One cannot expect to buy today and sell tomorrow at a profit. This sometimes occurs, but it is seldom the case. Time and constantly changing conditions of a favorable character are responsible for that elusive thing called "profit" in real estate transactions. With this in mind, great care should be taken to understand the fundamental conditions which surround a property before one invests in it.

Some men are considered lucky when they conclude a realty transaction that involves a substantial profit. Occasionally this is true, but more often the so-called "luck" has been inspired by a long and painstaking study of conditions applying to the property in question. It has been viewed from all angles, and due consideration has been given to many factors before it has been acquired Then time entered into the equation, and at the proper date the property was sold at a substantial advance in price and the reward due to vision and careful consideration came naturally.

Why urban land offers the most

Some of the principal reasons for expecting substantial returns to come from the buying and selling of real estate in cities are:

1. There is a natural growth of any new country where towns develop into cities within a short time.
2. The laying of a new hard-surfaced roadway; the building of a golf course; the discovery of oil or minerals; the building of a new industrial city by some large corporation; and the creation of a new harbor or a large irrigation dam often lend to low-priced outlying lands great additional value almost overnight. Watch for new improvements on a large scale; they carry profits in their wake. In addition to numerous atomic power plants and space installations, we may expect with confidence to see huge desalinization plants releasing vast amounts of water for industrial and irrigation purposes; pipe lines bringing vast amounts of water from the Pacific Northwest to the arid Southwest where the water will bring productivity to thousands of acres of fine soil; and jet-age transportation in huge planes traveling up to 2,000 miles per hour and carrying 400 to 500 passengers.
3. The rerouting of buses often gives to specific properties greatly increased value by reason of the creation of new transfer points. The extension of bus lines into new outlying territories nearly always results in the creation of new business centers where property values increase rapidly.
4. The location of an important industry in a new section of a city brings with it a demand for homesites, to be followed by the inevitable business district.
5. Street widening and street opening activities abound as investment possibilities. Channels of traffic are diverted, and new avenues of retail trade are created.
6. Demand for new store facilities in a business district of a rapidly growing city often results in properties being sold again and again at substantial profits.
7. Districts changing from homes to apartment sites often see substantial increases in value of land. When it is possible to house sixteen families on a lot where one family has normally resided, the value of the land, if properly located for such utilization, is greatly increased.

8. Development of lake, river, and ocean front property has been overlooked in many cities. After a community has passed a certain point in population, a condition of congestion begins to make itself apparent. If at this time a beautiful water front property, adequately served by a transportation medium, can be developed, it can be sold at a substantial profit.

9. Money has been made by keen-visioned men who have realized that outlying business neighborhoods can support a movie house, a market, or a bowling alley, and have proceeded to fill the need at the proper place and time.

10. Real money talks loudly. Often a substantial reduction in prices may be obtained when an entire transaction can be handled on a cash basis. It often is the one big inducement which will draw out the nearest thing to a bargain that an ordinary real estate market affords.

11. Favorable climatic conditions, such as those enjoyed by southern California and Florida, properly exploited, draw large numbers of people permanently to such territories. Many thousands who are advancing in age and are preparing to "retire," seek out such places, invest their money liberally, and create active real estate markets which continue to expand from year to year. Investments in such sections, if carefully investigated to the point where they prove warrantable, often show golden returns.

12. New outlying business centers are fertile fields for investment, especially if on heavily traveled highways leading to other important towns or cities. Surrounded by rapidly expanding home districts, the new business sites thus created are bid up by businessmen seeking to create new centers of trade.

13. Remember, the time to buy real estate that you may later sell at a profit is when there is a lull in the market. Buy at the low ebb, hold, and sell when activity is in full sway.

NINE

Starting Right in Buying
Real Estate

An inexperienced investor in real estate may encounter many pitfalls during his investigations of properties which may be offered him. Sharp practices are not unknown on the part of those eager to sell their holdings or those dealers who seek occasionally to act in an unworthy manner. A seasoned operator soon learns to recognize tricks of the trade which are practiced on the unwary. It is the newcomer, of course, who must be on his guard, and it is for his benefit that this negative side of real estate operation is considered.

"Caution" should be the watchword of the real estate investor, whether of limited or long experience. Unremitting caution and careful investigation will prevent the acquiring of real estate which may belong in the "cripple" class. Care must be exercised in examining the merits and demerits of property before a final decision is made.

Time taken to analyze a property thoroughly is always well spent. Do not be "high pressured" into closing a deal. Do not act until you are thoroughly satisfied that it is the property you want, and be sure you are getting the thing for which you are bargaining.

Pitfalls to avoid

In the first place, do not approach the subject of real estate invest-ment from the standpoint of looking for "bargains." There are few genuine bargains if the market you are operating in is normal. There may be many properties which may be classed as "good buys," but so-called bargains are rare. Do not be discouraged if you fail to find properties which offer astonishing returns at low purchase prices. If such appear, investigate such offerings just a bit more keenly than usual for there may be something radically wrong with them, and you may become a victim instead of an investor. You cannot get something for nothing in real estate any more than you can in other fields. Be satisfied if the proposition offers reasonably good returns, and then depend upon making a profit on your money through increase in value over a period of time and the utilization of the property for better and more profitable purposes.

Avoid dealing with irresponsible agents. They seek to make commis-sions and do not have your interests at heart. Select a responsible agent to guide you, and use your own good common sense in the examination you make into the merits of any offering. If in doubt, get reliable advice from an expert just as if you were ill or in legal trouble. If possible, investigate the general character and business dealings of anyone with whom you may not be properly impressed. Through your local realty board, bank, credit association, or friends, you can usually get information concerning anyone of consequence who is trying to sell you real estate. A little time spent in looking into the standing of the persons with whom you are dealing may save serious consequences later.

Do not sign any paper unless you thoroughly understand its import. Get advice. It is cheap at any price when a substantial deal in real estate is concerned. Be careful that your advice is not biased. If in doubt as to the value of a property for which you are negotiating, secure an appraisal from a responsible valuator.

Signing options, agreements, and similar papers may precipitate you into difficulty if you do not thoroughly understand them, and may involve expensive litigation.

Before paying any money, insist that the entire deal be placed in escrow to be handled by a referee in whom you have full confidence. The escrow instructions will provide that the real estate firm shall be taken care of in regard to its commission, and that the seller be fully compensated as regarding his interest in the transaction. Escrow agencies are now to be found in most cities. They are usually conducted in connection with title companies. If there is none in your community, you can escrow your deal with your banker, who will receive the purchase price from the buyer and disburse the funds to the seller after title has been properly passed to the purchaser.

Reputable real estate men welcome escrow transactions. If a real estate dealer balks at escrowing a brokerage deal, consider it a danger signal, and proceed slowly. If the deal is the mere purchase of a homesite, and the company is a responsible one, it is not necessary to escrow such a deal.

Weigh just as carefully the advice given you by your banker or lawyer as you do anyone else. The banker may desire to sell you securities or bonds. The lawyer may wish to earn a fee by revising contracts, or by injecting his own business advice when it is only his legal advice which is sought. Both bankers and lawyers are invaluable in real estate transactions, and for the most part they are unbiased and upright, yet real estate deals can be wrecked when bankers and lawyers get out of their proper spheres, and give biased or uncalled-for advice. You should make your real estate broker prove every statement he makes Treat other advisors the same way. Your money is at stake, and you want disinterested advice or none at all.

Do not buy property you cannot afford to carry. "Shoe-string speculating" consists of buying a piece of real estate with a small down payment, with the hope that it can be sold quickly at a profit before further payments fall due. It is a dangerous practice, especially if you do not have the money to carry the property in the event the anticipated resale does not occur. Many a man has lost his initial stake by buying a property he was not in a financial condition to carry once it had been acquired. Investigate the extent of the obligations you are assuming, and be prepared to carry them through. Secure the best terms you can and make the smallest down payment compatible with good financing, but once having acquired a property, be prepared to meet payments of principal and interest until a satisfactory disposition can be made of it.

Never buy property which has not a clear, marketable title. Never buy unless a properly sponsored title has been furnished by a responsible title company or abstractor. After the title has been presented for your examination, have it looked over, preferably by a lawyer who understands such proceedings, or insist on title insurance in the amount of your investment or more.

Do not allow yourself to be oversold If you have a certain amount of money with which to buy a lot, don't let some "high pressure" type of salesman sell you two lots when you know you cannot afford to own and carry two lots. Do not get loaded up with property you cannot afford.

Do not buy real estate without actually seeing it. Beware of the "long distance" deal. If a property is worth owning, it is worth going to see. Farms in distant states, fruit lands in Georgia, California, or Florida, ocean lots at seaside resorts, and cabin sites on cutover timberlands may sound interesting, but *never* buy unless you actually see them. Probably you won't buy them at all if you do see them and will thereby avoid a substantial loss. If a property is not worth the trouble of going to look at it, it isn't worth buying.

Don't acquire land in lotteries. One favorite plan of "get rich quick" promoters is to select a large tract of practically worthless land, prepare a fine looking map of it after subdividing it into small sites, and then issue tickets which are given away at fairs, movies, and other entertainments. A few days later every ticket holder receives an announcement that he has been the miraculous winner of a "free lot" which will cost absolutely nothing *but* the cost of an abstract and recording papers showing ownership. Charges of from $20 to $75 are made for these services. After the fee is paid, if one even takes the trouble to look at the so-called "bargain," one will usually find the lot is on a barren piece of seashore, a small tract in a distant cutover timberland, or so far from transportation that it is practically worthless. It is not worth owning, even if it costs you nothing. This is just another demonstration that you can't get something for nothing. Avoid lotteries.

Do not be rushed into a deal by the argument, "Well, if you don't buy this quickly, somebody else is going to take it." This is old stuff, and many fall for it, to their chagrin. Better miss one of these "bargains" than lose your money in a venture questionable in character. Few reputable agents advance such a reason for buying, even though it may actually exist. Be properly warned, if such a warning seems to be given in good faith, but be thoroughly satisfied that you want the property and are going to be satisfied with it before you part with your hard-earned money.

Understand what you are going to buy when you attend an auction sale of real estate. Many of these auctions offer "good buys" in real estate, but before the time the auction is held you should take a trip to the property, study it, and understand what you are buying. Reputable auctioneers advertise such auctions days in advance and invite investigation. Do not be swept off your feet at such a function, where the stage has been properly set to work upon the gambling instinct which every man possesses to some degree.

Beware of the arguments advanced by some persons when they point to the erection of a new railroad terminal, a park, a new pier, or a large municipal bridge. Only in exceptional cases do such projects permanently increase surrounding property values. Be thoroughly satisfied that the improvement is contemplated, underway, or completed, and is going to be of such a character as to increase the value of the particular property you are invited to purchase. A limited number of businesses may thrive near a terminal; an apartment overlooking a park may prove a profitable investment; certain activities may prosper near a new and important pier, and there may be some advantage in being located near the end of a new bridge, but the number of enterprises which can benefit by proximity to such improvements is usually so limited that a keen analysis of each project should be made before a final commitment.

Watch out for easements of one kind or another which may be attached to land you buy. Somebody may have the right to use part of the property for an alley, a pipeline, a passage or driveway, or some other purpose which may prevent you from developing the property to its best and highest use. These easements usually will be revealed in the abstract of title, as they must be made matters of record to make them legally binding. Always inquire as to easements and determine whether it, if it is attached to a property, will detract from its value. Many difficulties have arisen over easements, money has been lost, or advancement of property values retarded by their presence. If an easement is on record, a sales contract usually will include its acceptance, so it is wise to have a knowledge of such easements before signing a contract to buy a property.

It is not always possible to examine physical monuments which are set up to determine the exact boundaries of a property, but if such an examination can be made, it is well to do so. Also be sure to see that you actually have delivered to you the property you contract to buy. Mistakes often are made by a salesman pointing out a specific tract of land, and then discovering that another has actually been deeded to you when the deal is closed. Buildings are sometimes erected on wrong lots, and other difficulties ensue so it is wise to know that you actually have delivered to you the particular tract of ground for which you bargained and paid. If the property is a valuable one a survey is well worth while.

Determine the utility of a tract of land before you buy it. If it is a hillside, for instance, ascertain what it can be used for. If it is a gully, determine whether, within a reasonable time, enough dirt or refuse can be dumped there to make the land available for some definite use. If marshy land, ascertain whether building foundations can be provided in the event the water is drained from it, or that it can be filled to a proper level.

Be careful about buying small, irregularly shaped tracts of land. An acre of land, if it is square and has a street frontage, may be put to some profitable use. If it is a "shoestring" extending back hundreds of feet, with a width of only a few feet, there may be doubt concerning its profitable utilization. Very narrow lots in business sections are difficult to develop unless linked to adjoining properties. Shallow lots suffer from the same drawback. Land which may not have adequate access to thoroughfares, and which is thereby isolated from general use, may be difficult to sell at a profit.

Key questions to ask before buying

In buying buildings, the greatest care should be exercised to know thoroughly the exact structural conditions involved. Inquire as to the following:

1. Is the building properly adapted to the neighborhood and the land on which it stands?
2. Is it a special service structure for which only permanent use of a specific character will result in the maintenance of its value?
3. Is the building structurally sound?
4. Has it been erected and maintained according to the municipality's building code?

Be careful in buying property in a neighborhood with which you are not familiar to find out whether there are nuisances which may detract from value.

1. If a home, is there a public garage next door?
2. Is your neighborhood restricted against the quartering of livestock?
3. Does it adjoin a cemetery?
4. Are you next to a school playground where boisterous children may interfere with the quiet enjoyment of your premises?
5. Is there an undesirable factory emitting smoke, dust, smells, or gas in your neighborhood?
6. Do you, when the wind is in a certain direction, suffer from

odors from stockyards, sewage disposal, chemical, or rendering plants?

7. Are there unusual volumes of vehicular traffic passing nearby that may prove a nuisance?
8. If an unimproved lot, has it been filled in with rubbish or loose dirt so that a sound foundation is questionable?
9. Is the property subject to floods?
10. Has a building dry rot or termites?

There are opportunities to lose money which often may be avoided by careful investigations made before you have definitely committed yourself to take action. If you lose money, you can usually blame it on your own laxity, unless you are openly swindled, and even then a little consideration might have kept you free from difficulty.

Remember the watchword—*Caution!*

TEN

Types of Real Estate
Investments

Many times you have heard the statement, "Real estate is a great investment; they just aren't making any more of it." This is only partly true. The square footage of the land does remain constant, but the improvements and the uses to which various parcels of land are put do change with the times.

The last third of the twentieth century will witness many variations of real estate investments that were unheard of during the first half of the century. In 1900 and even in 1950 land was not needed for the installation of space ports and atomic power plants. Many states were unable to accommodate the sale of apartments in condominiums until the 60's when statutes in some states were revised to make such conveyances possible.[1]

Selecting real estate is a matter dependent upon the amount of money available for investment, the personal preferences of the buyer, the order in which various types of property are submitted for consideration, and, perhaps, just plain "luck."

---

[1] See Appendix for condominium forms.

The man who makes a study of real estate and considers his investment as a carefully-planned business enterprise, usually starts out with some well-conceived notions as to the type of property he wants. He seeks a particular kind because he is convinced that it best meets his personal requirements, that he can best handle it with funds at his disposal, and that it will pay him a greater proportionate return than any other realty investment. This man is more likely to succeed because he has a working knowledge of the merits of different presentations submitted to him.

Every town, every city in America has investment possibilities in real estate. Real estate men, trained to observe the evidences and possibilities of growth, and to judge the future by the past, hammer at men's doors pleading with them to accept opportunities to make money, but are often coldly turned away. Later, when a good deal is made which results in a substantial profit realized by another, there is regret that the opportunity was not seized upon at the time the offering was made.

Most kinds of real estate can be bought and sold at a profit. Some classes of property naturally afford greater profits than others, just as they involve greater investments and greater obligations in the way of improvements that make the land productive.

Residential property

Perhaps the simplest form of real estate buying is vacant lots in new subdivisions. There are certain times to buy and certain conditions to be observed, if land so acquired is to be sold at a profit. This is more fully discussed in a succeeding chapter, as it is the first type of investment many persons become interested in, and is the one that perhaps attracts the largest number of individual buyers.

Buying a house for other than personal use may result in the making of a good profit. Remembering that land usually increases in value with age, and that buildings suffer depreciation, care must be exercised in seeing that conditions exist that will permit such a property to be sold profitably. Sometimes an old home standing on a street which is gradually coming into use for business purposes can be purchased, rented as a rooming house or for semi-business purposes for several years, then torn down and replaced by a business structure. In buying such a house, remembe that the investment is substantially in the land itself, and that little value attaches to such a building. Its value, in other words, is absorbed in the cost of the land. Owners of such properties often demand full land value, and furthermore seek a replacement value, less depreciation, for the building itself. This, of course, cannot be considered as such a building is rapidly nearing the point where it is becoming inadequate to the location. Residences on business streets, which would cost thousands of dollars to build, or would be worth large sums if located in a proper environment, are practically worthless when the price asked for the land is taken into consideration.

The same principle applies to houses where a neighborhood is slowly changing from a single residential district to an apartment section. Such houses may be useful for occupancy for several years, but when the full value of land for apartment purposes is realized, the house itself cannot be given much value. Many appraisers arbitrarily give a value to such buildings an amount equal to one or two years' estimated or actual rental.

A profitable business is operated in many cities by persons buying old houses which are structually sound, remodelling and modernizing them, installing new bathrooms and kitchen equipment, and then reselling at advanced prices. This kind of business can be best engaged in by someone who understands building operations.

In many places, particularly in California, men and women buy lots, erect artistic homes, furnish and live in them for a time, then sell them completely furnished, moving to other houses. They constantly have places in which to live, and manage to make regular profits if the market is active. If a house does not sell, it at least provides a home in which to live, or which may be rented.

Building two-family houses on the same plan is popular in some towns and cities. An investor will erect a two-family house, live in half of it until an opportunity comes to sell it, meanwhile collecting rental from the other tenants. Such buildings meet with ready sale, and usually prove good investments for both builder and buyer.

Apartment buildings

Four-family apartments have been erected in large numbers in many cities. These have individual heating and air-conditioning plants, and do not entail janitor service. Each tenant looks after his own portion of the maintenance required, and about the only expense in connection with such a property is providing front and rear hall lights, the payment of taxes and repairs, and charges incidental to occasional decorating.

Larger apartment properties involve a greater outlay in cash and entail greater management problems, especially when heat, air-conditioning and hot water are furnished. In larger cities a great proportion of the inhabitants reside in apartment houses and pay rent commensurate with the quarters and facilities enjoyed. Due to congestion, individual homes slowly disappear from the centers, and even outlying sections of larger cities, and about the only place to reside is in hotels or apartment buildings. Thus there opens up a vast field for building development in housing the thousands who do not desire to maintain individual homes of their own in outlying sections. Condominiums in which families actually purchase apartments are becoming increasingly popular.

It is estimated that the gross rentals from centrally heated apartment buildings must represent from fifteen to twenty-five per cent of the property valuation to net an eight per cent return to the owner. Expenses involved are the purchase of fuel, hiring of janitor and repairmen, water, electric light for halls, gas for hot water boilers, insurance, taxes, payments of interest on mortgages and, if the property is managed by a professional apartment house manager, an allowance for that. There is a constant building, buying and selling of such apartment buildings in cities. Care should be taken in assuming such an obligation. It is well to consult a broker who is thoroughly familiar with such propositions before acquiring one as an investment.

Commercial property

A very popular and satisfactory form of building investment is the one that has stores on the ground floor, with offices or living suites above. These usually are built on business streets where values have a reasonable expectancy of increase. If such expectancy is realized, the rentals on the stores are likely to increase steadily, while the rentals on the second floor space will at least remain stationary, if they do not actually increase as time goes on. The average tenant on the upper floors of such buildings is easily satisfied as to accommodations and service. For the modest investor, the ownership of such a building usually proves profitable.

Large business buildings in prominent downtown locations are successful in the degree of relationship that rentals received bear to the cost and maintenance charges involved in such structures. It is significant that large structures in almost any city are monuments to their builders. Banks, newspapers, leading merchants, and wealthy individuals enjoy erecting monumental buildings for the purposes of self-advertisement, or to perpetuate their names. Large hotels and department stores are possible exceptions. Most of these buildings seldom pay more than a return equal to the current rate of interest on investment funds. The rentals received from the ground and second floors of a business building ordinarily should carry the investment and provide the profit. Floors above the second story in most buildings do not pay a return greater than a rate of interest on the investment, plus carrying and maintenance charges. Often a well planned and properly tenanted two story building will pay as great an actual profit as a ten or fifteen story structure adjoining it. This is not always the case, of course, but it is the usual experience. There are now skillful building managers, who by careful operation have changed conditions somewhat, yet the person or corporation erecting a large monumental building must stand ready to write off a portion of it to vanity, advertising, or civic pride.

There are a variety of special purpose buildings which often show good profits, but they should be carefully considered. Supermarkets have become immensely popular in recent years. Some of these ventures have not proven to be money-makers, although most have been successful.

Real estate developers early realized the value of providing modern playhouses for the showing of movies. The large cities have seen them built by the scores, while practically every village and town has a movie. Investment in enterprises of this sort should be carefully scrutinized. One great difficulty is that such a building is seldom convertible to other uses should it fail in its purpose as an amusement center.

Many cities have a Coney Island, or similar enterprise, where entertainment for the summer season is provided with roller coasters, dance halls, skating rinks, and summer park attractions. These parks, operating only four or five months during the year, in most instances, must earn substantial returns to be successful. It requires some close figuring to determine whether an investment of this sort will pay a fair and permanent return on the money.

To the investor who has ample funds, the central business district of a growing city naturally offers attractions. Retail business property can collect toll in a manner denied most other forms of real estate, and is approached only by outlying property of a similar character, situated for the most part in blossoming business subcenters.

Business sections offer the most in the way of land increment in any city. Business shifts in most cities come in, cycles. Districts outgrow themselves or expand, and new sections see new improvements erected, new values created, and higher rents received. Increasing and shifting population reflects itself in a constant spreading out of the congested downtown business area of any city, and as the expansion continues, new tenants pay an ever increasing scale of rentals for location.

Many who make it their business to buy and sell real estate specialize in one particular type of property. In this way they get to know all about their specialty. In Los Angeles a former lumber salesman took over an equity in a small apartment house from a friend who owed him money. He maneuvered about for a while and sold it, making some money. Liking the idea he bought another and then another. In several years he developed into a bigtime operator, controlling several million dollars worth of apartment house property and advertising that he dealt only through real estate brokers who sold all of his properties for him and many to him.

Another investor makes a specialty of service station sites. He will range about looking for corners on which stations will prosper. He makes a deal to buy a property if he can lease it to a responsible oil distributing company. Clinching the lease, the property goes to the new owner. Then follow the improvements, often financed by a company specializing in that kind of thing, repayable over a period of years out of rents. Now the owner has a going concern with a responsible lessee to pay him rent. This gives a service station corner a real investment value, so the owner goes out and sells at a profit and then buys another corner to do the same thing with over again.

In some of the larger cities some operators make it their business to buy unfurnished apartment houses, completely equip them with furnishings, make leases at rentals which make the investments profitable ones, then sell them to the highest bidders, usually realizing a neat profit on each deal.

Automobile congestion in large cities has developed a type of real estate buyer who seeks out some wealthy estate that owns a run-down piece of minor business property in a busy part of town where auto parking is needed. The estate is probably getting scarcely enough to pay taxes and often wants to get rid of its property. A low cash offer is listened to and later accepted. The buyer gets a few hundred dollars from a wrecker for an old building, paves the site which thus becomes vacant, and then leases the space to an established parking concern for a figure which pays a good investment return on the land, all building taxes having been eliminated. This has been done repeatedly in large cities. Of course, such a site must be bought at a right price to enable the new owner to make a profit.

In California and other west coast states where the weather is mild and where drive-in lunch stands flourish, many corners have been leased for long terms of years for such purposes. Some are on straight rentals, others on a percentage basis.

In eastern states, where there are always months of winter weather, it should be an easy matter to create a business constructing buildings for use for "drive-in" purposes such as laundry and rug cleaning agencies, shoe repairing, milk depots, bakery goods, magazine agencies, vegetable and fruit stands, and a host of other types which require a very short time to pick up and pay for. An "electric eye" device would open a front door for a car to enter and close the rear one in cold weather, while in fair weather the vehicular lane could be kept open. Similar enterprises are operating in California where, of course, the weather is not a problem.

The man who is alert, who has new ideas, who can do things differently, shines just as brightly in the real estate operating fields as in any other and probably makes much more money in return for his activity, providing he has the energy and funds to follow up and work out his ideas.

The time to buy real estate is NOW. If you have the money to invest, do not hesitate to take the necessary steps promptly to become a property owner.

ELEVEN

Things to Know About a
Property Before Buying

As time goes on, buying property will become more and more a matter for a cautious approach. Properties change hands time and again down through the years, and every change in ownership brings with it questions that must be asked concerning the property's marketability. This is especially true now in the last part of the twentieth century when matters of law have become so complex, especially those matters pertaining to the multitudes of loans available, the issuance and release of which create great quantities of paperwork.

For most persons the buying of a parcel of real estate is, perhaps, the supreme business event of their lives. This is certainly true of the first piece purchased.

There are so many ways by which deception may enter into a transaction and so many matters to be looked into as a mere business precaution, that a prospective buyer should give himself the necessary time to investigate carefully the merits of any property he proposes to acquire. He should himself, or through his agent, investigate matters fully, for "caveat emptor"—*let the buyer beware*—is still the watchword of persons who buy real estate.

There are many ways in which to secure information. Building records may be consulted; you may have a contractor familiar with building construction look over a proposed purchase; your trustworthy real estate broker should, out of his wide experience, be of great help in ascertaining that everything is in good order and as represented. Many matters do not come up at the time of sale to which direct reference may be made, yet some of these things require investigation before a deal is closed, and not after your money has been paid and you are irrevocably committed.

Fundamental factors

There are certain fundamental factors one should know about land and the acquiring of title to it, and there are many more things one should investigate about a building which is being purchased. Much information will be readily available and apparent upon investigation while other matters must be delved into laboriously through expert channels.

Is the property worth the price paid for it?

This is perhaps the most important question to be decided and requires a painstaking investigation either by the buyer or his agent. Property values in the neighborhood should be inquired into to determine that an exorbitant price is not being paid for land. It may be well to look up tax appraisals at the courthouse, although such appraisals are seldom, if ever, a true indication of value, as real estate is seldom taxed upon its full market value. If one is familiar with the ratio of tax valuation to true property valuation, it may be an index which will be useful in checking values. Delve into land values in the neighborhood through every available source, and be satisfied that the price is a reasonable one.

The federal government requires the buyer of real estate to furnish revenue stamps to be affixed to the deed at the time of recording in the amount of 1.1 per cent of the purchase price. From a survey of these stamps in the recorder's office, a prospective buyer can determine the amount paid for the property by the present owner, notwithstanding the fact that the owner has been astute enough to place within the deed the stipulation that the property was bought for "ten dollars and other valuable considerations." These stamps should not be considered foolproof, although most buyers do not have the courage to avoid what would be a serious offense by falsifying the amount of the sale.

If there is a building on the land to be purchased, greater difficulty may be found in ascertaining whether a fair evaluation is placed upon it. Realtors long familiar with real estate can advise concerning building valuations, or a contractor may be engaged to furnish a more detailed appraisal. In every community there are professional real estate appraisers who for a fee will go out and render an appraisal of properties you may be contemplating. Some buyers are perfectly willing to pay the small fee the FHA appraiser charges, simply for the purpose of finding out how much the property is worth. Such appraisals as this cannot be had for unimproved properties as a rule, although a revision of the FHA lending program as of 1967 does allow FHA loans on raw land for development purposes.

Has the property a marketable title?

That is a matter which will sometimes be passed upon if the deal is being handled in escrow with a title company. Part of such an escrow service often consists of making a careful search of the title and rendering to the buyer an opinion as to the marketability of the title If there is any doubt as to the validity of the title, have the matter carefully passed on by a lawyer, for it may cause endless trouble later. Do not be persuaded to accept a property suffering from a defective title This may be cured sometimes by a title company issuing a title insurance policy, which usually is a sufficient guarantee to satisfy an average buyer.

Are there restrictions, easements, rights of way, etc., provided for in the title to the property?

Nearly all subdivisions have definite sets of restrictions which extend for from fifteen to fifty years or more before expiring. A buyer should be familiar with their terms. Likewise provision may be made for easements and rights of way over any kind of property. If there is reason to believe that such easements may prove onerous, a careful inquiry into their provisions should be made *before* one buys, rather than afterwards.

Occasionally large sewers, built below ground and across a property, may prevent construction of adequate foundations for a building planned for the location. There may be an old provision that someone has the right to drive a cow across the rear end or side of a property, which prevents its use for a building's location. A title search will reveal the presence of these restrictions, easements and rights of way, but by the time title search is available to all concerned, a buyer may be committed to the purchase of the property and may be forced to accept restrictions and easements which he would not have accepted had he known at the outset of their presence.

Are there hidden assessments against the property?

Prospective buyers should realize also that with the tremendous growth of cities which has required them to extend services out many miles into what once were suburbs, there are a number of liens that might be held against properties which are not placed on record at all. Among these are front-foot charges for sewer lines which are laid alongside unimproved properties. Until recently (largely since the 1960's), property owners who had holdings en route to the outlying subdivision being improved and served with city utilities just sat back and enjoyed the increment their properties gained by virtue of the fact that these utility lines were laid in the streets alongside. Cities now have mastered the art of front-foot charges assessed against the property owners. This front-foot charge cannot be collected by coercion, but it must be paid nevertheless when and if the property is developed and the developers desire city water and sewage services. Many an unknowing buyer finds that the property that looked so good is assessed may thousands of dollars in front-footage charges. These charges *never* come to light in a title examination.

Paving liens come under this same pattern. Many cities do not place paving liens on record. Nevertheless, they must be paid by the developer when he asks for city services.

Are all taxes paid up to date of purchase?

Every buyer should know that delinquent taxes never appear in title examinations. The state of tax payments on property can only be ascertained by going to the tax collector's office and having the records examined. Never accept property without having the tax certificates showing all taxes paid from previous years. If the seller agrees to prorate the taxes for the present year, or even if he should graciously suggest that he should pay the taxes for the present year entirely, the examination must still be made for delinquent taxes from past years.

Is the property financed in such a manner that the buyer can comfortably carry it within his means?

Properties which are loaded with first, second and even third mortgages, payments on all of which fall due monthly, quarterly or semiannually, often become a very serious burden, and in the end may mean the loss of the buyer's equity through his inability to meet the fast recurring obligations. Understand exactly what financial burdens you are required to assume, and hesitate to carry a load which may be beyond your financial strength.

Do you know exactly the size and boundaries of the land you are purchasing?

If there is any serious doubt, insist that an accurate survey be made. If the seller will not pay for such a survey, it may be money well spent to have it done yourself before you pay him good money for something clouded with doubt. You may avoid trouble later in developing or reselling the property if this problem is settled once and for all before you become the owner of it.

If improved, are the buildings adequate to the land? If not, are you paying too high a price?

There should be a reasonable relationship between the value of improvements and land. In the case of residence, the house is usually worth from three to four times the value of the lot. In business buildings, the ratio differs according to character and locality. In important downtown sites, a large building is usually about the same value as the land. The determining of adequacy is one almost entirely of judgment. If you are not qualified to judge, consult someone who is.

Is the property properly financed?

It is most important that you know exactly the financial conditions surrounding the transaction you are about to consummate. Do you know definitely the rate of interest to be charged on the balance which will remain after your cash payment is made? Is the mortgage, or the second mortgage, of a character you are financially able to assume? Will the holder of a mortgage call your loan and force you to refinance the proposition at a time when funds are difficult to obtain? Have a very definite understanding regarding these matters before you commit yourself to proceed with a deal.

If the property is of a rental character, such as an apartment building, or a store and office structure, have you been furnished a careful statement as to actual rentals, length of leases, and a statement of actual expenses to check against the income?

Check the rentals, if necessary, by personally consulting tenants. If there are written leases, insist on seeing them. Too great care cannot be taken to prove to your own satisfaction that the rentals represented meet the acid test of careful investigation.

Is the property subject to floods, tornadoes, or any special attack of the elements?

This is important only in sections of the country where such devastating influences prevail. It is well to consider the question, however, as frequently land which looks good in summer is subject to overflow of creeks and rivers in the winter or springtime, and great damage may be done, the expense of which must, of course, be borne when the new owner takes possession.

Are there special fire hazards?

Possibly the building itself is a firetrap or may be located alongside or near such a structure. Perhaps the building stands alongside a facility employing large-scale combustion as part of its normal operations.

Is the section affected by stockyard or other disagreeable odors?

Many a person has moved into a neighborhood when the wind was in the right direction to blow such odors away, but has discovered a few days later when the breeze was coming from an opposite direction that foul smells made the district an almost unbearable place in which to live. Do a little investigating on this subject before closing your deal.

Does the property you propose to buy consist of a so-called butt or key lot?

The first lot on a street, in back of a corner lot which fronts on another thoroughfare, is known as a butt or key lot. It is risky to buy such a lot for residential and sometimes for business purposes, although not so much so as in former days when the owner of the corner occasionally decorated the rear of his lot with a stable. Nevertheless it is dangerous, for your building may be set against one or more neglected garages or storage bins. Furthermore, the corner lot may be given over to business purposes now or at some future date, and an undesirable condition may be maintained which will cause a serious depreciation to your property. Whether the key lot is vacant or improved, give full consideration to the consequences which may follow if you acquire such an investment.

Is the property affected by undue noise from factories, or smoke and fumes from passing railroad trains or automobiles?

A visit to the property at different times may reveal some startling reasons why the owner is anxious to sell, and by the same token indicate to you very good reasons why you should not buy that particular property.

Attention should be directed to seeing that there are no streams of noisy traffic on heavily traveled highways nearby which may interfere with the rest of those who are to use the newly purchased property for residential purposes. With vast increases in the uses of automobiles, trucks, buses, and otner rapidly moving vehicles, there have come increases in traffic noises along and near all heavily used arteries of travel.

Is the property likely to be condemned for a street opening, a park, public building, or for some other public or quasi-public purpose?

It is unwise to buy a lawsuit, and that is what you may do when you acquire a property in the pathway of public or semi-public improvements. Municipalities and railroads possess the right to condemn a property, set a price upon it by court action after expensive and distasteful litigation. Let the other fellow carry such a burden, and do not be drawn into purchasing a property, the possession of which may be limited in time.

Are the sewers installed, are they adequate, and do they connect with proper sized main trunk systems?

There are two common types of sewers: sanitary sewers which carry away sewage from bathrooms and kitchen sinks to proper outlets, and surface sewers which are designed primarily to carry away surface rainwater from land. Sometimes sanitary sewers are unlawfully connected to sewers designed to care for surface drainage only, and difficulty will be encountered later by having the sewer disconnected, and the new owner compelled to undergo considerable expense in installing either a septic tank or connecting with a sanitary sewer some distance away.

Is an adequate supply of pure drinking water available, and is the pressure sufficient?

In many new subdivisions which are just beyond a city's limits, and therefore, beyond its inspection control, water mains are installed by subdividers. These systems later become inadequate because of the large number of houses which must be furnished with water. In such sections it may be found that the water pressure is sadly deficient and that new water mains later may have to be installed. This means added expenses and inconvenience.

Are foundations sound and stable or do they show evidence of cracking and sagging?

Care should be exercised in looking into the merits of a building's foundations for if evidence of deterioration in this part of a structure is discovered, serious difficulties may occur later. Foundations, for the most part, are usually adequately built and require little attention. There are occasions, however, when this is not so. Structures erected on hillsides sometimes slip from place. Earthquake tremors occasionally make foundations insecure. Occasionally inadequate foundations have been placed under a structure, and they may require strengthening. Make a careful inspection of foundation work under any building you plan to acquire.

Has the property adequate fire protection?

Most cities and towns do offer adequate fire protection for all buildings within their limits. Occasionally, however, and usually on the borders of large cities, there are certain unincorporated territories which have only such fire protection as may be afforded, through contract, by some other municipality. This kind of service may be far from satisfactory, and your house may burn down before one of these "hired" fire brigades reaches your building. Make certain that you have adequate fire protection whenever building a structure or acquiring one.

Have buildings been erected on filled land?

In some sections a builder may fill in a ravine because a street has to pass over it. On such filled ground substantial buildings are sometimes erected before the land has settled thoroughly. These buildings may crack, or even collapse. Be sure that you are not buying such a questionable investment, for you may discover that a perfectly good-looking structure has started to slip, crack, or actually crumble after a rainstorm that has caused the ground to settle or wash away beneath the foundations.

Is the building infected with termites or dry rot?

In many sections of the country, wood-boring termites create great damage in the underpinning of frame structures, eating away wooden portions of foundations and even walls and attics at times. Considerable structural damage, which is not even apparent on the surface, may be suffered in this way. If termites are prevalent, always have a termite inspection made of the premises. Repairs are not difficult to make and if the infestation is discovered in time, the damage may easily be repaired and will not necessarily be very expensive.

Dry rot, likewise, attacks buildings in certain climates and locations. This is a type of fungus disease which attacks timbers. Whole sections of a wooden structure near the ground may be affected. Here again, inspection by an expert will reveal whether a structure is free.

Is there a garage in connection with the property you propose to buy? If not, is there a place to build one?

Automobiles nowadays are regarded as necessities by most persons, and the availability of proper storage facilities should be ascertained whether the property is of a residential character or otherwise. It pays to spend a few dollars more and secure such accommodations, for if you do not use a garage, you can probably rent it.

Is natural gas available for cooking, and is the price reasonable?

Gas for cooking is almost as necessary as electricity for lighting a home. Don't be content on being told that, "Gas is available." You may find it is "bottled" gas which is never as desirable as natural gas.

Is adequate and reasonably priced transportation furnished in the neighborhood in which you propose to buy property?

This is important, for transportation is to land what blood is to the human body. Accessibility is created through a proper street system and adequate means of transportation over such thoroughfares. If a property is too far from a bus line to be conveniently reached, its salability may be seriously affected, should one seek later to dispose of it. The owning of an automobile does not necessarily solve the problem, for a new buyer may not own a car, or a member of the household may not have one. If there is not adequate transportation, a future sale may be lost.

Are stores, schools, and churches within a reasonable distance of a home to be acquired?

If not, great inconvenience will be suffered, and the property may not be sold at a profit. On the other hand, too close proximity to such places sometimes affects its sale.

Are telephones and electricity for lighting available?

If not, the value of an improved property is certain to be affected. Telephones and electric lights are essential to common comfort in homes these days, and nearly everyone demands that they be available for use if needed.

Care should be taken to ascertain, if possible, whether the building to be acquired has been properly wired for electricity in conformity with good practice and the regulations of the local building code. Presence of temporary electric wire extensions and homemade fixtures may serve as a warning to look further for violations of the code and possible fire hazards.

Is television reception good?

In a day when practically every household has a television set (usually one color set and several smaller black and white), it certainly pays to find out about TV reception. Some localities require expensive antennas for good reception, while still others require the signals from the TV stations to be brought in by cable. Check out this factor carefully, because a home without good TV reception is a real "lemon" regardless of how fine it is in every other respect.

Is the roof of the building in good shape?

Poor workmanship, and the incessant wear and tear of the elements can be innocently hidden in a roof which needs repairing. If possible, determine the character of the roof of any building before buying it. This may seem a trivial thing, but replacing a roof is sometimes an expensive operation.

Are windows weatherstripped?

In cold climates this is important. Weatherstripped windows not only retain heat but they also keep out heat and dust as well as moisture in the form of excessive rain and snow.

Is the plaster cracked?

Defective workmanship in a building may be revealed through cracks in the plaster. The structure may have been "roughed in" during wet weather. When lumber later dried out, excessive contraction took place and plaster throughout the structure may have cracked badly. In a home this is far from desirable.

Is the heating and air-conditioning system adequate and in good repair?

In the modern space age, air-conditioning for most sections of the country has become almost as important as heating. Usually these modern systems work in unison within a single installation—the furnace and cooling coils are housed in the same unit while the compressor for the air-conditioning unit is somewhere outside the house. Furnaces usually last many years, but compressors usually have a life-expectancy of about five years. Thus, you should know how old the compressor is, or you may find that you will have to buy a new one a few mothes after acquiring the property.

You should always check the tonnage of the air-conditioning unit and ascertain whether it is capable of doing the job. Many people advertise their houses as "air-conditioned" when all they have is a window unit or two. Never be persuaded that a watercooled unit (utilizing evaporating water for the cooling process) is in any way comparable to the refrigerated air unit. It will be worthwhile to have an air-conditioning expert examine these facilities including the duct work because this is definitely a matter for experts, and a matter where a foolish mistake could be very costly.

Is the plumbing system in good repair, and is it modern?

You won't need to tear a building apart to determine this, but some casual glances may reveal the deficiencies in the plumbing of any structure. Many a buyer has discovered later that the supposed bargain he acquired contains leaking plumbing which ate up a great deal of money before being placed in a good state of repair. The plumbing system of any building should be carefully scrutinized before a deal is closed.

Particular attention should be directed to seeing that sinks, bathtubs and other fixtures have proper shut off valves, otherwise it may always be necessary to cut off the water supply at the street main in order to make even minor repairs which call for water to be turned off in any of the numerous faucets throughout the building.

Do the interior walls of the building indicate the presence of dampness?

Such a defect may be due to poor structural work or some other cause. Damp buildings are not healthy or pleasant to live in, and they should not knowingly be purchased. Great trouble may be encountered in curing the difficulty, and usually the effort is not worth while.

If farm property, is the land subject to overflow? Is it tilled? Has it been fertilized? Is the soil sweet and tillable? Is it underlaid with shale or rock? Is the territory subject to extended droughts? Have soil bank allotments been set up? Are there governmental crop restrictions or subsidies?

A whole chapter might be written on what to look for in buying a farm. Cheap land, merely because it is cheap, and has no other redeeming features, may be dear at any price. The greatest care should be exercised in buying land for the purpose of cultivating and raising crops. Many a city man has hurried to the country to buy a farm, noticed some attractive trees or a pretty view, and promptly signed up as a new owner. Later he has discovered many things he should have inquired about before buying. Often he quits and sells out, thoroughly discouraged and disgusted with rural life, largely because he did not take the proper precautions to make an investigation as to the merits of the land offered. He may discover, for instance, that what he thought was a lowland meadow in summer, is a dank swamp in the springtime, and that all he can raise is sourgrass. The land oftentimes is so wet and soggy that it cannot be plowed until midsummer, and crops seldom mature upon it. He may discover, in attempting to set out an orchard, that a foot and a half below the surface of what looks like a perfecty fertile field there is an underlying stratum of shale or rock that will not permit the roots of trees to penetrate it. He may find that it will be necessary to spend a small fortune in labor and materials to underdrain with tile every field he proposes to use. He may even find that, in going into a new country, the summers are excessively dry, droughts prevail, and that nothing ever matures to a state where it can be harvested and marketed.

Guidelines

Many a modest fortune has been lost or hopelessly wrecked through lack of careful inquiry. There are pitfalls for the unwary which may be avoided only through unceasing vigilance. Hence, it is wise in buying property to observe the following general conditions:

1. If at all possible, compel a seller to prove every claim made.
2. Don't be rushed headlong into a deal before being satisfied that every representation is correct.
3. If you are not qualified to pass upon matters which may be strange to you, take steps to secure proper advice from an unbiased third party, even to being prepared to pay for it. A little money spent this way may save much cash and trouble later.
4. Weigh well every argument why you should buy, and be thoroughly satisfied that what you do buy is substantially what you want and what you are paying for.
5. If not satisfied, have the courage to demand full information about any questionable feature. In many deals the things mentioned in this chapter will not present themselves. However, you should be properly posted so that if a problem appears, you are able to recognize it and protect yourself accordingly.

TWELVE

Residential Income Property
Investments

Income properties, embracing types
of multiple dwelling structures ranging from duplexes to large apartment
and hotel developments and condominiums, depend for their success as
investments upon three primary elements:

1. Location
2. Construction
3. Management

As a community develops from the stage of being a town and shows
signs of becoming a city, there appears a demand for multiple dwellings.
There are families that cannot afford to rent houses and furnish them, or
who find such quarters larger than they need. They prefer to rent
furnished or unfurnished suites, and the demand for such accommodations is met by the erection and operation of double houses, small apartments of four, six, eight, or more units, and condominiums. Later, as the
city grows and the demand continues to increase, larger apartment and
hotel properties are provided.

Modern suburban districts are developing their skylines too. But these high-rise buildings are not office buildings as in the downtown district of yesteryear. Rather, they are apartment and condominium complexes.

The condominium is an idea revived from many years back and has become a huge success. These apartment buildings are most often developed by some form of syndicate, and the apartments so developed are planned as the homesteads of the owners who are able to reap the benefits of apartment dwelling as well as of home ownership. It is often the case that some apartments are rented, and some are sold outright.[1]

Location

The question of location is a relative one. A good location for one type of building, catering to a certain rental demand, might be entirely inadequate to that required for another kind of accommodation. The success of any venture often depends upon the judgment exercised in choosing a location. It takes a considerable amount of knowledge of territories in general for one to make up his mind just where to establish his enterprises.

The first thing for a prospective builder, promoter, or owner to do is to make up his mind concerning the type of tenancy he wants to provide with accommodations. The lowest income group occupying multiple dwellings naturally pays low rent and does not always take the best care of property. The element of physical depreciation, wear and tear, is always greater among low-income renters than among the tenants who occupy higher-grade properties. Likewise, the loss through unpaid rentals may be higher in the low-income group. Offsetting this is the fact that there are a great many more tenants in this low-income group and the demand for suites will always be greater while loss from vacancies will be less. Services furnished need not be as elaborate, and the quarters themselves can be much less attractive and cost less.

Unfortunately, there are very few large and successful multiple dwelling developments provided for the low-income groups that are not associated with the idea of public aid through funds provided for slum clearance projects. For the most part buildings have run down from a higher class of occupancy and have finally wound up by taking in anyone who can continue to pay the ever-declining rents.

In recent years efforts on the part of governmental agencies have been directed toward the encouragement of large-scale multiple dwelling projects. These have started with praiseworthy hopes of furnishing excel-

---

[1] See Appendix for condominium forms.

lent accommodations in new buildings at considerably lower rentals than those charged in old run-down tenements. It has been altogether too frequently the case, however, that when such new projects were completed it was found to be necessary to charge much higher rents than at first announced and almost on a par, in many instances, with rentals charged for much finer and higher grade accommodations. The result has often been, therefore, that structures intended for low-income tenants have been filled with families of consiredably higher means, and the persons for whom relief was intended continue to inhabit the slums. Efforts to subsidize multiple housing developments so that the low-income tenant can really live in them have been made, but they are always subject to vehement protest from taxpayers who consider such procedure unfair. By and large, it seems likely that many of the low-income groups will continue to occupy run-down properties.

Nevertheless, low-income housing developments under government subsidy promise to be with us for a long time to come. In 1967 the census indicated that there were 22 million people living in slums while only 21 million were living on farms. The Department of Housing and Urban Development is speeding up the machinery for offering municipalities and various other govermental groups various helps in the process of clearing the slums. Most of these housing units are developed under non-profit "housing authorities."

The selection of a site will usually determine the class of structure to be erected upon it, for each neighborhood will meet a certain demand. Erecting a fine structure in a poor neighborhood that will not support it is just as foolish as erecting a cheap tenement in a fine neighborhood. A site should always be in conformity with the type of structure one wishes to build and own. If a mistake is made, the project will quite rapidly adjust itself to the type of tenancy the neighborhood demands. If too good a type of structure has been erected, lower rentals than those justified by the building's cost will be offered and paid. Of the two evils it is probably better to have a relatively cheap building in a good neighborhood than an expensive structure in a cheap district. Deviation to any great extent either way is unwise.

Construction

Construction will have a tendency to adjust itself to neighborhood levels. Building codes in most cities now require fairly good and uniform building construction. Most builders aim to make their apartments "ultra-modern" in that they install every new and useful device or piece of equipment to attract, serve, and please tenants. This includes swimming pools, color TV, automatic ice-makers, self-service elevators, and air-conditioning.

It is usually wise to have a multiple dwelling erected under the direction of a capable architect. He will save money by giving to the structure elements of design that only a trained student of construction can furnish. Through supervision he will see that a good construction job results, that architectural harmony prevails, and during progress of the work he will do much to expedite matters and complete work within reasonable time limits.

Changes in types of construction are constantly being made. New materials and equipment are incessantly appearing upon the market. These should be taken advantage of if they add to the service, appearance, and livability of a structure. General finish and workmanship should be on a par with the quality of the building to be constructed. If a $75 rental is expected from a unit, naturally it will not be finished to conform to another unit for which $150 is to be charged. There is such a thing as running up expense that will not be warranted by rentals to be received when the premises are occupied. An architect must keep his work and charges in full conformity with the income to be expected.

Management

When an apartment property is finally completed it becomes subject to, and definitely affected by, the element of management. If it is a small two-, four-, or six-family structure, it may well be handled by an owner since management problems in small properties are extensive. If it is a large and expensive property, then it will be necessary to place a capable manager in charge. There are many such managers now available in cities where these larger units exist.

Poor management will sometimes ruin an otherwise successful property. There may be a large number of fine units rented to excellent tenants, but if halls are left dirty, if employees become careless about their appearance, are uncivil and otherwise lack courtesy, if other essential details are neglected, it will not be long before tenants begin to move elsewhere. The most finely constructed and equipped apartment structure in the country may prove a financial failure under poor management.

Cleanliness and orderliness are important above all else. Keep floors well swept and polished. Renew decorations and window shades before they become worn. Keep the building in complete repair. Do not permit carpets, furniture, and equipment to become untidy and shabby. Proper upkeep of a property is not abnormally expensive, but it is one of the most important things that must be done if tenants are to remain happy and satisfied, and pay the rents demanded.

Two- and three-family structures are to be found in almost every city in the country. Some are old houses remodelled into two or more units. Many are occupied, in part, by their owners who secure rental from one or more of the suites to enable them to maintain the property and to meet interest charges, amortization of mortgage, and taxes.

Considerable saving can often be effected through two-family construction. Two five-room cottages on separate sites may cost $9,000 apiece, a total of $18,000. Yet two equally good five-room units may be built as parts of a duplex and completed for $15,500. In the latter instance the same land is used for both and the extra cost of one site is eliminated. There are fewer walls to build as the two units merge into each other. Likewise plumbing and wiring can be centralized and money saved there. Frequently half of a duplex will rent for just about as much as would a single family dwelling of the same size.

There must be a proper relationship between the price paid for a site and the cost of a building erected thereon. In properties totaling in cost over $60,000 the site should not cost, usually, more than about one-fourth of the amount expended for the structure. Over $60,000 the relative cost of the site will lessen as the size of the building increases. There is no exact ratio, but it is never wise to permit the land value to become too large a proportion of the enterprise. A $200,000 apartment structure might well be erected on a site costing, say, $35,000. If the structure is being included, the land cost can naturally go much higher.

Recognizing the fact that the demand for expensive accommodations is less than for cheaper ones, great care should be exercised in not over-building with higher priced units. It not only costs more to build the higher class buildings per rental unit, but it likewise is more expensive to furnish and operate them. There must be elevators, switchboards, day and night clerks, and managers in many instances.

In recent years there has been a distinct tendency to cut down the size of unfurnished flats in most cities. The call for six-, eight-, and ten-room suites in apartment buildings is lessening constantly, except possibly in New York. When accommodations under four or five rooms are offered, the general practice is to furnish them. Many buildings filled with "singles" and "doubles" have no larger units. A single consists of a good-sized living room, with an in-a-door bed, a combination kitchen-dinette, and a nicely equipped bathroom. A double has the same rooms and also a separate bedroom equipped with twin beds or a single double bed.

Improvements in architectural practices in recent years have had a tendency to disguise multiple dwelling units and in many instances make them look like large, private dwellings. This is particularly true of two- and four-unit buildings which often can scarcely be distinguished from private residences. There has been an inclination on the part of some architects to use new and rather startling styles of modernistic architecture, but this has been checked in many instances by a disinclination on the part of mortgage concerns to finance such a structure on the assumption that it is often difficult, if not impossible, to resell some of these unusual architectural monstrosities.

In many cities codes require that all buildings higher than three stories be equipped with elevators. These may be self-operated or run by elevator operators. This naturally adds expense to building maintenance. There seems to be a distinct disinclination on the part of most tenants to climb more than two flights of stairs. In those cities where four-story buildings operate without elevators, the rentals on the upper floors are always considerably lower than for floors below. Then again, most building codes in cities require fireproof or semi-fireproof construction for all buildings more than three stories in height. This adds very definitely to costs.

Automobile congestion in large cities has, in recent years, resulted in building code provisions requiring that a garage be furnished with every apartment containing a kitchen accommodation. This means that considerably larger land sites must be provided. Congestion of streets in apartment house neighborhoods in large cities, due to the number of cars owned by tenants who have no place to park them, has become a serious matter, and recent provisions that garages must be built with all new buildings have been the result. This garage rule does not apply to hotels.

Apartment house ownership is a fertile income-bearing field. Such structures earn the largest returns the first five or six years of their lives. As far as an increase in land values is concerned, a site under an apartment building becomes fixed in value the day the land is improved and it seldom increases. Likewise, the building suffers depreciation through obsolescence the day it goes into service. What a property earns must come through rents and not increment in property values. There are many hazards in this field, and the experienced operator usually maintains that if he does not earn 12 per cent net on his investment annually he is not getting all that is coming to him. In good times such properties may earn much more; in dull times they undoubtedly earn less.

A type of multiple housing which may be found in some of the larger cities is known as the bungalow court. This consists of a series of small three-, four-, or five-room cottages grouped on a large site. These units have the advantage of more privacy than the usual apartment house affords. They also have some land about them that may be gardened if tenants desire. These bungalows often bring more rental than do similar sized apartments, but a disadvantage is that they cost more to produce per rental unit and also cost considerably more to maintain. Land taxes are usually higher.

One of the hottest investment opportunities is the motel. With tourism at an all-time high, it seems that there is no end in sight for the need for accommodations for the traveler. To be competitive, the motel must be modernistic in design and equipped with the very latest building paraphernalia, including television in every unit. Where these motels prosper there is great danger competition may become so keen that their building is overdone and profitable operation thereby ruined. In investigating such a project, an investor should take great pains to ascertain the percentage of vacancy throughout the year. It may be as high as 50 per cent or even higher. Motel enterprises may be profitable investments. Occasionally they become liabilities to their owners.

Expert appraisers usually give apartment properties an economic life of from thirty to forty years. Of course, fading values in this class of property, as in other, may be recaptured by careful maintenance, rebuilding, and refurnishing periodically. From a mere physical standpoint, many hotel and apartment buildings might be sound for one hundred years, but it is obsolesence that bears down on a property after fifteen, twenty, or twenty-five years. A program of complete remodelling and refurnishing may carry the enterprise on for fifty or sixty years. Always remember that physical real estate improvements wear out. Only the land is imperishable, although its utility may change from neighborhood influences steadily at work throughout the years.

A good investment may occasionally be created by purchasing a large, well-located house and remodelling it into two or three living units. Frequently, the site alone is worth the purchase price. Considerable money must be spent in remodelling and rebuilding, but the owner will have a place to live and one or two rental units to help carry the property.

Some operators in recent years have sought out old multiple unit structures that remained in well-located areas. These have been bought cheaply and remodelled and restyled throughout. Such structures have been soundly built but have become outmoded—suffering from obsolescence, as the appraiser terms it. Their rent earning capacity has sagged, and possibly a lower-income type of tenant has taken possession. Completely overhauled rentals often can be raised and the property revived. In years to come there will be much similar activity, particularly as properties begin to wear out and need expert attention.

Little need be said about the gigantic apartment house developments of New York, Chicago, Washington, and Los Angeles because these are operations the cost of which run into the millions, promoted by experts of long standing. The man who intends to make it his business to promote and build apartment properties on a big scale might do well to take a long swing about the country and make a study of the methods followed in connection with many of these huge operations. Large insurance companies are directly sponsoring and financing some huge developments in New York, Los Angeles, and elsewhere, feeling they can earn larger returns on their funds than by spreading them in loans on property. Such action speaks well for the stability of this form of investment, on which millions have been made in the past and on which doubtless equally large fortunes will be made in the future.

There always remains the problem as to whether a prospective owner should build a new property or acquire one already in operation. Only a survey of the field will determine this. With the unionization of labor throughout America, building costs have gone up. It might be better in some cities to search out a good property, purchase it, and modernize it if need be, reestablishing it on a higher earning basis. In another city, if the need for new apartment accommodations seems apparent it might be wise to build. Only familiarity with a city and its conditions can reveal this.

Summarizing:
1. Before buying or building, study your city, its needs for apartment accommodations and the trends of residential development.
2. Preferably deal through a wise and experienced broker who knows the apartment house field. His guidance will be invaluable and he will save you many times any commission he may get for selling you a property.
3. Remember the three important factors: (1) Location; (2) Construction; (3) Management.

4. See that the cost of a site is in reasonable proportion to the amount to be spent for a building.

5. Ascertain, at the outset, the size and general character of the investment you wish to establish and then explore the field.

6. Determine whether it may not be wise to buy an established building and revitalize it rather than go to the trouble and expense of erecting a new one.

7. Remember that new apartments make their greatest profits in the first five or six years and then deteriorate. Also that complete remodelling and refurnishing may make them almost as good as new. The wise operator should set up a reserve to do this work periodically if he intends to retain a property over a long period of years.

8. Don't overextend yourself. Don't get too much of one kind of property. Pare down your encumbrances steadily so that when a business recession appears you can be as free from debt as possible. More investors have been ruined by being overtaken by debt in a recession than in almost any other way.

THIRTEEN

Investment Merits of Business Property

Business property, especially that situated in outlying business shopping centers always has been, and probably will remain, the highest type of real estate investment.

More relative value is represented in this kind of real estate than in any other. Values in the downtown sections of large cities, and many smaller ones, extend to fabulous figures, sometimes as high as $50,000 per foot front. Even in outlying business areas land values will often reach several thousand dollars per foot front for choice locations.

High-powered retail organizations such as those represented by large department stores in which millions of dollars are sometimes invested, as well as outstanding stores that are units of nation-wide chains, bid for the best locations, where the greatest number of customers can be attracted and where the highest volume of retail sales may be registered.

Rental income

Rent is a relative proposition. If a merchant decides that he can pay six or seven per cent of his gross sales income as rent, there is no limit to the amount of rent he can and will pay if he can still maintain the ratio to his gross income. If a merchant can establish a record of $100,000 in retail sales for a year, he has no hesitancy in agreeing to pay $6,000 annually in rent. If a larger establishment can sell $1,000,000 worth of goods a year, a rental of $60,000 is reasonable. The subject of the relative amount of rent a merchant can afford to pay has been studied quite extensively by real estate experts. It varies between cities as well as with the type of business.[1]

Many large downtown business properties are owned by corporations, that form of holding title being in the favor of the large interests involved. Valuable real estate holdings are often favored by estates and occasionally by well-to-do individuals who have faith in commercial realty as a form of investment. In outlying areas, however, individual ownership is more generally the rule, and when properly selected and managed, such real estate is often found to be more profitable than many a gold mine.

Depression years saw visible shrinkage in downtown values in many cities, yet the depression was far less than in most forms of investment, particularly stocks and bonds. Rentals were curtailed in many cities, but for the most part the central business areas survived remarkably well. With the coming of better times rentals again advanced. Therewith, it became necessary for many owners to modernize their properties to enable them to get the most income from them. Business buildings, like all forms of physical property, wear out. Worse, they suffer keenly from obsolescence or out-of-dateness, which, if not remedied, slowly throttles their earning capacity. Vast rehabilitation activities in recent years have been apparent in the downtown sections of most cities. Face lifting and remodelling of buildings in shopping centers has been equally apparent. A wise investor, looking for a bargain, can often spot a property which needs only a major remodelling operation to make it pay handsome returns.

Co-operative efforts, promoted by live brokers, often result in the syndicating of retail properties which are promptly worked over into modern units and again occupied at increased rentals. Such developments in past years have been sponsored by outstanding promotional enterprises such as the Fifty Associates Co. of Toledo and Boston; the American Real Estate Co. of New York; the Trustees Companies of Seattle, Portland, Los Angeles, and many others. These were stock companies which, promoted under expert guidance, followed a general program of selecting well-located business properties, rebuilding or remodelling them, and then

---

[1] See Appendix for percentage of rents to gross sales.

filling them with new aggressive merchandising outfits which were able to pay big rents and thereby greatly increase property values. Possibilities of this kind may be found in most cities throughout the country all of the time.

The investor who desires to enter this business property field can do no better than to select a business property broker in the city in which he desires to operate and then to examine the downtown and outlying sections, seeking those spots which seem to offer the most promise. These may not necessarily appear to be the most attractive as of the moment. They, in all probability, need a better type of building than currently exists to enable them to attain their highest and best use. They should certainly be in the pathway of future business development to insure them long life, and they should have inherent in them all the virtues of first-class business property investments. Frequently all that is necessary is to get rid of tenants, put a complete new front on an existing building, modernize its interior somewhat, and then proceed to select new tenants who belong in that particular location. Often an enterprise of this kind will prove a magnet in drawing the best business district toward it, being engulfed and uplifted in the course of the operation, with values magnified over the course of a few years.

Business properties, as such, include not only the high-powered retail establishments to be found in any live community, but also office buildings, theaters, amusement enterprises of all kinds, garages, hotels, and so forth. They may be bought or sold outright, leased for terms of five, ten, or twenty years, or for ninety-nine years. To buy outright often involves the expenditure of large sums of money. To lease for short terms means that it may be difficult sometimes to amortize building improvements over the term of the lease. To lease for ninety-nine years sometimes requires the expenditure of considerable sums for building improvements and the assuming of rental obligations which extend far beyond the life of the person signing the lease. All have their merits—*also their hazards.* The investor must recognize what they are and decide the manner in which he intends to proceed..

Location

Just how is an investor to ascertain what is the most advantageous location in which to place his funds? Here again reliance must be placed on a seasoned Realtor who has had long and wide experience in this field. Such a Realtor will have been a student who has been tracing the trends of the city's growth for years, examining the earning capacities of a wide variety of individual properties, and who knows the background of individual ownerships so that, when a property is placed on the market, it can be acquired at a satisfactory price for a new owner to proceed to revamp the premises for a higher and better use and incidentally increase its income and value.

Traffic counts are sometimes resorted to for ascertaining the volume of pedestrian traffic. A large number of individuals passing a given point may give certain evidence that a property is well-located, but if the passers-by do not enter the stores and purchase, such traffic is of questionable value to merchants. Crowds hurrying to railway stations, piers, public buildings and places of amusement must be studied closely to ascertain whether they will enhance a property's value by patronizing a tenant doing business there. Traffic counts have their value and are worthwhile in some instances, but sometimes they do not indicate faithfully all of the facts unless they are made by operators who understand the merits and weaknesses. Traffic counts are usually taken between 10 and 11:30 A.M. and between 2 and 4:30 P.M. Restaurant operators will sometimes count all day, figuring that they will attract a proportion of any traffic going by. If a district is being tested for a men's store only men are counted. If for a women's enterprise only the women are checked and these are analyzed as to age, type, income, character of social importance, and so forth.

Availability of tenants

An investor, before acquiring business property, likes to be convinced that tenants are available for expensive premises when such are acquired and conditioned for retail use. The principal and best rent-paying tenants are those representing chain store enterprises. Chain store merchandising has come to stay in America, despite its effect upon individual shopkeepers and the efforts of politicians to kill the chains through heavy taxation and regulatory measures. The chains are always competing with each other in 100 per cent retail districts for locations which they rent at figures no other type of merchant will attempt. The chains usually want ten-year leases, often longer, and on a percentage basis of their gross sales. They will promptly pay liberal rents, will not pioneer in new districts except in unusual instances, will install costly improvements in the way of fixtures and equipment and will definitely enhance a property's value through their occupancy.

The hottest business venture of the last few years has been the discount house These are to all practical purposes, department stores which occupy suburban sites for the most part where acres of parking space are available. The secret of these enterprises is their high volume, which gives them the possibility of cutting prices considerably below that which smaller stores can afford. Many of these are chains, but some are locally owned.

Aside from chain store tenants, there are many individual merchants who are responsible and who are always eager to secure first-class accommodations, paying current rents for them. Such merchants also like to operate on percentage leases, but they sometimes present problems to the property owner since it is sometimes harder to check on his sales than the chain store lessee. The chains have worked out elaborate sealed cash register systems which assure a landlord that he is receiving his rental on a percentage basis of the actual business done

The real estate investor who combines the instinct for selecting logical locations and the promotional ability to follow through with buying and improving such choice locations is the investor who usually makes the most money in the realty field. Through long experience and the exercising of mature judgment, he will unerringly be drawn to a section of a downtown area or some suburban shopping center in the outlying section of a city and realize that a certain piece of property has a future if treated in a definite manner. He will study the problem carefully and then act. A site is acquired, old equipment removed or revamped for new and better uses, and finally filled with rent-paying tenants who place the stamp of success upon the venture. A property which may have cost $50,000 or $75,000 is retained as an investment or sold at a handsome profit, and the funds worked over into another deal.

An operator in business property must have extensive knowledge and experience about financing such enterprises unless he has sufficient money to handle the deal himself in its entirety, which is seldom the case. Nor is this often desirable, as the property probably has to be financed anyway before it is sold.

In developing business property an operator must acquire a wide range of information about the requirements of different types of tenants. A department store usually needs several acres of space, often in a building five or six stories in height. In most instances such an owner will try to develop his own premises rather than rent them. The chain stores operating on a nation-wide basis prefer usually to rent. Modern variety stores usually demand a width of 100 feet and a depth of about 150 feet, if possible.

Stores catering to women's and men's wear of all kinds, grocery chains as well as hardware stores, restaurants, and similar enterprises require facilities for parking automobiles, which has greatly complicated the problem of existing merchants in practically all cities. More and more the use of the automobile is increasing, and one can only speculate as to the number to be found in use ten, twenty or thirty years hence. Parking space therefore is absolutely essential for use in connection with most retail stores. This can be provided in new building enterprises, but the problem has not as yet been solved in regard to stores which were erected some years ago. Co-operative efforts sometimes result in the acquiring of vacant parking spaces nearby. In other instances, parking operators are subsidized by merchants agreeing to pay for customers parking up to a certain length of time. A shrewd investor will always geep this important subject of auto parking in mind when considering the acquiring of a property. It may bear no important relation to his project in some instances, while in others parking facilities may be most necessary if an enterprise is to prove successful.

An investor will do well to remember that his principal rent-producing space is situated directly on the ground floor, except in times of booms when rentals may ascend to such abnormal figures that business tenants, in self-protection, are forced to occupy basements or second-floor spaces. Basements can occasionally be rented for poolrooms or storage purposes, but in ordinary times basements often remain vacant. After the Cuban crisis in 1962, practically every available basement was stocked as a fall-out shelter by Civil Defense.

Second-floor space is suitable to some extent for office use, beauty parlors, and so forth, but retailing cannot be very well conducted there because customers seem to have a distinct aversion to climbing stairs except when bargains are available or there are escalators.

From time to time there seem to be epidemics of different types of business property developments. Some years ago it was service stations. Then came the miniature golf courses, followed by roller skating rinks, later by ice rinks. Then came a period of building bowling alleys with billiard rooms. The old time corner drive-in market with a butcher, grocer, and vegetable dealer was succeeded by supermarket development. Remember the established principle applicable to all of these splurges in building promotion: "Exorbitant profits breed ruinous competition!" When a rush of building activity associates itself with any particular kind of patronage, always keep an eye to windward on such developments and *get out* of the enterprise if competition threatens a collapse or at least a definite lowering in rental returns. The investor who can, through far-sightedness, realize when some influence is going to affect a property in an unfavorable manner, will have a chance to dispose of it or alter it before the change occurs and probably save himself a considerable part of his investment.

Recent years have seen a big growth in the number of movie theaters throughout the country. With the legitimate theater succumbing to vaude-ville, which later was driven out by the movies, many theaters underwent changes in use, some of them winding up as garages or storage warehouses. Some still endure and have occasional use or have been modernized for use by the present-day moving picture business. An old-time theater with its towering stage in the rear to accommodate scenery and rows of elabo-rate boxes as each side of the auditorium costs several times as much as the new compact modern movie seating the same number of persons.

While theatrical enterprises and the premises they occupy are of considerable importance from a real estate standpoint, an investor should always remember that such buildings are, for the most part, single-purpose structures, and that once the demand for an individual enterprise begins to dwindle, the value of the land involved also begins to spiral downwards. There is nothing quite so hard to rent or sell as an old-time theater which has seen its usefulness disappear, while the building still retains a large element of value from the mere standpoint of reproduction cost. Only a major operation in remodelling will solve the problem, and frequently such an expenditure is not justifiable.

In sections of a city which are going through a transitory stage from average utility to that of locations for high-powered retail trade, the leasing of vacant corners for service station purposes is often profitable. Leases of five or ten years sometimes permit corners to "ripen" in loca-tion and use value so that later they may be the sites of important retail enterprises, in the meantime earning substantial returns from responsible tenants. Corners at crossroad intersections of rapidly developing vehicular highways may, in the course of a few years, develop from mediocre service station sites into sites for large important business structures.

In this day of super-highways, freeways, and controlled-access high-ways the investor cannot simply think in terms of acquiring highway frontage property or even corner properties where two highways join

It is often true that an investor will rush out to these places and buy, only to find that the particular traffic flow pattern ruins his chances of success. With controlled-access roads such as our interstate highway system, properties which border these access roads are of relatively little value unless an exit is conveniently located.

To be successful in acquiring business properties on highways, the investor must study every detail of the highway plan; he cannot afford to guess about it, or he will be left high and dry with the traffic whizzing by and drivers unable to stop even if they wished.

Some shrewd investors make it a business of teaming up with a practical real estate man of experience and standing. They supply the money and the real estate man supplies the opportunities and often the brains to develop them. Sometimes this takes the form of a syndicate, or in other instances a corporation, where individual financing is more or less limited. The good business "buys" come to the attention of the broker first. If he engages in operating as well as in brokerage work, he may pick these offerings up himself. If he is unable to do so, he will refer them to some wide-awake investor who is waiting for a broker to show him a way to make money and to take the broker in on the deal if the latter cares to join. The practical knowledge of an all-round real estate man is often extensive and of unusual value to the investor, particularly if the latter is not thoroughly seasoned in all of the details of real estate promotion.

Real estate brokers who have become wealthy have graduated from brokers to operators. Most brokerage businesses pay only a good living to those engaged in them. The profitable business is in buying and selling. If a broker-operator, or an investor associated with him, has access to all of the good buys which drift from time to time into a well-organized and conducted realty office, there will be found many excellent opportunities for profitable placement of funds. When a recession does occur, however, the broker or investor who engages in more or less speculative enterprises should watch carefully to see that he is not left with properties on his hands which are not thoroughly seasoned and fully paid for.

A real estate operator, necessarily a student of trends, will always make it his duty to watch the drift of retail business. Business periodically shifts to new locations in almost every growing city. If the operator can detect the direction and speed of such movement and intercept it with worthwhile purchases of properties which will later ripen, he will be on the high road to financial success. It takes courage and resourcefulness to follow the trend and take advantage of it, but that is the operator's business and chance for profit.

Likewise, the real estate oroker is the most likely person to develop into a speculative operator. To own a property is an advantage, if it has been rightly bought. If a broker has confidence enough in property to offer it to a client, he should have just as much confidence in buying it himself, if he can do so. Of course, no broker can buy all of the bargains which come to his attention. He can find choice ones from time to time, however, to make operating a most profitable sideline.

Elements of success

When there is an ascending market in real estate, an operator should not be afraid of a mortgage on income-bearing property which has seasoned sufficiently to be in a position to carry itself and pay a profit to the owner. While one should not become a gambler, it is wise to have faith enough to proceed calmly under the burden of a reasonable encumbrance. As the ascending market begins to level off, which usually takes several years, then is the time to get the property as nearly clear from debt as possible so that if a recession is encountered, the earning power will carry it through the low ebb.

A real estate investor to succeed, therefore, should:

1. Be a keen student of real estate, particularly of property development trends and uses. He should read everything available on real estate.
2. Have sufficient funds to make substantial payments even if he finds it advantageous to encumber the property he is buying.
3. Be willing to let time elapse so that the property will ripen for use before he seeks to sell it.
4. If not thoroughly seasoned in real estate investment technique, be wise enough to associate himself with a practical real estate broker of experience and standing.
5. Use his imagination in ferreting out possible uses for property which the average owner is overlooking.
6. Watch for technological and business changes which may result in a demand for real estate wherein it becomes employed for higher and better uses, thereby increasing the value.
7. Have the courage of his convictions and nerve to follow them through to logical conclusions.
8. Spread his investment funds into several ventures rather than putting all of his eggs in one basket.
9. Watch the cycle of real estate activity and know when values are increasing and when, possibly, a recession may occur.
10. Not be afraid to take a profit when a fair opportunity occurs. Thousands of greedy owners are caught by recessions with

properties on their hands which they could have sold at fancy profits if they had not demanded impossible prices.

11. Creep before he walks. He should win his spurs by consummating small deals before plunging into the big ones which take more money, involve greater risks, and require more skill and experience.

12. Be willing, occasionally, to take a chance—but a smart one!

FOURTEEN

Profits in Non-Urban Real Estate

Land situated on the circumference of a growing city advances most in value. Property lying in between, while not always stagnant, is often sluggish in its movement, and the increment to be realized from it usually is less.

On the outskirts there usually is activity in promoting new subdivisions, creation of new business districts, and the gradual absorption of farm land for the further expansion of a city. This trend of suburban development reflects itself out for miles beyond the limits of a town or city. The size of a city and the rapidity of its growth will influence the extent of the demand for suburban property.

Suburban acreage has made fortunes for men of vision who have gone out in advance of the demand, secured possession of well-located tracts, and then held tl.em until the insistent call for subdivision or business has made itself felt. Land bought at from $200 to $1,000 per acre in or near large cities and held for investment frequently has sold at prices ranging from $3,000 to $5,000 per acre a few years later.

Highway acreage

Buy such land on main, heavily traveled highways if it is possible. If improved transportation facilities extend out at some future day, so much the better.

Be sure to make proper inquiry concerning the nature of future highway improvements alongside the property you may acquire. Many people are misled, thinking that a super highway by its very nature provides contiguous properties with ready access. On controlled access roads, traffic can leave the mainstreams only at designated exits. Then too, a cloverleaf or a multi-level intersection may leave your property stranded forty or fifty feet below the elevated traffic.

A variety of means have been taken by owners to make property on such main highways help to carry itself. Sometimes a gardener is given a lease on the land, if suitable for such purposes. Occasionally a greenhouse development will help carry such land for a few years. Frequently there is an opportunity on corner properties to make leases for service station purposes. An old dwelling may be rented for a suburban roadhouse, dance hall, or restaurant. In some cities such land has been made to pay its carrying charges by the building of tracks for horse and auto races. Such enterprises must be conveniently located to cities, but cannot indefinitely afford the investment necessary as land becomes increasingly valuable for residential, business and manufacturing purposes.

Recreational land

Devoting attractively situated land to use as summer camp sites is now common in many localities near cities. For a comparatively small rental, a camper is permitted to erect his tent and use the land for several months during the summer season. This brings in a small revenue which helps to pay carrying expenses of land.

A popular method for holding land for future development is to acquire a large tract, organize a golf club, and lease the land for a term of years. Cases may be cited where groups of investors have formed golf clubs, invited in their friends, used close-in acreage for a few years, and following the development of such land with homes, have acquired other tracts farther out in the country for new club sites.

One subdivider has promoted a lake front development some miles distant from a large city, where hundreds of lots were sold in conjunction with the opening of an eighteen hole golf course. This course is to exist for a term of years. The subdivider is then at liberty to cut it into home sites if he desires to do so. The golf club is the attraction which really is selling the proposition, and the subdivider will, through the golf club membership dues, easily carry the land until there is a demand for its more intensive utilization.

Farm land

Small farms ranging from five to twenty acres, if conveniently situated and in the line of a city's development, may profitably be acquired and held until such a time as they can be subdivided for the erection of homes The carrying charges on such properties usually are much less than the increase which comes in the value of the land each year. When it is remembered that an acre of land can be cut into three or four ordinary sized city lots, the selling value of such property, when properly improved, readily can be recognized.

Ordinary country land, purchased by one who expects to operate a farm as a going concern, must be bought on an earning basis. The price paid must represent an amount equal to the capitalized yearly income of such a property. During World War II, when foodstuffs were in great demand and high prices were being paid, farm sales were brisk and high land prices prevailed. Immediately following the war, when the demand for food for export to foreign countries dropped off, the price of farm land sagged, although the drop was temporary. All of this indicates that a farm is currently worth a price on which an investment return can be earned.

Nearly everyone, at some period in his life, longs to own a farm. We have suffered from the "farm bug" ourselves and have been through the mill. A farm of fifteen acres, six or seven miles beyond the limits of the city, was acquired at $125 an acre. Seven years later, after a fine brick pavement had linked the farm with the city, it was sold at $600 per acre, plus a profit on the improvements which had been added to the property. The place was sold at that particular time, not because of the profit offered, but because a questionable development was projected nearby. It was a case of knowing when to sell.

So much depends upon the individual character of a property its surroundings, price, and availability for future city development, that it ıs difficult to give other than very general advice regarding the purchase of farm land. The chief difficulty with outlying property is tha it is subject to no restrictions worth mentioning. One can have very little knowledge as to the probable character of development which may come five, ten, or fifteen years later. The neighborhood may become an exclusive one, or it may degenerate into a very commonplace sort of section. One must use his own judgment in this respect and try to visualize the future. The better the class of development it promises to be, the more you will have to pay for the land when you buy it, but the more you will likely realize from its resale at a future date.

Effort has been directed in recent years toward the orderly development of suburban territory. Groups of property owners controlling land near growing cities have followed a plan of incorporating a village covering a considerable area of suburban land. Following incorporation, an engineer is engaged who carefully plats out the entire area included within the village limits. Streets are laid out on paper, having in mind the best utility of the land concerned. These plans are definitely adopted, and property owners in selling their land know exactly what can be done in the way of future development. This immeasurably improves the territory and results eventually in a much higher type of development than would be enjoyed if a definite platting plan had not been followed..

One man who has made considerable money by acquiring and selling farm lands near a large city has followed two definite plans. In one instance, he buys land in considerable quantities, assembling several adjoining large farms in some instances. He plants fruit trees, places a superintendent in charge, and after several years they come to a bearing state, thus providing a revenue to carry expenses Another plan, which he has found quite successful, is unique. He will note a farm attractively located and in the central pathway of development. He will inquire from the owner the price wanted for it. The owner, in all probability, will ask somewhat more than the land is worth. The investor then suggests to the land owner that an option for five years be given at the price quoted, the investor agreeing to pay all taxes on the property. This sounds attractive to the farmer because not only is he promised a higher rate of return in five years than he is entitled to at the time the option is given, but also he is relieved of the necessity of paying taxes. The farmer overlooks the fact that the increment to the land in five years will doubtless be much greater than the price he has asked. When the five years expire, the investor arranges to assume ownership of the land if he has not already contracted to sell it to someone else at a substantial profit.

If you desire a lot on which to build a modest home, don't go way out in the country to buy it just because the lot happens to be cheap. In all probability, it is dear at the price you are paying for it. To live comfortably, a homeowner requires water, sewer, electric light, gas, and other conveniences. Why not pay a little more money for land which has these facilities rather than acquire a lot in a half-baked subdivision which, in all probability will afford but a scant return on the investment if at some future time you desire to sell.

Remember that it ordinarily costs no more to erect a home on a well-located city lot than it does out beyond the city limits, where few comforts are obtainable. Many a man answers a call to the country when in reality he should stay right in the city. It costs money to own and pay the carrying charges on land and to install new improvements on land away from city development. Unless you want to let yourself in for possible hardship and serious inconvenience, be wary about rushing out into the country.

This leads to a brief consideration of that more or less fortunate type known as "gentlemen farmers." You know the brand. It is represented in the story of such an individual who bought a fine hog in April for $16. He sold it in October for $18.

"Why, you darn fool," exclaimed a friend on hearing of the incident. "What did you do that for?"

"Well," said the gentleman farmer, "I had the use of it all summer, didn't I?"

Many wealthy men take a whirl at the game. They buy expensive land, often paying excessive prices for it, erect fine buildings, secure high-grade livestock, drift along for two or three years until they become amazed at the cost of their hobby, and then pass the property or to another gentleman farmer who proceeds to learn his lesson.

These men often do a great deal of good in raising crop and breeding standards and in setting examples to other farmers in keeping their properties in fine shape. They seldom make any money at the business. If you would be a gentleman farmer, go into the project with your eyes and pocketbook wide open. The farm will last just as long as your money.

Let it not be understood that it is impossible to make money in farming. The exception will be found in the man especially fitted by education, training, and environment who fits into the picture, likes his work, and is successful in the farming business just as he would be in any other walk of life.

It is also true that in the last twenty years, farming in some sections of the country has become big business with the owner-manager sometimes knowing little or nothing of the actual mechanics of growing crops. Instead he is a businessman who employs well-trained foremen to operate his extensive acreage. Success in farming has become not less a matter of growing crops, but certainly it has become more a matter of marketing these crops.

Special uses

One would scarcely think it possible to make money in cemeteries, yet such developments when properly managed and when there is real need for them prove quite successful. A large acreage is bought at a comparatively low price, cut into very small lots, and sold over a period of years. Mausoleums are erected, and crypts are sold or rented, giving additional revenue. Successful cemetery enterprises have been promoted in many sections of the country. If asked to participate in such a plan, investigate thoroughly.

Summer resorts, established at particularly favorable points, have been instrumental in some instances in returning substantial profits to their promoters. Those resorts which have water facilities of some sort usually prosper most, for in the summer season people like to be near the water. Such enterprises can be made more profitable when a subdivision is promoted in conjunction with them. Examples of such developments may be found around small inland lakes, situated not far from the larger cities of the country. Here amusement features are provided, hotels and cottages are erected, and a thriving business is done during the summer season not only in catering to those who come for just a few days' recreation, and who for the most part live in hotels, but also those more permanent patrons who buy or build cottages, and return year after year to meet old friends and neighbors.

FIFTEEN

Investing in Vacant Lots

Money can be made by investing in well-located vacant lots. Incidentally, money can be lost in buying *certain types* of vacant lots. Any non-income producing property can be either an asset or a liability, depending upon the ingenuity and acumen of its owner. A merchant may have a fine line of merchandise on his shelves, but if he foolishly locks his doors and goes away for a six months' vacation, he cannot expect to show a profit on his balance sheet at the end of the year. There is a fundamental difference between the commodity under discussion and the merchandise of the average storekeeper. Vacant lots are generally situated in or near a growing city and increase in value commensurate with growth in population, whereas the average nationally advertised staple merchandise brings as high a price in Rising Sun, Kentucky, as in Chicago.

How lots are created

In discussing the question of making money by investing in vacant lots, let it be assumed that the examples which are cited are in a typical large city. Acreage is acquired by a subdividing company, allotted into restricted residential lots and sold in an intensive campaign by salesmen who canvass selected lists, or who canvass from door to door. The retail

113

selling price of lots is usually figured on the rule of three, or four to one—
that is, the entire tract is marked for three or four times the cost of the
original acreage, assuming that the subdividing company has not paid an
exorbitant price for its acreage, but has wisely bought property that is
accessible to transportation, or in line with future transportation extensions.

The majority of the lots will be sold on land contracts, with a cash
payment of from ten to twenty-five per cent, the balance to be paid in
monthly installments of one or two per cent of the sale price. This payment sometimes includes interest on the deferred balance, or the interest
is payable at semi-annual periods, in addition to monthly payments. What
is the possibility of making a profit from a lot so purchased? There, of
course, will be a wide difference of opinion.

Proper management

By proper management, a profit can be realized from such a purchase. But what is meant by proper management? It means the exercising
of sound business judgment, the same as is required in the management of
any merchandising business. The selling prices of lots in a new subdivision
are generally at figures which represent all the traffic will bear, because
there is considerable expense entailed for advertising and selling costs,
including commissions to salesmen, sales superintendents, general managers, collection costs, shrinkage due to defaulted payments, mortgage
financing costs, installation of improvements, and other expenses. Consequently, the purchaser of such a vacant lot must not expect to make a
profit immediately. He should look at his investment as a long compulsory
savings enterprise, just as he would regard the purchase of savings and
loan stock or life insurance. He should not be carried away by the enthusiasm of some "high-pressure" salesman into the belief that his particular
lot is going to be resold in three or six months at a handsome profit. It
simply is not being done, except in the isolated case where some unlooked-
for public improvement brings a rush of people into a neighborhood. In
this discussion, only the average case is considered.

Factors that effect value

Experience has shown that the chief factor creating increases in value
in vacant lots is the arrival in the locality of people and houses. Transportation facilities and schools themselves do not make values or create
population. Every new house erected on a street adds a certain definite
value to every vacant lot in the block. Experience has also shown that the

average new subdivision requires a period of from four to eight years from the time it is originally marketed before resale of individual lots will show much of a profit to an owner.

The first several years after a subdivision is placed on the market, the individual lot owner is confronted with competition on the part of the allotment company. It has the remaining unsold lots which it can continue to offer at prices somewhat below what the individual owner can quote.

The average buyer does not care to pioneer. He likes to be where other people are located, and consequently he waits until a few houses have been built in a neighborhood before he makes his selection of a homesite.

A striking analogy can be made between vacant lots and children. You cannot expect a boy of tender years to do a man's work. Neither can you expect a lot of tender years to pay you a profit such as you might expect from a mature piece of property. The problem therefore resolves itself into the question of analyzing your merchandise to determine the proper selling time to get a maximum profit. It is necessary, too, to analyze local conditions to determine just when is the adolescent period of your property, so that you will not be foolish enough to carry it through into the period of final maturity, or even past the time when you should realize your maximum profit.

Like the youth who is still in school, your vacant lot is a constant expense, because of the ever-present tax and interest expense. Special assessments develop for street paving, sewer and sidewalk construction, and sometimes discourage the lot owner from persisting in the completion of payments on his contract. Often he becomes so burdened with other responsibilities that he sells the property at a sacrifice to get rid of the millstone around his neck. Do you give away your boy just because he is expensive to maintain? Not at all! There is a personal element entering into that problem which makes you put your shoulder to the wheel to enable the boy to complete his education. Then he goes to work with the enthusiasm and energy of youth, because he has been managed and directed properly. Do the same for your vacant lot, and it should pay you a profit.

When to buy and sell

There is always a time to buy and a time to sell. Most of the big things in life come from small beginnings. It is an interesting fact that many a wealthy owner of real estate got his start through acquiring, by compulsory saving, a small equity in a vacant lot which, when sold, gave him working capital for other and larger real estate investments. In the course of years he may have sold the lot at actual cost, but nevertheless he acquired a habit of thrift through his compulsory saving enterprise, which taught him the rudiments of operating in real estate.

Now, let it be assumed that you have a couple of thousand dollars in the bank with which to buy a piece of property. You inspect several income-producing properties, but are overwhelmed by the burden of mortgages that must be assumed in the event of purchase, so you turn your attention to a well-located vacant lot in a fairly active section. To buy wisely one should study the flow of demand in the general territory and analyze sales and transfers to determine where the buying is. Then buy just slightly ahead of the present activity. Buy when the majority wish to sell, and sell when the majority are anxious to buy.

The general season for the sale of most vacant lots in most cities is from March 1 to July 1, and from September 1 to Novembe 1. Therefore, buy in an off-season, say in the month of July. Having ascertained from a reliable broker who knows the locality thoroughly, and who can quote definite, authoritative figures as to actual sales, as well as asking prices— for actual sales are the best criterion of lot values– then proceed with the negotiations.

How to choose a lot

Assume that the purchase is to be made strictly for investment, and not as a combined investment and home location. It is difficult for the average buyer to visualize the future growth of a territory, and his judgment is usually warped by a desire to pick a location such as his own personal desires dictate for a home location for his family. Cover ground carefully, select a lot that lies slightly above the sidewalk level, preferably with a gentle slope to the rear, so that drainage is away from the house rather than towards it. If the lot is attractively wooded, without too many large trees where the house will ultimately stand, it may be particularly desirable as many people prefer wooded lots to shadeless ones. Corner lots are desirable but should be about one and a half times as large as inside lots, because you have to set the house back from both streets. Avoid "butt" lots which lie directly behind a corner lot. To do this you must know which way the house on the corner will be facing if it has not already been built. It should be easily accessible to schools and on a street where at least a house or two of good design have already been erected, establishing the type of development for the street.

If you buy a lot from an original owner, who has become tired of carrying it, so much the better, for if the lot has changed hands several times, at least several profits have been taken, and commisions paid. It is well, also, to find an owner who has some good motive for selling and does not require too great an outlay of your cash.

Assume that you buy a lot for $3,000, with a down payment of $800 or $1,000, the balance to be paid in the form of a mortgage of six or eight per cent interest, the entire principal to be paid in two or three years, or possibly a small payment the first year and increasing payments during the second and third years. You now have salable merchandise that can be carried for a year or so with very little expense, until such a time as the flow of demand which you have anticipated has an opportunity to reach the property in question. In the interim, keep in touch with the asking prices of neighbors. Your broker is constantly on the lookout for a purchaser who will be attracted by interesting financing and who can pay you your equity in cash. Be satisfied with a reasonable, legitimate profit and endeavor to make a "turnover" as quickly as possible.

Investing in merely one vacant lot may hardly justify your devoting your entire time to the study and analysis of the territory surrounding your particular property. Consequently, it is the part of wisdom for you to select a competent and reliable broker who knows the territory, and who can prove a record of sales where profits have been made for other customers. If others speak well of him as to his integrity and the workmanlike manner in which he handles his deals, you will make money by trusting him and indicating frankly that you do trust him. You should not ask him to do your deciding for you, but use him as a means of securing reliable information and as a contact with the party from whom you are buying, or to whom you are selling. A broker, with your whole-hearted co-operation, invariably can make better deals for you in both buying and selling than you can do yourself in dealing directly with an owner or buyer.

Do not seek to "milk' the last nickel out of your property. Be willing to sell at a price where the buyer is securing a good deal either as a location for his home or as an investment. Do not refuse to accept a small actual cash profit if the percentage of return on your invested capital is great. Do not try to cut your broker's commission. If you pay him his commission gladly and willingly, being a normal human being, he will enjoy working for you and will bring you many interesting propositions which otherwise he would present to persons whom he considers better customers.

Do not disparage a property to a broker before you have seen it, but always be willing to investigate. Although you may look at many properties which you do not buy, you will quickly accumulate a fund of information as to conditions, prices, and sales which will give you a standard of comparision with which you can substantiate or reject the statements of your broker.

If you are buying in a territory that is just beginning to show marked activity, you can sometimes afford to pay the market price or even slightly in advance of the market price, if you can get reasonable terms, enabling you to carry the property through to the period where it will give you the maximum of profit.

Just a word of caution about holding vacant lots too long. Keep always in mind the idea of quick turnover, and because a market is rising rapidly, do not be hoodwinked into the idea that it will always continue to rise. Many people carry property through its period of adolescence into the period of final maturity and then find themselves in a stagnant market where they can only sell at a price much lower than they actually have been offered. This results sometimes when their cupidity is aroused by the fact that they are frequently asked for prices on their property, and they acquire the feeling that they have something of exceptional merit.

It is always unwise to hold a lot until it is "boxed in" by houses built on each side of it. The moment these houses are built, the process of deterioration begins with them; and unless you dispose of your "boxed in" lot very soon, you will suffer a loss. No one wants to build a home between two houses that are beginning to show signs of age. You will find yourself forced to sell to one of the neighbors for purposes of enlarging his property, and he will not pay competitive prices for this acquisition.

The buyer who can afford to pay you the greatest profit naturally is the ultimate consumer who desires to build a home on the lot he is acquiring. He buys for location because of schools, bus lines, or friends in the neighborhood, and he usually pays cash because he gets a construction loan for his house and necessarily must clear the lot before going ahead with his building operations. He is the ideal buyer. He usually buys a short time before he is actually ready to build, and at a time when money is easy and no difficulty is encountered in getting a construction loan. Every so often banks and savings and loan companies "tighten up" and do not freely grant construction loans. Thereupon, the lot buyer who is figuring on building a home decides not to buy, and consequently a prospective purchaser is removed from the market. Then is the time to buy instead of to sell.

Money can be made in the buying and selling of vacant lots, but the amount that can be made out of a given capital investment is directly proportionate to the accuracy with which one keeps a record of costs, to the ability and activity of the investor and his broker, and to the degree of judgment that is exercised in managing the capital invested.

SIXTEEN

Buying a Lot as a Homesite

Acquiring real estate for a homesite
is a trying and perplexing task which should not be undertaken too lightly.
Be prepared to spend considerable time and don't be in too great a hurry
to close a deal unless you are thoroughly satisfied with what you are purchasing.

Finding the best site

When buying a lot, there are a few fundamental principles that should
be kept in mind. Perhaps the most important of these is *location*. Some
deem the price the all-important feature, but poor judgment is often shown
in choosing a cheap lot for a fine home. Remember that a house costs
about the same to build anywhere, and that the value of your property
will depend upon surroundings, accessibility, and general desirability as a
home.

It usually pays to spend a little more on a lot to insure its being in a
neighborhood where the property will increase in value. Consider the
locality for healthful features, school facilities, and the general character
of the neighbors.

Around every city throughout the country, developments open up which are, for the present, far beyond the city limits. They are bought at a ridiculously low price, yet the owner may expend an amount equal to the price of his lot in gasoline during a single year. Hungry for land he buys a lot, pays on it until the realization slowly comes to him that if he has to spend so much for gasoline and time going to and from his work, he should certainly have more land as an inducement to live so far from the city. Many realty men recognize this fact by subdividing their properties beyond the city limits into small farm tracts of from one to five acres, for which there is always a demand. Ten or twenty years from now such property will have "arrived" for homesites and will then be worth the money asked for lots. For the present, however, the homeowner would do well to consider the size of his plot of land when it is located far from the city.

Around every large city there are a score of these developments which have "gone dead," as real estate men say. Usually lots can be bought within the city limits at nearly as cheap a price, when improvements are considered.

It is an axiom among real estate dealers to avoid buying what is termed "butt" or "key" lots. For instance, there may be a main street with a good corner lot formed where a side street joins it. In the rear of this corner lot and facing the side street the tract is again subdivided. The first of these lots is the "butt" lot. It is directly in the rear of the corner lot. If a building of any kind is built on the corner lot it will adjoin the "butt" lot in all probability. There are so many objectionable features that it is usually wise to avoid buying such a property, especially if the corner lot remains to be improved.

It is scarcely necessary to advise the home builder to avoid lots near mills, noisy shops, saloons, garages, or drive-in restaurants.

This leads directly to the question of restrictions. It is usually wise to buy in developments where property is adequately restricted. Property restrictions are the safest sort of land insurance. Few people build and fail to insure their buildings, but some people buy with absolutely no insurance as to what the future of their land will be. Land sometimes costs more, but in the long run the extra cost is offset by increased value. Restrictions frequently fix the minimum cost of residences, the distances back from the street line, the exclusion of flats, multi-family houses or stores, thus confining the entire district to single family homesites. Where one can afford it, it is always wise to demand as many restrictions as possible for one's own protection. The higher the class of the property, the more stringent the restrictions imposed.

Be careful to get good transportation facilities to your home. Bus lines operating on some streets are frequently more desirable than on others, because of the territories they serve. These must be considered in the price the dealer asks for his lot. A lot worth $1,500 on one bus line is possibly worth $2,000 on another, so great is this influence.

It pays to deal with reputable development companies. They make a scientific business of handling property, especially new tracts. Better terms can be secured for making payments, and one can hold a company to its agreements better than he can an individual who has perhaps left the city or state. Be convinced, however, that the company is reputable and that the development is not a mere land speculation in which the company's main interest is in getting rid of its lots instead of building up a desirable neighborhood.

It pays, also, to dc some preliminary studying before buying a lot. Read the real estate advertisements in the daily papers, note the location of lots and prices asked for them. One gradually acquires a knowledge of values and where desirable neighborhoods are located. Take a trip out to the allotments you become interested in before you approach the agents. You will soon be convinced whether the propositions they have to offer will interest you.

Questions to consider

To epitomize some of the many problems that must be considered, Walter R. Hagedohm, Los Angeles architect, suggests that a lot buyer ask himself the following fifty questions about any tract of land he proposes to acquire as a homesite:

1. Is the neighborhood homogeneous in character and promising for future development?
2. Is the property protected from inharmonious land uses by zoning and building restrictions? What are the restrictions?
3. What are the restrictions covering style or price of house or houses in area?
4. Is it in danger of encroachment by buildings of other uses which are detrimental to residential property, such as factories, etc.?
5. Is the property so located as to be free from danger of flood, fire, subsidence or erosion?
6. Is the property in a fire area where you are prohibited from burning trash or lighting incinerators in the dry season?

7. Is the property filled ground or natural terrain? Is there danger of earth slippage?
8. How accessible to schools, churches, shopping centers, and recreational facilities?
9. Will children have to be driven to school every day or can they safely walk the distance?
10. Is transportation available at low cost or is a second car necessary for the family?
11. Is property on a minor street or major thoroughfare? (It should be a minor street.)
12. Is site sufficiently convenient in case owner changes place of employment in future? (In case he wishes to sell?)
13. Is area subject to freaks of weather? (Cold winds in winter or unusual heat in summer.)
14. Will location be satisfactory to owner in event his fortune should increase in a few years?
15. Are telephone rates the same as metropolitan rates, or must all calls be made through long distance or toll exchange?
16. What are general assessments against property in area?
17. Are sanitary sewers at property line, or must cesspool or septic tank be constructed? (How much additional cost?)
18. Are utilities at property line or must they be brought in from a distance?
19. Is property in the area already approved for FHA loans? (Consult local FHA office to make sure.)
20. What is condition of street paving; will it require resurfacing in the near future?
21. Can you drive your car on property or must garage construction be a result of costly road building or concrete construction?
22. Will it be necessary to construct terraces, exceptionally long steps and walks?
23. Will foundation costs be excessive because of slope of land?
24. Can building material be hauled onto site or must it be carried?
25. What is the natural direction of drainage? Will water run down on your building site?
26. Is property sufficiently large to permit ample window space on all sides of house?
27. Will it be possible to achieve a pleasing view from the house?
28. Will there be space for recreational and gardening area behind house or room for small outbuildings?
29. Will the house have to be specially planned to preserve trees now on property?

30. How much planting of trees and shrubs will be necessary?

31. What is the state of soil and how much treatment will be necessary for planting?

32. If tract is bare now, will you like it as well after houses are built on street? (Suburban atmosphere will be gone.)

33. Is there rental property nearby? (It seldom enhances values.)

34. If there are houses already on the street, how old are they and in what state of repair?

35. How will those houses look when your own is 10 years old? (Visualize neighborhood for future.)

36. If street is winding, what is the shape of your lot? Will it require special planning, such as key or pie-shaped lots?

37. Are surveyors' stakes on corners, or will you have to pay for a survey?

38. How far away are friends and relatives? Can they exchange visits often?

39. Do you know anyone in the vicinity? Ask them how they like the neighborhood.

40. Will your wife be afraid to stay alone at night, in case property is in an undeveloped tract?

41. Have you decided upon the general style of house you want, and does the lot fit this style of construction?

42. Has your architect seen the property?

43. Has your entire family agreed favorably upon the site?

44. In spite of price asked for property, what is its estimated appraisal value? (You'll need this information for FHA.)

45. Who holds the title to the property, and how much effort will be required to deliver it clear?

46. Will it be necessary for a lawyer to handle details of clearance, and who will pay his fee?

47. How much time will be required to clear title and get tax receipts? (Must have this to apply for FHA loan.)

48. Is salesman a licensed real estate salesman or property owner?

49. Can he produce printed contract of sale guaranteeing delivery of clear title, payment of back taxes and assessments? (Verbal guarantee is worthless.)

50. Is the price comparable to prices on lots of similar area you have looked at previously?

SEVENTEEN

Buying a Single Family Dwelling

The purchase or building of a dwelling is usually one of the most important events in the lives of an average family. For the first time probably, they are called upon to face an important financial problem, for the buying of a home calls for a substantial down payment, to be followed by regular contributions each month to carry and amortize the debt being assumed. Having hurdled the down payment, the monthly payments take on largely the aspects of rent, although a good portion of the monthly contribution is applied to the debt, so that the premises may be wholly owned in ten, twenty, or thirty years. The first thing for a family desiring to own their home is to save for the down payment.

Financing

Thanks to the modernization of financing programs under which dwellings are now developed and sold, the United States has a system created under the auspices of the United States government known as the Federal Housing Administration, created for the purpose, *not of actually lending money on real estate,* but simply *guaranteeing repayment of such loans.* It has become possible to purchase a lot and build a house, the entire enterprise costing not more than $15,000, wherein the down payment is not more than 3 per cent or $450. Properties costing more than $15,000 can be acquired in the same way by a down payment of 7½ per cent of the next $5,000 up to $20,000, and then of 20 per cent for the next $10,000 up to a maximum of $30,000 on a single family dwelling.

When an FHA loan is desired, the procedure is to contact a bank, building and loan association or some other institution and secure a commitment on the development of a definite lot or on a completed dwelling, as the case may be. The application is considered and approved, and the deal is concluded. Information concerning any part of the FHA plan may be obtained from almost any lending institution. A rigid system of appraising, planning, and building insures the buyer of fair values and good construction. This type of guaranteed governmental financing has vastly widened the field for home owning in recent years, and it seems likely that it will be further extended as time goes on. There is the danger, indeed, that it may go too far and put home ownership on a basis where a buyer may acquire a dwelling with scarcely any equity in it, which is not wise for one does not keenly appreciate something he gets for practically nothing as much as when he has to make some sacrifice.

Entrance of the federal government into the home building field, to the extent that it guarantees mortgages, has brought a great change in financing plans now followed by banks, insurance and mortgage companies as well as private investors who lend money on real estate. Second mortgages have practically disappeared in real estate because first mortgages cover so large a proportion of the value that there is little equity left to be covered by second liens.

Ownership vs. rental

"Shall I own or rent my home?" is a question that puzzles many, but few persons attempt to analyze the reasons they may have for arriving at a definite decision.

The subject to be carefully considered must be viewed from several major standpoints:

1. Sentiment.
2. As a means of compulsory saving.
3. As an investment proposition.

From the standpoint of sentiment, there is only one answer, and that is that as soon as possible you should own your own home. Around the word "home" are woven all of life's sweetest sentiments. Pride of ownership is enjoyed to no greater degree in any other possession that comes to mankind. It anchors one to his home town, and makes a good citizen of a man or woman as no other influence can hope to do. A home owner takes a greater pride in the way his city is maintained and built. Home ownership is the bulwark of the nation, the citadel of family life. A nation of home owners will always be a contented and prosperous people, each family eager to do all it can to build up a community and make it a worthy and pleasant place in which to live.

Many a man who has met with great success in investing in real estate learned his fundamentals by purchasing a home. It has been truly said that the saving of his first one thousand dollars is one of the hardest things a man ever does. Many a man has saved this money because he has been eager to go in debt to acquire a home. Starting with a down payment of five hundred or one thousand dollars, he has set up a savings program of a compulsory character that has resulted in a few years in the securing of a sizable equity in real estate. Knowing that the payments on mortgages and taxes are coming due regularly, he has organized his affairs in such a way that when he bent himself to the serious task of setting aside funds for investment purposes, he has found it easy to follow a steady and consistent plan of saving.

As one's standards in other things in life change with advancing age, so do one's standards of a home change, and it is often only after two or three homes have been purchased, and disposed of, that a man acquires something that begins to meet his ideal. Hallowed by the intimate scenes of family life, his heart clings closely to his home and makes him fight harder for success than if he had continued a mere renter of property.

Having acquired enough money for a down payment on a home, the young married couple begins looking about for the home of their dreams. Nowadays homes are sold on the partial payment plan, and almost anyone's purse can be satisfied. Do not hesitate to go in debt for a home. Things will work out right in the long run. It is amazing the way the payments will be taken care of and the mortgages reduced as the seasons go by.

Most persons do not save willingly and consistently. They need the burden of a mortgage to teach thrift in saving for old age and the proverbial "rainy day." If a man has a fairly steady job and enough money to make a down payment, it is a good policy to begin looking for a suitable home. Better terms, as far as payments are concerned, will usually be secured from regularly established companies which make a practice of building and selling homes on the partial payment plan. Upon the depositing of a comparatively small down payment, the complete home is at your disposal.

For many years following World War II, people had a mania for home ownership. However, there is good evidence that this obsession is waning somewhat. The high rate of movement of families as they pursue their jobs has somewhat dimmed the traditional obsession of Americans for homes of their own. Hence has come the tremendous upsurge of apartment complexes. This is certainly not to say that those families that are able to put roots down are oblivious to the values of home ownership. Once a family becomes permanently located, the old urge seems to return.

A few reasons why one should own his own home if he is permanently located or even relatively so:

1. Home ownership gives a stability to one in a business way, for credit is more readily extended to a home owner than to renter.
2. Your ability to care for your family is best evidenced by the possession of a home.
3. One has more confidence in his ability to encounter the storms of business and domestic existence when a home is at stake.
4. If you have a sudden call for capital, or are in dire distress, money usually can be realized if you have a home to pledge as security.
5. A home purchased on a payment plan encourages the cultivation of thrift and its continuance throughout one's lifetime.
6. You get pleasure in tinkering about and fixing up your own premises, which effort naturally would not be willingly expended on rented property.
7. The investment, if taken under proper conditions and from a responsible source, is absolutely safe.
8. Ownership of a home strengthens domestic relations. It will make a wife and mother happy and contented in a way nothing else can hope to do.
9. It furnishes the proper environment in which to raise a family. Children learn new ideals and responsibilities in a home owned by their parents, an element usually absent when property is rented from month to month.
10. It prevents embarrassment to parents who have children, and who are refused accommodations in rented premises, whether it

be a house or an apartment. The home owner can snap his fingers at the would-be landlord no matter whether he might be beneficent or inconsiderate.

Homes should be acquired and used to live in, not to hold for investment purposes. It is significant that in recent years the number of individual houses for rent in the cities of this country has greatly diminished. Most accommodations available are in the form of double or two family dwellings, and apartments or flats. With the necessity for intensive housing accommodations, due to increasing prices of land, and soaring building and maintenance costs, it is seldom that the owner of a house which may be rented for family use realizes much profit on his investment. The result has been that the number of landlords who rent individual houses has greatly decreased. Were these landlords to keep actual account of receipts and expenditures, and figure a reasonable rate of return on their investments, they probably would sell their single houses and reinvest in more profitable forms of real estate.

Does it pay to own a home? Isn't it cheaper to live in an apartment where heat service of all kinds is furnished? Doubtless to the person who can with convenience live in an apartment and be satisfied with that sort of a home, it may be cheaper, but the charm of home ownership, however, can never be enjoyed in an apartment, particularly if there are children to rear.

Don't enter blindly into buying a home. Analyze carefully the burden you are assuming. Do not be alarmed if you find that buying a home is a slow operation, for it is indeed well worthwhile.

Do not buy a home merely as an investment, although under some circumstances it later can be sold at a profit. Consider it a duty to yourself and an obligation to your wife and family. Consider your home your life anchor, and go about this business as early in your married life as you can.

There was a time when it was considered smart to pay one's debt on the home as soon as possible. Nowadays, however, many people consider it wise to keep the cash equity as low as possible so as to make a sale easier should one decide to move either to a new town or up the social ladder to a larger home in a more exclusive neighborhood.

Buying a home offers a problem which the circumstances of each family must justify. Home ownership carries with it benefits and burdens which must be carefully weighed one against the other. It is very similar to the problem that presents itself when the consideration concerns the number of children desirable in any family. From an investment standpoint children often are a liability, as far as the actual expense of rearing them is concerned. But obviously, dollars and cents are not the primary consideration where children are involved.

Construction features

Having made up one's mind to buy a dwelling and having settled the financing of the down payment, the selection of the site follows. This has been fully outlined in another chapter. If the property is an improved one, steps must be taken at once to analyze the neighborhood and become satisfied that the building meets the requirements of the buyer and that it is well constructed. If the property is financed under an FHA guaranteed loan, it will usually be found to be well built. If not, extreme care should be taken to inspect the premises, looking for these main features:

1. Are the foundations adequate? Are they built to resist dry rot and termites? Do they show any slippage which would indicate the presence of filled ground? Are there plenty of vents? Is there good surface drainage?

2. Is the structural frame of the dwelling adequate and sound? Are upright timbers the proper size to carry the weight? Are the cross timbers the full normal size usually employed, or has the contractor skimped by putting in 2 × 6's instead of 2 × 8's or 2 × 10's?

3. Is the floor plan acceptable? Are the rooms of suitable size and arrangement? Can the floor plan be amplified by adding more rooms?

4. Does the woodwork show evidence of having been installed by skilled mechanics, or are there gaps at corners where joints should closely fit so as to almost defy detection of their presence?

5. Note the type and grade of plumbing and the manner in which it has been installed. Good plumbing, properly installed, may last almost a lifetime. Poor piping and fixtures may have to be changed after a few years.

6. Look over the installation of electrical fixtures and see if they are adequate in number and of good grade. Note particularly the presence of plug outlets for floor lamps and appliances, their location and number. Note if provision has been made for lamps at the front and rear doors and over the garage entrance. Many electrical outlets are needed in a home, and if they have not been installed you will probably have to do so.

7. Inspect the kitchen carefully. Look at the plumbing fixtures.

Note the quality and quantity of the drainboard about the sink and the manner in which it has been installed. See where the range is situated and note whether there has been adequate space and connections provided for the electrical or gas refrigerator. What laundry accommodations have been provided?

8. Note particularly the heating and air-conditioning arrangements. See if there are registers or other types of outlets in every room. Inspect the furnace and air-conditioning equipment and observe whether it is of standard size and of good grade and adequate for the service expected. Carefully inspect the hot water heating facilities which are to be used, and see if the tank is adequate in size, in good repair, with glass-lined interior.

9. Look over the interior decorations of the house, noting the wall coverings, the color and manner in which woodwork has been finished, and whether the entire treatment is pleasantly harmonious and restful.

10. Inspect the roof. If the house is not new, have it carefully examined. Roofs last only ten or fifteen years in some climates and then have to be renewed. Note the type and quality of roofing and ascertain, if possible, whether it has been properly installed. Note also whether there are adequate vents under the roof, if such vents are customarily installed in that climate. Leaky roofs cause a lot of trouble to interior decorations and cause a house to deteriorate structurally.

11. Inspect the lot aside from the building improvements thereon. Will it require the expenditure of considerable time and money to improve it? Has it a sprinkling system? Is it subject to floods from neighboring lots? Is the soil adequate? What is the condition of the shrubbery and trees, if any? What are the general possibilities of improving the entire vacant area for garden use?

12. Observe the distance to neighbors' houses, from both the house itself and the lot lines. Will the neighbors' television or squalling babies or barking dogs be annoying? Is the lot fenced, has it hedges, or is there a "spite" fence on one line?

13. After satisfying one's self about the foregoing, which are but a few of many factors that must be considered before acquiring a home, the prospective buyer should carefully weigh the entire subject of *location value*.

Location value

Location value includes the perplexing but important problems of adequacy and proximity of transportation, schools, churches, libraries, shopping districts, as well as the presence of public service facilities such as telephone, mail delivery, electricity, gas and water, paved roadways, and the character and number of neighbors.

When one decides to build a new dwelling, there are several approaches to the problem which must be considered. These include:

1. Employment of an architect to design plans and enter into contracts for the erection of the dwelling, while at the same time employing the architect to give the building expert supervision during construction.

2. Contacting a professional building company which furnishes plans or makes them to order, proceeding with the erection of the building, its completion, and delivery to the new owner.

3. Securing a set of so-called "stock" plans or plans acquired in various ways for a building it is desired to duplicate. A contract may be made by a prospective owner with an individual builder or a series of contractors on different parts of the work. This is somewhat hazardous unless a thoroughly honest and competent contractor supervises the entire arrangement. Building a home is a highly specialized job which the average person is scarcely competent to do without proper supervision.

4. Building the house yourself, by hiring skilled and common laborers to do the work under your direct supervision. Unless you are experienced and know how to proceed, this is fraught with much danger and expense, although you may, of course, save an architect's fee and a builder's profit.

If you plan to build you will have to select one of the foregoing methods of procedure.

Volumes could be, and have been, written about planning houses. Individual ideas concerning type of architecture, arrangement of rooms, design, quality and quantity of interior finish, selection of lighting, plumbing, heating, and air-conditioning, equipment to be used, and a host of other ideas are involved. Anyone planning to erect a home would do well to go into a huddle with himself some months in advance of actually proceeding and clarify in his mind all of the problems involved. The subject is too vast to cover adequately here.

Before acquiring a home, whether by building or buying one, it might be well to give consideration to the purchase of a dwelling which is not absolutely new, or even a few years old. It will be found, in many cases, that an older house can be bought at a saving of from twenty-five to fifty per cent under the cost of erecting a new one of comparatively the same square footage of floor area, and it will also often be found that the location advantages of the older house are vastly superior at the price than those offered in the absolutely new dwelling.

The older house is a structure which is probably settled and seasoned, and in a neighborhood which has been developed in beauty and utility over a longer period of time than a new one. Trees and plantings are mature. There are few ugly vacant lots. Every form of public utility is available. A home two, three, or five years old is often more dependable than the new one which has not yet been tested. Weaknesses, if there were any, have been discovered and corrected. The average dwelling will develop and show its inadequacies within the first three or four years of existence. Settling and shrinkage, if any, will have taken place and been remedied. For some reason or other the original owner wants to sell and move elsewhere. In many instances such a house can be bought far below its reproduction value and can, with the expenditure of a little money on decorating or remodelling, be made into a home which may far outrun the expectations of the couple who seek to plan and own an absolutely new structure. Investigate this subject of acquiring a house already built and adapting it to your needs. Discover whether you cannot save considerable money and actually get a much better situated and seasoned dwelling than by buying a lot in an outlying neighborhood and erecting a new building with all its attendant construction problems.

What you should know before buying

The prospective home buyer should carefully consider his ability to pay for the type of dwelling he has in mind. There is a relationship which should exist between the value of the site and the cost of the building thereon. There is also a very definite relationship between the amount which should be spent for a home when monthly payments are to be supported from income.

The average family, no matter what its income, should operate on a budget, setting aside certain sums monthly for specific uses. Broadly, these include general living expenses, welfare (which embraces education and recreation), and savings (which include putting money in the bank, or what is just as important in earlier years, the investing in a home).

The United States Savings and Loan League of Chicago, Illinois, has prepared a booklet entitled *What You Should Know Before You Buy a Home*. It contains tables to help families determine the amount they should spend for a home. One of these tables is reproduced on page 136.

INCOME

Total Income . . . . $_____

(Omit wife's income from this computation if, for any reason, the wife's income will prove temporary.)

Total wage or salary deductions such as withholdings for income taxes, retirement, social security benefits, hospitalization insurance, etc. $_____

(Subtract the second figure from the first.)

You Total "Take Home Pay" is . . . . $_____

EXPENSES

Monthly savings budget $_____
Food and clothing . . . $_____
Medical care . . .   . . $_____
Life insurance . . . $_____
Recreation . . . . . . $_____
Utilities and fuel.   .. $_____
Transportation   . . . . $_____

All other expenses (membership dues, contributions, charge accounts, installment purchases, etc.) . . . . . . $_____

(Add these up.)
Total Expenses . . . . . . $_____

(Subtract Total Expenses from Take-Home Pay.)

Your Income for Housing . . . . $_____

Thus, the amount of money you can afford to pay for a roof over your head, or your Income for Housing, is $_____ $_____

Appeals to women buyers

What are some of the compelling influences which urge people into home ownership? It is well known that women do over 80 per cent of all the family buying and they are very influential when it comes to purchasing a home. It is the women, therefore, the house builder seeks to impress with various devices. Outside of the obvious "musts," recounted heretofore, here are some of the things that have a strong appeal for women house buyers and which encourage them to purchase:

1. Clever window treatment—the corner window, picture window, bay window, or studio window that streamlines a house into the latest style.
2. Two closets in the master bedroom—and shelves instead of so many drawers, with different widths to take care of various sizes of objects.
3. Window stool or window shelves at least five inches wide on south and east windows to accommodate plants. Stools on steel casement windows may be used, too, as window seats.
4. A motto over the fireplace or a gay bit of Dutch tile in the kitchen; a spice cabinet above the stove; mirrored shelves in a dressing room; mirrored mulls on twin windows. Mirrors create impressions of space.
5. Unusual uses of wallpaper. Women prefer plain wallpaper but they love borders, gaily papered closets, and beautiful ceilings Women, it is claimed, always look at ceilings.
6. A summer house in the backyard. This requires a few yards of concrete, rough timber and screen. It will have more appeal if built with a small fireplace in one end. Women particularly like summer or tea houses, but they must be screened!

The appraisal system used by the Federal Housing Administration for the valuation of dwellings which have their mortgages insured under that plan, is probably the most comprehensive one in existence. The checklists utilized by FHA in assessing property are comprehensive and exacting, all of which is to the benefit of the buyer to assure that he knows what he is buying and that he gets what he pays for To show the concern FHA evidences toward complete appraisals and their desire that the buyer be forewarned of many contingencies, parts of FHA Form No. 2800 are included in the Appendix, along with instructions to home owners.

Jesse B Blue, FHA valuator, has compiled an excellent list of "don'ts" to be observed in connection with planning one's home as follows:

Some "don'ts" in planning your home

1. Don't set your house back from the street a greater or lesser distance than those of your neighbors unless the contour of lot requires it.
2. Don't crowd the sidelines and leave less than eight feet between your house and the nearest existing or future allowable structure.
3. Don't place your garage further from the house than neccessary to provide easy and safe accessibility for your car or cars.
4. If your neighbors on each side have their driveways on the east, don't place yours on the west.
5. Don't enter your garage from an alley unless there are advantages to more than offset the disadvantages.
6. Don't construct a ribbon driveway.
7. Don't build your driveway so narrow that an average driver has difficulty in keeping a car on it or that it becomes necessary to put bumpers on the side of your house.
8. Don't place a garage in such a location that it detracts from the appearance of the main building. On level lots don't build a garage which projects out in front of the house.
9. Don't plan an exterior design which is out-of-date, unbalanced or inappropriate to its surroundings. Don't build an English type of house in a block where all other homes are of Spanish design, and vice versa. Don't build a two-story house in a neighborhood of one-story bungalows, and vice versa. Don't build a 25-foot house on a 50-foot lot or a 30-foot house on a 60-foot lot. Use your lot width to spread your house out.
10. Don't waste space in hallways and special-use rooms.
11. Don't face a rear living room on unsightly conditions existing over your rear yard fence.
12. Don't plan room sizes or shapes that are difficult to furnish.
13. Don't have any rooms without plenty of light, and on the other hand, don't cut your wall space up with windows and doors so that you have no place for furniture.
14. Don't build a narrow and deep kitchen.
15. Don't make your living room a hallway.
16. Don't put your laundry in an attached garage without direct access to it from the kitchen.
17. Don't construct a garage on the opposite side of the house from the kitchen and service porch.
18. Don't put the bathtub under a window, the toilet against the living room wall, or the lavatory away from natural light.

19. In houses over 800 square feet, don't limit your dining space to the kitchen.
20. Don't build porches if they add nothing to the appearance or comfort of the house but result in darkening important rooms.
21 Don't omit cross ventilation in all principal rooms, if possible to secure it.
22. Don't install corner windows unless the advantages offset the disadvantages.
23. Don't use up valuable exterior corners with closets and service porch.
24. Don't install doors that are too narrow, and don't hang them so that any two clash against each other.
25. Don't put your front door where a stranger can't find it, and don't leave the entry unprotected from rain and weather.
26. Don't place your bathroom door where, when opened, this room is exposed to view from the front entry door, the living room or dining room.
27. Don't build "kitchenettes" in homes—provide the necessary room and conveniences for a family that really wants to live in the house.
28 Don't place the drainboard along an inside wall.
29. Don't make the only access to a bath through a service porch or bedroom.
30 Don't build corner fireplaces without good reason.
31. Don't install wall heaters behind doors.
32. Don't build a one-bedroom house without providing in your plan for the economical addition of a second bedroom.
33. Don't create an unattractive living room in order to have a rumpus room. In other words, don't build a house around a rumpus room.
34. In a one-story house, don't have the rooms on different levels unless warranted by contour of the lot.
35. Don't install an ironing board that can only be used from one side.
36. Don't build more steps up to the front door than the contour of the lot requires.
37. Don't build steep and dangerous stairways to basements or second stories.
38. Don't build a single garage smaller than 10 × 20 or a double garage smaller than 17 × 20.
39. Don't have over a 20 per cent incline on any part of your driveway.

40. Don't wait until the house is finished to find that your closets are too few and too small. Don't build "tunnel" closets, the kind that are 2 feet wide and 8 feet deep.
41. Don't build until you have studied the effect of sun, light, and prevailing winds on all rooms and the outlook from all windows with respect to view and privacy.
42. Don't build at all until you have planned a good house.

EIGHTEEN

Industrial and Water Front Properties

Opportunities exist for profitable investment in industrial, warehouse, and water front properties, but frequently puzzling, even hazardous, factors will be found in connection with their acquisition, development and sale. Before entering this field much study and investigation should be engaged in by an investor or speculator if he is to operate successfully and profitably.

Broadly speaking, industrial property is lacking in merit as a speculative medium. This is because, in part, most industrial property is not acquired until a period just before its improvement and ultimate use. Some concerns occasionally will look into the future and buy acreage adjoining their plants some time in advance of actual need, but when they do so they usually depress prices to points where sellers fail to make much speculative profit.

There are broad bands of property about the borders of most industrial cities which may be classed as potential factory acreage. It may still be used for raising crops, but in many instances its proximity to industrial activity and the hope of its early sale result in its lying idle, producing nothing but weeds. Such land, in large part, is not in active demand. It may have railroad or even water frontage or may be on a good truck high-way, yet the demand is not urgent enough for anyone to acquire and improve it Usually it is farm land out of use for agricultural purposes. The owners ask too much for anyone to buy it for purposes of cultivation, and industrial activity has not reached out to demand its use. So there it lies, many parcels in competition with each other, subject to sale only on the basis of the cheapest price asked for a parcel of it. Some industrialist may be willing to pay $300, $400, or $500 an acre for land which is normally worth $100 an acre for raising crops, but such land is often withheld for such a long period between the time of convertibility from one use to another that profits fade when actual carrying charges are considered.

It may be seen, therefore, that a speculator is seldom interested in owning land of a character that develops into actual use so slowly. An investor may see potentialities of use some time in the future and may assemble several hundred, or thousand, acres of such land for ultimate resale. A sudden industrial development in a community such as a war boom may result in considerable activity in industrial lands. Creation of single large new manufacturing enterprises may likewise cause a demand in a specified district. For the most part, however, large areas of industrial lands can scarcely be considered very much worthwhile as speculative units.

Selecting the site

It has become the practice in most American cities to locate industrial activities on "the other side of the tracks." Here warehouses and small factories of all sizes, designs, and values may be found. Owners sometimes find they possess lands in such districts and decide to improve and either sell or rent them. Here again they run into difficulty—that of financing building improvements. Despite the fact that industrial activity is an important background of a city, local financial institutions are often loath to finance new structures unless they are for specific owners who have ample backing, or unless an owner of a site puts considerable money into such a building himself and has it rented in advance to a desirable and responsible tenant. In some ways banks cannot be blamed for their lack of desire to finance industrial units, for during a recession there is nothing that seems less salable than an empty factory building for which there is no tenant in sight. Factory space in most cities usually exists in advance of actual needs and, as such, units are of a single purpose type that can seldom be used for other than industrial purposes.

There was a time some years ago when it seemed almost imperative that factories be located on railroad trackage, if manufacturing operations were to be engaged in. With the advent of auto trucks this necessity disappeared to some degree. The manufacturer of large heavy units of production still needs trackage, as does the fabricator of many products produced through mass production. Many types of goods may now be produced in factories, however, that can be delivered to freight stations and to wholesalers and consumers by means of truck service. This has brought into productive use large areas of land not fronting on railroads but having proximity to paved roads as well as accessibility to various types of public services such as gas, water, electricity, telephones, and transportation.

A basic requirement of a business property is that it must have adequate frontage on a commercial thoroughfare. It is usually valued on a basis of such foot frontage. Industrial property, however, is usually valued by its square foot area, and the necessity of street frontage is not so important. In fact, if a factory property has a sufficient amount of frontage to permit the location of adequate offices and allow proper egress and ingress, that may be all the frontage it needs, provided there is a sufficiently large area of interior land for development purposes.

A buyer of industrial property should, at the outset, make sure that a site has adequate public service facilities. A modern factory must have water, gas, postal, telephone, electricity, transportation and sewage facilities, although the latter may often be taken care of by the building of a separate sewage plant or a series of septic tanks for the particular development. Likewise it must be approached over paved roads. It must not be too far from residential development where workers may live at reasonable rentals. While automobiles permit workers to live at considerable distances from a plant, there is always a demand on the part of many workers to live nearby. Unless reasonable housing facilities are within walking distance of a plant, there may be difficulty in securing adequate labor supply.

The demand is usually for well-drained level or slightly sloping land for industrial use. Occasionally a type of industry will use a tract irregular in topography where refuse which accumulates from industrial processes may be dumped, as in the case of steel and iron mills. Swampy, marshy land is usually taboo.

Industrial cities are often located on banks of rivers or lake or ocean harbors, thus affording water front lands on demand. Due to their comparative scarcity, prices are often quite high. The most desirable type is where such water frontage is also served with railroad facilities and where the depth of water is sufficient for the draft of large vessels. Such land often requires the expenditure of large outlays for wharves and docks, as well as dredging operations, but this is usually warranted by reason of the prices obtainable. Before an investor acquires this type of site he should obtain costs of improvement to see whether the expense is warranted in view of the price to be realized for the completed property.

Filled-in water front property is not as desirable as natural soil of clay, rock, or some firm quality. Difficulty of installing foundations for docks, warehouses, machinery, and other improvements is much greater where filled-in land is encountered. An investor should also ascertain whether a site is subject to flood waters during springtime, when it might be entirely under water and of little use to anyone, despite elaborate and costly improvements.

As contrasted to ordinary industrial property in cities, water front land is usually priced on the foot frontage of a navigable stream or harbor.[1] This is so because of the necessity for dock frontage along which vessels may tie for loading operations. Large and important real estate developments of this character may be found in all ocean and lake front cities. A notable one is the Bush Terminal in New York City.

The location and its relative advantages as to depth of channel, trackage, and general utility will measure the value of a water front property. If frontage in a locality is limited, the price naturally will be much higher than if there is a quantity. The age and importance of a harbor will also definitely affect price.

Climatic conditions may have much to do with the usefulness and value of industrial water front property. A city on the Great Lakes, for instance, may see water front property cut off from use by wintry conditions for four or five months each season, while an equally advantageous site in the far south or in Los Angeles, in southern California, enjoys all-year services accompanied by ideal climatic conditions.

In buying industrial property, the subject of an available labor supply should be seriously considered. Sometimes a manufacturer should scarcely consider accepting a site free of cost if he is unable to obtain the quantity and quality of labor he requires in his factory. A location with an abundance of cheap efficient common labor in one locality might be useless to a fabricator of goods who requires skilled labor of a higher type.

---

[1] For a detailed study of the valuation of water front property, see Chapter 23 of Stanley L. McMichael, *McMichael's Appraising Manual*, 4th ed. (Englewood Cliffs, N.J.: Prentice-Hall, Inc., 1951).

It will be found that there is a differentiation in both usefulness and value between industrial sites on one railroad as contrasted with those on another. A line bringing in a supply of coal from distant mines will not be as desirable as a railroad which connects directly with other large neighboring cities and which engages in a general shipping business. The importance of a railroad line and its attractiveness to shippers generally must be considered and investigated closely.

In prosperous times, when business is active, important enterprises have been promoted in many of the larger cities by the acquiring of well-located sites and the building thereon of large factory buildings, subdivided into many small units of various sizes, which are rented out and which are furnished with power and shipping facilities. These are sometimes called "incubator buildings" because small industries are born there. Here a manufacturer may rent 1,000 square feet of space or space many times that size. It enables him to get a start, later expanding into his own plant. These rental units often prove profitable for a promoter, but care must be taken to see that one is not loaded with a lot of space which may go idle as the result of a depression. Sometimes an empty factory of considerable dimensions may be sub-divided and used in this manner.

Industrial buildings are sometimes to be found on the very edge of business districts where a commercial area expands and converts into business use such factory units. This means the employment of the factory space for commercial purposes, thereby developing it into higher and better use and creating new value for an owner. Scouting about with this thought in mind, one may occasionally see an opportunity to make a purchase and convert a property into new and better uses.

Occasionally a factory may be found right in a business section where it has become engulfed by business advancement. Judicious remodelling of such premises for commercial use will frequently earn a great deal more than when it was employed for its original purpose. Warehouses in the pathway of business development may likewise be improved by being remodelled into stores, automobile display rooms and similar establishments.

An industrial building located on a main commercial thoroughfare, even though somewhat far removed from business neighbors, may be converted to business uses and tenants secured who will conduct retail businesses there. It may require a new front for the factory building or the entire premises may have to be remodelled to make the structure suitable, but that may be found to be well worthwhile.

An owner of a large vacant area of land located not far distant from active industrial development may do well to investigate carefully whether it may not be wiser to use his land for a residential development for those employed in the already existing factories, rather than to enter actively into competition with other factory sites which are awaiting sale and development. Employees must live, and if a pleasant subdivision can be made of such land, it may bring an owner a better return than if it is employed for industrial purposes. Living near industrial enterprises these days does not involve the unpleasantness which existed when factories belched great clouds of smoke and cinders over an entire neighborhood. With the widespread use of electricity generated by water power, many factory neighborhoods are just about as clean and fit to live in as in some restricted sections. Smoke condensers, too, have removed the threat of dense clouds over home areas.

It is interesting to note that in 1968 all auto manufacturers were required to install devices on auto muffler systems to cut down on air pollution from engine exhausts. Much more legislation is forthcoming concerning air pollution, a major problem of the last part of the twentieth century.

Before buying land with a view towards its use for industrial purposes, it might be well for an investor to visit the chamber of commerce, the city planning commission, and similar fact-finding agencies to ascertain, if possible, whether more factory land is desirable in that area. Even when you have a tenant calling for a site with a new building, it may be found that a plant already in existence may be bought and adapted for use more cheaply than a new one can be produced. Surveys are made from time to time in almost every city, and there is always a considerable amount of factual information in the hands of certain agencies, available to those who are interested.

In some of the larger cities catering to industrial activities and where a number of railroads are in operation, so-called "belt lines" have been constructed around the city, connecting with all the various lines. This enables a shipper to tranship to any line via the belt line. Property located on a belt line itself often shows a value of from twenty-five to one hundred per cent over sites located on individual railroad lines. Where a belt line intersects with a main outgoing thoroughfare extending from the center of a city, there may be corner sites which have great additional values as locations for warehouses or particular types of mercantile or industrial enterprises. Such sites may have not only railroad sidings, but frontage on business thoroughfares as well. In one instance such a site was employed for use by an automobile agency which received its wholesale shipments through its back door and retailed them through the front door.

Don't overlook the possibility of reconverting large abandoned plants into multiple unit industrial developments to be rented to members of small users of manufacturing space.

Industrial districts

In periods of great business activity, it is occasionally profitable to plan and develop industrial subdivisions where sites ranging in size from half an acre up are made available with transportation facilities in the form of railroad sidings for the larger units and street facilities for trucking for the smaller units. An operation of this kind often requires an original site embracing hundreds of acres of land. In this connection one Chicago authority says that the development of an industrial district falls naturally into four progressive steps:

1. The assembly and purchase of the raw land.
2. The installation of street improvements and essential facilities.
3. The sales promotion and location of industries coupled perhaps with a plan for financing building construction.
4. The establishment of various forms of permanent service.

In selecting land for an industrial district or in deciding to develop existing holdings for that purpose, this authority contends it must be clearly held in mind that success depends upon whether the property has potentially the elements vitally essential to successful plant operation. The most important of these are:

1. Railroad facilities.
2. Express, parcel post, and mail service.
3. Labor supply.
4. Bus transportation.
5. Water supply.
6. Drainage and sewage disposal.
7. Ample electric light and power supply.
8. Industrial gas supply.
9. Favorable topography and sub-soil conditions so as to avoid excessive costs in filling, grading, and construction of foundations.
10. If located at a seaport, an inland lake, or railroad shipping point, the matter of dock frontage and accessibility for boats must be considered. Unless these elements are present, the undertaking is almost certainly doomed to failure.

An industrial operatoi oi broker can make money occasionally by observing the plight of a misplaced industrial ənterprise and correct the fault by relocating it in a proper environment. Likewise, it may be found that a plant has outgrown its facilities or is using an old-fashioned, worn-out factory structure which should be replaced with a new one. The thoughts and activities of the manufacturer himself are often centered on a business and its processes, so that he has not been impressed with the need for better plant facilities.

It is important for an operator of factory properties to know the amount of investment which a specified tenant or industry may assume. One concern may be able to pay $2 per square foot for its site while another outfit, operating on a much smaller scale and on a lesser margin of profit must be satisfied with a location costing one quarter of that amount per square foot. To place a concern on land too expensive, or not good enough, may possibly spell disaster over a term of years.

NINETEEN

Long-Term Leaseholds as Investment

Long-term land leases have been successfully used for centuries in both Europe and America as mediums of investment—*but not speculation!*

The time is so recent, and in some cases the losses were so great, that one still remembers the vast amount of speculation in ninety-nine year leases which unfortunately took place during the boom days. Despite such speculative leases, however, long-term leases do offer much of value to the real estate investor bent upon developing building projects in areas where high-priced land prevails.

For instance, if you were interested in securing possession of a certain tract of ground for use in your business, and the owner of the land offered you the land at a satisfactory price, but demanded no money payment for it, simply asking you to pay him for a stated period of time an amount of money equal to the interest on the sum which you would otherwise invest in the property, what would you do? Naturally you would accept his offer. In doing so, you would be taking a long-term lease on the property, and following the basic principle underlying such contracts.

"Here is my land," the owner in effect says to you. "Take it, improve it, and use it for ninety-nine years. Pay me in rental a sum of money equal to seven or eight per cent on its value. Of course, until a building is erected to serve as security for the payment of rent, I shall require you to give me a bond equal in amount to at least two years' rent and taxes. I don't want your money. In fact, I want to lend you the full amount necessary to gain possession of my property. Just as long as you faithfully live up to your contract, the right to the use of the land is yours. We will incorporate this agreement, together with other protective features, in a ninety-nine year lease instrument, and you can proceed to use the land for your business, or any other legitimate purpose."

Is it any wonder that long-term leases prove attractive to investors who can, at comparatively small expense, gain control of land in rapidly growing sections of a city?

The legal right to use land, undisturbed by anyone, is after all the very essence of land value.

Long-term leases are useful in large cities where values steadily mount, and where it is sometimes difficult to muster sufficient funds both to buy land and erect large buildings. Fortunes have been made in this type of investment by reason of enhanced values in land and bonuses which have been paid for leases.

Benefit to the lessee

The chief benefit accrues to the lessee by reason of the fact that future increment to the land belongs to him. For instance, a property having a frontage of 100 feet, worth $1,000 per foot front, leases for $100,000, with a rental of $6,000 per year. It is not improbable that in from five to ten years, the property will reach a value of $2,000 per foot front, showing a profit of $100,000. The tenant, if he desires to do so, can sub-lease the property for $12,000 yearly, pay $6,000 a year to the original owner and retain the other $6,000 he receives annually as income. If he does not desire to sub-lease, he may sell his interest in the original lease for $100,000 , and if the property is actually worth $2,000 per foot, he will have little difficulty getting that sum.

Values in business districts in some cities have a way of bounding upward within a few years. Property owners who do not wish to wait for this increment, or who are unable or disinclined to finance improvement, often are willing to lease their land and let the investing lessee reap the accumulating benefits.

It is true that the lessee has to pay taxes and other carrying charges on the land, but if it is located in a growing territory, it has a way of paying out handsomely. If the land is not so located, *it should not be taken under long-term lease!*

The ability to use borrowed money honestly and skillfully often represents the chief factor in the success of many men. Under a leasing arrangement one has the opportunity, by simply furnishing an adequate bond, of gaining control of valuable land which can be properly improved and made to pay handsome returns.

There is a decided advantage in leasing land rather than assuming a financial burden in buying it outright. Mortgages have a way of falling due when an owner is least able to meet the obligation. If the mortgage is defaulted, the land owner is likely to lose his entire investment. If he could cure his trouble by simply continuing to pay the required interest, his difficulty would be greatly minimized. This, of course, is exactly what the lessee does under a long-term lease. As long as he pays his rent regularly and lives up to the other covenants of his lease, he remains firmly in possession, and nothing can dislodge him or prevent him from enjoying the use of the land or whatever increment comes to it.

If vacant land cannot be reasonably expected to increase in value to the extent of at least five to ten per cent per year, it seldom should be considered a fit subject for a long-term lease unless it is adequately improved at an early date. A long-term lease should be taken as an investment *and never as a speculation!* One should have some satisfactory use to which one can put the land. This can be accomplished by erecting a structure for your own use, or by promoting a building, space in which can readily be rented at a profit to responsible tenants. With a definite outgo with which to be reckoned, it is most desirable that there be a definite income with which to pay expenses. There are some tracts of land in growing cities where this can be figured almost to a certainty, and it is these parcels which attract the investor who wishes to assume a ninety-nine year lease.

Advantages and disadvantages

Merchants in actively growing cities are rapidly learning the advantages of leasing property for a long term. Most business leases now are for five and sometimes ten years. Property owners hesitate to grant a longer term becouse they desire to participate in possible increment. If they tie their property up for twenty or twenty-five years at a set rental, they preclude the possibility of sharing in the increased values which they later may obtain. Buildings will depreciate and change in style, and when the lease expires the building goes back to the owner, and often is a cause of constant expense. By leasing for a long term, the owner gets the building off his hands, while the new tenant is in a position to spend money on improvement because he knows he will remain in possession for a time sufficien'v long to permit the amortization of the expense.

Be warned, however, against taking ninety-nine year leases where land and building together form the capital value. For instance, a tract of land worth $50,000 may have thereon a building worth the same sum, or at least the property will rent for a sum today which may bring the owner a net return of $8,000 a year. Therefore, the owner demands that rental under a ninety-nine year lease. To accept such a proposition is hazardous in some instances, for the building may depreciate very rapidly in value, and in fifteen or twenty years it may become practically worthless. The land may increase in value, of course, but unless there is a certainty of its increasing more rapidly than the building depreciates, the proper way is to buy the building at an appraised value, allowing for depreciation and obsolescence, and then to lease the land on its market value for the full term. A depreciation fund should be set aside to reproduce the capital value of the building when it must be torn down or remodelled. Then the entire investment remains intact, and the lessee does not find himself in the position of paying $8,000 a year on land which may not have reached a $100,000 value. The fund which has been accumulating can be applied toward the erection of a new building, or remodelling the existing one.

Improved property is sometimes offered for a ninety-nine year lease on an income basis that may seem attractive. Unless the building has a life of at least forty or fifty years, the project should be carefully scrutinized, for the possibility is always apparent that changing conditions may require its destruction long before the land beneath it increases in value enough to wipe out the loss which attends its passing. The income may seem inviting, but it must always be remembered that buildings depreciate while land usually advances in value. The safest procedure is to lease land, and either buy or build the physical improvements.

Occasionally it will be found that ground can be leased when it is impossible to buy it. For sentimental reasons owners decline to part with land they own, but will listen attentively to proposals that it be placed under a long-term lease. Gaining possession this way is advantageous to the lessee, and land which otherwise might continue to lie idle becomes the subject of immediate improvement and made to pay its way. Choice parcels of property are in this way put under lease to investors who sometimes reap substantial increment as time progresses.

One should understand the fundamentals of long-term leasing before engaging in such operations, or should secure the assistance of an agent who makes a specialty of this kind of business. There are many safeguards to both lessee and lessor, which should be incorporated in a modern ninety-nine year lease. Any document which is to control the destiny of an expensive piece of property for a century or more should contain every possible safeguard which is fair to each side concerned.[1]

To summarize:

1. A long-term lease is a good investment if the rental paid represents a fair capitalization of the present market value of the land.
2. The lessee benefits by his ability to control the land for a long term and be assured that he can amortize the cost of improvements which may be added to the property.
3. The lessee gains through possession of increment which comes to the land, which should be located only in such a territory as may reasonably be expected to increase in value in the years to come!
4. If the land is improved with some kind of a building, the land may be leased, but the building should be purchased at a price which may be amortized over a given term of years.
5. A lease on land which has substantially increased in value may be sold for a cash bonus, or the land may be subleased at a higher rate of rental return. In large cities where leased land has greatly increased in value, sub-lease may follow sub-lease many times.
6. Leasing should be entered into with a full knowledge of existing conditions, which should warrant a steady increase in values over the term of the lease.
7. Consider a long-term lease an investment—*not a speculation!*

---

[1] For a detailed study of the entire subject, obtain the book Stanley L. McMichael and Paul T. O'Keefe, *Leases: Percentage, Short and Long-Term,* 5th ed. (Englewood Cliffs, N.J.: Prentice-Hall, Inc., 1959).

TWENTY

Subdividing Land

During the last third of the twentieth century, America has become a land of cities, some old, others distinctively new. Time was when a city could be developed only by a slow evolutionary process; many cities have been centuries in the making.

But now we have new cities that spring up almost miraculously—sometimes around a new industry, sometimes just because a developer has the foresight to envision their existence. Many new cities are forming from the overflow of other larger neighboring cities.

Operators all over America have accumulated a great deal of money marketing homesites, transforming raw acreage into subdivisions by formulating attractive but definite plans on paper, submitting them to expert engineers, laying out streets and main highways, and completing improvements of the property ready for retail sale by the installation of pavements, water and gas mains, sewers, and electricity for lighting.

American towns and cities during recent decades have developed in an unprecedented manner. There has been a steady drift of population from rural districts to urban centers, necessitating the furnishing of extensive housing accommodations, and this has necessarily meant the creation of many new subdivisions.

There is a general rule used by subdivision operators that raw land properly developed should sell for from three to five times the cost of the original acreage. Formerly it was estimated that the land cost one third, the improvements and sellings costs represented one third, and the other third came to the operator as profit. In recent years, the rule of four or five to one has more generally prevailed, allowing one fourth for land cost, a fourth for improvements, a fourth for sales and overhead costs, and a fourth for profit. There is no strict rule that can be followed, however as varying conditions change the problem. Some subdivisions are highly developed with expensive improvements, while others are furnished only with water, light and sewers. When a demand for lots is very active, sales costs are greatly reduced, and the expense of financing is minimized as the property does not have to be carried very long.

General principles

The first problem the subdivider encounters is the choice of land, priced so that it can be sold profitably in competition with existing subdivisions in a given area. A few general principles to be observed in this connection are:

1. Land for a subdivision should be chosen first on the basis of an existing or an immediately available population of prospective home owners. A majority of the subdivisions that have gone sour have done so because there were no customers available.
2. It is definitely not enough that there be a tract of land beautiful to behold with rolling hills, trees, and scenic splendor. Only people can make a subdivision.
3. At the same time, in the presence of a population of prospects, the subdivisions that have good topography and good location will prosper beyond those that do not.
4. Facilities in the way of public improvements such as water, electricity, pavements and sewers should always be available. Gas for heating water and cooking is a great boon and helps sell lots. Telephone service and mail delivery are also necessary.
5. It may be well to buy a large tract to begin with, because the purchase of other acres once the subdivision has been started is sure to be prohibitive inasmuch as property values will rise enormously. At the same time a developer does have to demonstrate good judgment not to get in over his head. If large amounts

of land may be acquired at prices paid in that area for farm land, considerable portions may well be acquired *providing the developer has financial backing to make it possible for him to carry the land until the market rises.* Even so, the land should be developed in parts, not all at once.

6. The operator, in choosing the land he plans to sell at retail, should analyze his market to determine the class of buyers who will bring him the most profit on his enterprise. It is sometimes a question of selling to a lower socioeconomic class of people rapidly and with modest profits, or on the other hand, selling at much higher prices to a considerably higher class of people at a not so accelerated pace.

7. Land which is gently rolling, or possessing lake or river frontage, may be profitably used for medium and higher priced lots. Although improvements may cost more to install, the charm lent to the property by a little picturesqueness later will sell lots at higher prices.

Obtaining the best price and terms

Having given due consideration to general fundamentals underlying the selection of land for subdivision purposes, the next step is to acquire it upon the best price and terms possible. Sometimes an operator can afford to pay a higher price for land if he succeeds in securing favorable terms of payment. Most owners usually ask enough for their property, and some have the notion that because land fully or partly improved adjoins their holdings raw acreage should bring as much as the improved property. They forget that many expenses are involved in the development, sale and carrying of a subdivision enterprise, which is a credit risk the same as other lines of business.

Most subdividers buy their new holdings through brokers or through special scouts whom they employ to comb suburban territory for tracts suitable for development. Some brokers specialize in this sort of business. If an owner of suitable land for developing is approached directly by a known subdivider who is operating successfully in a community, the owner is likely to ask a prohibitive price. If a broker or private scout casually approaches an owner, a better basis for price and terms can invariably be established.

Many operators fail because they take on too much property to subdivide. The more successful ones plan to develop just enough to sell out in one or two seasons. When a large property is taken over, only an amount is improved that may reasonably be expected to be sold in a single season.

Except in southern and Pacific coast cities, subdivision operations are most active from May to November. There is a distinct lull during the winter seasons, though many operators work out special plans to permit them to continue operations unabated throughout the year.

Subdividing land is a complicated business, and cannot be entered into and profitably carried on without a great deal of specialized knowledge, and this should be kept in mind by the investor in outlying acreage who has visions of the city engulfing a piece of property and absorbing it at high prices. There are many risks just as there are certain gains resulting when the operation is thoughtfully directed.

Assuming that the price is a satisfactory one, the matter of terms must be given careful attention. Most subdividers do not actually invest a great deal of cash in properties. The reason for this is that the operator seeks to reserve most of his available cash for the installation of the necessary improvements and overhead of selling expense. Many an operation involving a $50,000 or $75,000 tract of land has started with an investment by an operator of $5,000 or $10,000, the land owner taking back a mortgage on his property and agreeing to release lots from under the so-called "blanket" mortgage as they are sold.

Under such an arrangement, the land owner releases small parcels on the basis of the value the single lot bears to the value of the entire acreage, plus twenty per cent. This can be worked out to a cent mathematically before sales begin. The land owner not only receives a down payment, but he also benefits by the expenditure of money by the operator in installing improvements and setting up and placing in operation a selling organization for the disposal of the land. This plan has worked out successfully on many occasions, and as the sale of the land progresses, the operator clears away his underlying mortgage and reaps his profits from the sale of the residue of the lots.

Land for development purposes seldom is purchased outright. In some instances, subdivisions have even been taken over by operators and sold out without any down payment to the land owner whatever, all security coming to that person by reason of the substantial sums of money spent on improvements before sales actually were permitted to begin and transfers made.

Some large and successful operators invite investors to join in their deals, arranging to have such investors buy a property outright, and then paying them back the actual price of the land plus forty or fifty per cent of the profits accruing from the transaction, which still leaves the operator a comfortable profit.

It is generally conceded that most of the larger subdivisions take at least five years to completely sell out, and it is maintained that any mortgage on the property subject to release clauses should extend for that time, the subdivider being required to make annual payments in reduction of his indebtedness, in addition to the amount received by the original land owner upon the release of individual lots. Usually release payments are merged in the specified amount the operator is responsible for each year.

Layout and planning

Modern subdivisions, even the humblest, are now being laid out quite differently from those of a generation ago. The old rectangular plat, resulting in a series of square or oblong blocks, has changed to permit the installing of slightly curved or winding streets, which give character and charm to a neighborhood.

Pavements in strictly residential neighborhoods do not need to be more than thirty feet in width, and sometimes even less. Sidewalks are laid in conjunction with curbs so there is no lawn between them. This allows of a wider tree lawn which can always be better taken care of by a home owner.

Many cities have planning or platting commissions which pass upon plans for a subdivision before work may be started. Violation of any of the rules of the commission are met with a refusal to connect public service facilities with those furnished by the municipality. A sewer which has no outlet beyond the boundaries of a property and water mains which have no pumping station to supply water are of little use to the subdivider or his customers, so he is eager to have his property plat approved, and consequently he obeys the regulations set forth.

Most platting commissions now require cross streets in a subdivision at least every 1,000 feet apart. This permits vehicles to be turned at these intersections. Too many cross streets involve the needless use of land.

Costs of installing improvements vary greatly in different cities, but the cost per lineal foot per lot in the average sized city will probably be about $25, including hard surfaced pavements and other modern improvements. On a fifty foot lot, it may be seen that the sum of about $1,250 must be expended, regardless of the original cost of the land, selling and other expense, and not forgetting an additional amount to represent a profit to the operator.

Lot sales

Establishing lot prices in a subdivision is a difficult matter and one which can be accurately solved only after considerable experience in operating. A close study of competitive property must be made as to prices being received. If priced too low, there is no profit in the operation. If too much is asked, the operator fails to attract buyers, which is just as disastrous to his project.

The same psychological condition which prompts department stores to sell articles at 98 cents or $2.98 is taken advantage of by the subdivider who finds that he can sell more lots at $995 and $1,950 than he can at $1,000 and $2,000 for the same lots.

It is claimed that the operator who handles the inexpensive class of home sites makes more money in a season than the one who markets high-priced property, but this theory is open to considerable discussion, as it has been disproven many times. The thing to do under most circumstances is to develop the property in conformity with the neighborhood and the class of people who are expected to buy there, and then charge the cost plus a reasonable profit.

Many cities will not accept plats of subdivisions where lots have a frontage of less than eighty feet. This is a wise rule for it does away with congested conditions such as are found in many sections of large cities where lots originally were cut as narrow as fifteen or twenty feet. These can be improved only with "row" houses, which are out of style and definitely undesirable.

Platting commissions now insist on orderly subdivision of land. Often they lay out definite plans for future development, extending out into the open country. Main and secondary highways are laid out on paper, with open spaces for street development such as may suit the operator's convenience. In his plat, however, the subdivider is not permitted to install dead end streets, and he must link in his thoroughfares to existing streets or ones to be installed later. By this plan the operator in buying property knows definitely the limitations to which he will be subjected.

Expenditures for a sales force average about fifteen per cent of the cost of a subdivision. Salesmen draw from six to fifteen per cent, according to salability of the property. Superintendents and crew managers get from three to five per cent, and a general sales manager receives from two to three per cent. Advertising, done mostly in the daily newspapers, in most cities averages five per cent. Other incidentals usually bring the sales up to thirty per cent or more.

Most subdivisions are sold on the partial payment plan, from ten to twenty per cent of the cost price of each lot being required at the time the contract is signed. Subsequent payments are made on a basis, usually, of one or two per cent a month, with interest on deferred payments of eight per cent. Interest sometimes is waived for a year or more, but it is buried in the price of the lot just the same. Cash discounts sometimes are given to buyers who wish to pay outright for properties they acquire.

Most modern subdivisions have careful restrictions concerning the use of the land. Houses must be of at least a certain price; must be set back a given number of feet from the sidewalk; must remain a given distance from side of a lot; no outbuildings except garages may be erected; only low fences may be built, and other conditions are definitely set down so the territory may develop in an attractive manner. In some high-grade properties, house plans must be approved by the realty operator before work can proceed. This is done not only to have an orderly architectural development, but is sometimes used to keep undesirable persons out of an area, as house plans submitted by them will be rejected on one pretext or another.

The better the class of restrictions, the higher the prices charged and obtained for lots. Operators have found that high-class development pays; that the average individual desires to live in a well-regulated locality, and that he will pay for the protection which rigid restrictions provide.

Some of the most successful operators will not permit the installation of alleys in their developments, maintaining that alleys furnish a dumping ground for rubbish and litter which should not be allowed to accumulate. Alleys in downtown business sections, however, are most essential for loading and unloading merchandise, as automobile parking regulations in cities are constantly tightening up, and it is difficult for merchandise to be carried into a business building through the front door or sidewalk elevator entrance.

Many of the better grade subdivisions restrict against the erection of multiple dwellings of any sort. Others permit two-family, four-family, and larger apartment buildings in certain sections where they may act as buffers against undesirable neighborhoods which adjoin the property.

Zoning laws have been adopted in many cities where the use of buildings in certain localities is definitely regulated. Such laws tend to enhance and stabilize property values, and when reasonably conceived and executed are a benefit to any community. They are especially valuable in preventing encroachment into residential districts of undesirable buildings, such as public garages, taverns, and similar enterprises.

Property restrictions in subdivisions range from twenty years for cheap developments up to 100 years for very high-grade enterprises. The more rigid and the longer the restrictions run, the better the class of building development which usually may be expected to take place.

Operators are interested in seeing the values of individual lots increase, as it enables them to sell their remaining holdings at better prices. They always encourage and frequently help the financing of building operations, as new homes assist greatly in the sale of property because the section takes on life and individuality. Many operators build houses to establish the character of the neighborhood, and it is interesting to know that the standard nearly always is steadily maintained. The most successful operators all build extensively, making profits on both their land and the houses they sell. This is the highest type of subdividing and the one on which most money can be made.

After a property is partially built up many sales will be made through residents who have built homes for themselves. They have friends and callers who become interested in the locality. Operators keep in close touch with homeowners in subdivisions which are selling out, and many valuable tips and much assistance is secured in this way.

There are investors in many cities who buy acreage and pay the cost of developing it themselves, giving a contract to a sales organization to dispose of the lots. A commission of from twenty-five to thirty-five per cent is paid for this service. A difficulty with this plan is that after the cream has been skimmed off and sales become harder to make, the selling agent may lose interest and is likely to shift operations to a new field, something he would not do, of course, if he had a personal stake in the property.

Tag end lots in a subdivision usually are difficult to sell. So are "butt" lots. Since the coming of the automobile, corner lots move more readily than formerly, as it is convenient to drive into one's garage from a side street. The noise and lack of privacy attendant upon living on a corner lot, however, and the increased cost of improvements and taxes make corner lots difficult to dispose of, especially as most operators add from ten to fifteen per cent to the price of such properties.

Subdividing property is a highly specialized business, requiring considerable capital. Unless an investor is willing to make it his principal business and devote his entire time to it, it may be said that money can be made more easily and quickly by operating in other kinds of real estate. If he desires to specialize, however, it is often an excellent field in which to make money.

The trend in subdividing land is definitely toward the aim of creating self-contained small cities or cities-within-cities. Instead of dividing a small tract into a number of homesites, a very large tract is acquired and divided in such a way as to anticipate every need the new community might have as it grows, and to capitalize on those needs that will develop along with the subdivision. Thus, the land is divided to allow for a shopping center, parks, church sites, multi-family units, condominiums, etc. One of the most critical needs of a growing community is schools. Clever operators offer the school officials land within the subdivision at a low cost so as to assure the success of the subdivision.

TWENTY-ONE

Operating in Real Estate

Creative genius commands the supreme price paid for the efforts of men in their life's work. The reward to the individual possessing this rare characteristic who uses it properly is not only sure and certain but also commands favorable recognition from everyone. The opportunity for demonstrating this genius is to be found in every field of endeavor. It may be an inventor who presents the world with a useful invention, or one who directs his energies to the development of new ideas in social service. Often it may be a businessman who by reason of his foresight is able to promote or conduct a commercial enterprise better than his fellows, instilling new ideas which force the business to the front.

The creative genius in the real estate field finds his best opportunity in the development of properties which he may acquire either for himself or as the promoter of a syndicate of investors. He may be fortunate in possessing enough capital to enable him to conduct his operations alone. More often his unique ability will produce the rewards which, by careful investment, grow until he himself becomes a capitalist able to command large resources.

The broker who represents the buyer and seller and unearths opportunities for realty investment often stands as a genius, but usually his training and function require him to serve as an intermediary and to act solely for others. The owner of capital is often satisfied to let his money work for him, relying upon the ability of others to make it increase. But the operator lives by his brains; his foresight and ingenuity furnish the incentive which creates out of a rough vacant area a new business center, or causes land formerly unused to develop into a use wherein it not only serves the community and fulfills a definite need, but also provides satisfactory profits for the operator.

Operators who plan and erect buildings help develop cities and increase the desirability of the locality as a place in which to live. He is the operator who builds a fine theater behind a row of stores, utilizing a worthless back area, and providing thereby entertainment facilities for many thousands. He is the operator who lays out and finances new subdivisions where people may erect beautiful homes.

The operator in real estate has demonstrated his worth to the community. In former years he was little appreciated and often was considered unnecessary. He was often a real estate speculator, buying to sell at a profit, mortgaging everything to erect a building, always facing discouragement from his friends who frankly laughed at him. Operating is now a recognized business worthy of the best talent available.

What it takes

The essentials for successful operating in real estate are foresight and imagination, honesty and square-dealing, a thorough knowledge of the broad basic principles which underlie the growth and development of cities, with particular reference to the section wherein one intends to operate, a knowledge of the peculiarities and habits of people, and last but not least a power to attract capital to finance enterprises. Behind it all must be sound business judgment to steer around hidden rocks which may mean disaster to promotions.

Not everyone can become an operator. There are many who have not the essential qualifications for such a career. Likewise there are those who may have qualifications which, when properly directed, result in profitable ventures.

Types of operators

How is one to gain the knowledge necessary to embark on this interesting and profitable field? This can be done by a close study of the conditions as they were and are now in thickly populated sections; by watching keenly the shifting of business neighborhoods in cities; by keeping track of the increase in population and its sources, and the increase of wealth and commerce and their sources and distribution; by endeavoring to see where history will repeat itself and anticipate it, and by studying methods of financing real estate and profiting by the successes and mistakes of others. The successful operator must thoroughly know his city, he must correctly anticipate the needs of its people and then have the courage and understanding which will carry him through to a successful conclusion of the enterprise undertaken.

The city, for example, may be in need of a new street to connect a residential section with a business district. A close study will reveal this condition. Convinced of the need, the operator will proceed to option the necessary property to extend the street, at the same time acquiring sufficient land upon both sides of the proposed thoroughfare so that when it is opened, he will be able to sell as frontage upon the new street, land that was formerly the rear yards of lots fronting upon other streets. He will assist in fathering the necessary legislation through the city council, and when the street is opened, his reward will come from providing new facilities for travel which will enhance the value of his holdings adjacent thereto and permit him to sell at a substantial profit.

In one middle western community, a real estate operator visualized the need of the community for new and better places of amusement. Selecting a location upon the city's principal business thoroughfare not far distant from what was then the established retail shopping center, he obtained long-term leases upon several tracts of land at prices below the values of nearby land. Promoting and constructing a building containing two theaters was his next endeavor. In laying out his project, he radically departed from what was the recognized plan of theaters and built the auditoriums over 300 feet back from the property line, utilizing the street frontage for retail store purposes and affording access to the auditoriums with long entrances attractively designed and elaborately furnished. What was formerly waste land he converted into highly profitable commercial space and still had the use of the high-priced street frontage for store purposes. His profits on the transaction were large, and by his foresight he caused others to invest large sums in new buildings nearby and soon created a new business and theater district.

Important street intersections in business districts beckon for constructive endeavor, particularly when located near a residential district inadequately supplied with neighborhood shopping and amusement facilities. Often an old building designed for a special purpose such as a church, market, or skating rink will afford opportunity for a wide awake operator to remodel it for more constructive and profitable use. In one city, a former clubhouse having a large gymnasium stood abandoned on the main street for many years until a merchant saw the possibilities of utilizing it for his particular business. He acquired the land and in turn sold the vacant land fronting on the street for enough to remodel his building and leave him a fine profit, reserving an entrance through the large modern building which was later erected in front of the old structure.

An interesting promotion on the part of another operator involved the use of land situated in the rear of commercial buildings fronting on two important parallel business thoroughfares. One of these streets, however, was about twenty feet lower in grade than the other. The operator acquired control of buildings fronting on both streets, cut through adequate entrances and then erected a "double deck" movie house. The upper theater had its entrance from one street and the lower one was entered from the other. Both streets furnished patrons for this unique theater in which the same film was projected on both levels at the same time. This gave double earning power to a tract of rear land which up to the time of its improvement in the manner noted was practically valueless.

Since building costs have increased so largely during recent years, there has come into existence a type of operator who makes a practice of acquiring old mercantile buildings, rehabilitating them, cutting large store units into smaller ones, and greatly increasing the rentals thereby. In one city a ground floor store which was bringing $20,000 per year rentals was subdivided into nine small units and made to earn $90,000 per year. The cost of making the alterations was nominal.

Another type of real estate operator engages in the erection of apartment houses in small or large units. Financing is done through mortgages, and the operator himself usually has little money in each project. Many small operators in the larger cities erect one or two buildings each year and dispose of them at a nominal profit which frequently represents only a good salary for superintending the work. More ambitious schemes, of course, are worked out from time to time and result beneficially to the locality where the new enterprise is situated and, usually, to the promoter himself. Operating in this field has become a specialized business and needs careful study and unceasing attention to details. The inclination to overbuild in the apartment field is ever present and this naturally involves hazards which must be carefully considered by the investor who is attracted to this branch of the real estate business.

Some operators give attention to the erection of single homes and duplexes in wholesale lots. They buy blocks of improved lots from sub-dividers and proceed to build up street after street with dwelling houses which are sold at nominal but satisfactory profits. By applying the principle of "mass production—small profits" they are successful in making a good living out of the business. These men are frequently referred to as "speculative builders." They perform a distinct service in furnishing an adequate supply of housing accommodations for a class of buyers who have only small amounts to pay as their initial deposits on the purchase of homes.

A favorite plan of operation in many cities is to take advantage of the natural inclination of businesses of a similar character to group themselves in neighboring districts, or in buildings equipped to meet their requirements. Large projects have been promoted in different cities where special buildings have been erected for the exclusive use of physicians, lawyers, insurance agents, dentists, textile dealers, jewelry manufacturers, millinery supply firms, and many other lines which find it advantageous to operate in close proximity to each other.

Many realty operators have directed their attention to supplying garage facilities in congested districts. Some unique plans have been worked out for the utilization of unused land located in the rear of business streets for the storage of automobiles. This land, when once improved, earns large returns on the initial investment which, usually, is relatively small.

In the congested downtown areas of the larger cities, enterprising operators have erected high-rise parking garages. Cars are quickly moved to any level by means of ramps or elevators. Where land is at a premium, the only way to go is up.

Another use to which rear land has been placed in some cities is the construction of arcades containing many small stores between business thoroughfares. This should never be attempted except between two heavily traveled thoroughfares, otherwise there will be no flow of pedestrian travel through the arcade, and it will be impossible to rent stores as merchants will soon find they cannot make a living. Given the proper setting, however, an arcade can be made to produce a large and profitable return.

A unique promotion by the Van Sweringen interests some years ago in Cleveland is worthy of attention. A $60,000,000 passenger terminal serving a number of railroads was so planned that practically all the space in the huge building was made to produce rentals, train facilities being located in the basement which had been excavated so all trains entered at lower levels. Stores fronted on several of the adjoining thoroughfares, a 1,000 room hotel occupied a portion of the site, and the remaining building space was used for offices and similar purposes.

Important promotions have been worked out by foresighted operators in connection with summer resorts and country clubs. These have been the magnets which have attracted many people who have purchased summer cottage and permanent homesites in such neighborhoods.

Almost every large city has a high grade subdivision with a nine or eighteen hole golf course in connection. Some of the finest residential lots are grouped about the golf course itself which often furnishes a vista particularly pleasing to those who desire to erect exclusive homes. From the operator's standpoint this is good business for by giving enough land for a golf course, an additional price may be added to adjacent lots to more than pay for the donation of land and leave a handsome profit besides. Small parks serve the same purpose.

As cities grow in size, downtown business property becomes increasingly valuable and more difficult to obtain. It is the natural instinct of the skilled operator to in some profitable way utilize every square foot of land which is not earning a return. He will spread out on his desk a map of his city's business district, study it carefully, note where land remains vacant, plan a profitable enterprise which can utilize the waste land, and then acquire control of the necessary property with this promotion in view. When the improvement is completed the operator has not only made money but has performed a definite service for his city by literally obeying the sentiment of the biblical injunction to make two blades of grass grow where one grew before.

Genius leaps beyond precedent and is not dismayed at the failure of others to accomplish what is clearly a sound and logical purpose. Genius, however, must be fortified by a thorough study of the fundamental principles which have contributed to the successes or failures of others. Just as the manager of a department store, in the face of accepted opinion to the contrary, will sometimes move his business into a new and untried location, pioneering frequently with satisfactory results, so will the realty operator when convinced that his analysis and study of conditions is correct, press forward with his project in the face of adverse criticism.

With real estate values and building costs at high levels in cities, the operator usually finds that in order to promote a venture he must secure financial assistance from others.[1] Syndicating, consequently, has become customary, and speculative investments in real estate are divided among a number who are willing to stake a limited amount of capital upon the judgment of the operator. The syndicating operator must be able to command the respect and loyalty of men with money who will rely upon his opinion. He should never solicit support for his plans until he is reasonably certain that he has analyzed conditions so thoroughly that he cannot only convince others of the correctness of his judgment and the soundness of the contemplated project, but also be assured that his plans will not miscarry because of some small hole in the dyke which he has not discovered or has neglected to stop up. This care his syndicate associates not only expect but demand of him. His integrity, sincerity, and good faith is that of a trustee in whose control is placed substantial sums of money for a profitable investment.

Integrity is fundamental. The operator may need financial support from banks and other money-lending institutions before his enterprise proceeds very far, and he must be able to secure this support promptly and at not too great a cost. Failure may be excusable, but dishonest and sharp practice can never be condoned.

Genius is frequently displayed by operators in methods adopted for financing enterprises. For instance, one man became interested in the possibilities of an old building located on a downtown corner. He found that it had been erected upon leased land. The terms of the 99 year lease on the land provided for a reappraisal to fix rents in ten-year periods. Inquiry from the fee owner disclosed a willingness to convert the reappraisal lease into a graded lease with fixed rentals. The operator thereupon sought the lessee and obtained an option for the purchase of the leasehold estate and the buildings at reasonable valuations. Before closing the deal, however, the operator negotiated a contract with the land owner converting the reappraisal lease into one with fixed rentals upon a basis higher than were being paid at the time but much less than the actual and potential value of the property. The purchase of the leasehold was

---

1 An excellent form of syndicating agreement may be found in the Appendix.

then consummated, and financing effected by a mortgage for the amount of the purchase price necessary to acquire the interest of the original lessee. All of the operations in the transaction were made carefully to enmesh the various phases, and no risk was taken by the operator as he did not proceed to buy the leasehold estate until he had arranged for definite rentals, nor until he had the entire project successfully financed.

It is one thing to buy property and entirely another thing to sell it. Little profit is usually made until a sale is effected, so that one who knows how to buy properly makes a sale much easier if he acquires property at a price which makes possible a profitable sale. Not much money, ordinarily, is made from actually operating a building. The greatest returns await those who are able to profit from the increased land values which come from the growth of cities and the business districts therein. To a competent building manager there is usually a fair interest return upon the money actually invested in a property, but fortunes are seldom made from this type of operating except where property acquired in a location before it has come into favor benefits substantially from a shift in a business district.

Care should be taken by an operator to provide for a thorough bookkeeping and accounting system which should disclose all items of income and expense in connection with the operation of a property. Adequate reserves should be provided from the rentals obtained from commercial properties to take care of ground rents, taxes, interest requirements upon mortgage loans, depreciation, repairs, maintenance costs and operating expense. Nothing will discountenance an operator as much as failure to meet his obligations when due.

Do's and Dont's

In operating in real estate:

1. Do not plunge into an enterprise until you have thoroughly investigated it.
2. Do not be driven to make a decision by a persistent broker or owner who merely desires to make a commission or profit.
3. Do not expect to buy at the bottom of the market and sell at the top.
4. Be satisfied if you make a satisfactory profit in a reasonable time. Let the other fellow have his profit too.
5. If your judgment has proven wrong and you see losses ahead, be willing and courageous enough to take your loss before your ship sinks.

6. Be honest with your associates if you are a syndicator. Never misrepresent a property in negotiating for a sale. Do everything to inspire confidence not only in your ability but, most of all, in your integrity.

7. Rely upon competent advice. Do not attempt to act as your own broker, banker, lawyer or architect. Men who have specialized knowledge along these lines will make you more money and fully justify the fees charged. Sound advice is always cheap, no matter what it costs. Do not seek to get advice without paying for it. Free advice is usually worth no more than what it costs.

8. Having assembled your facts, made your studies, and consulted your experts, make your own decisions and stick to them until proven right or wrong. One swallow does not make a summer, nor does one loss spell total failure. Courage is vitally essential to success in any business, and particularly is it needed in realty operating.

TWENTY-TWO

Exchanging Real Estate

Whether the real estate market be good or bad, there is always a considerable amount of exchanging of real estate being done. Man's trading instinct is at the bottom of most real estate ownership, for while a property may be bought as an investment or for actual use, it will promptly be sold if the owner feels he can realize a satisfactory profit.

Those who acquire real estate may be divided, broadly speaking, into two classifications:

1. The investor, who buys land to hold for personal use or the investment return he can collect from its rental.
2. The trader, or the restless type, who, once he has bought a property is constantly seeking to sell or exchange it for something else, at the same time bettering his position either by making a direct profit or building up his equity. This is the chap who develops into the busy speculator during a real estate boom if he can muster the funds to operate on a large scale.

Exchanging or trading real estate requires a peculiar sales psychology, and the fact that most realty salesmen fail to have it results in comparatively few outstanding examples of successful traders, although almost every type of realty broker will at times consummate trade deals.

A considerable amount of the property which gets down to the trading level has something wrong with it. It lacks adequate income, or it is "crippled" in some respect, such as being located in an undesirable neighborhood or in the ownership of someone who is in distress and must dispose of it. There are legitimate trades, where one person has a property which fails to meet his needs which he successfully exchanges for another type of holding that he can use. In such an exchange one side may pay the other an extra sum in cash or execute a mortgage or second mortgage to enable equities to be evened up and a deal consummated.

How exchanges are made

Exchanges are executed in connection with almost all kinds of properties. A common type of exchange is a city home for a country estate or a farm. The owner of the farm or estate has grown lonely living out in the country and seeks the bright lights of the city. The city dweller has become weary of the roar and turmoil of metropolitan life and longs for the quiet solitude of rural life. Here is the setting for a natural trade. If equities are not equal they can be balanced with the giving of a mortgage or the payment of cash.

There are always persons who seek to move elsewhere. The man who owns two houses and a small apartment in Cleveland is eager to go to Arizona on account of his wife's health. Someone in Arizona who owns a furnished apartment and who used to live in Cleveland or a neighboring city, has developed an urge to go back to his old haunts. Here again is the making of a trade. It may be difficult to match up and adjust equities, but the clever trader will maneuver around until it is done and he gets his commission in cash, an equity in some kind of a property, or notes extending over some months. "Eastern" exchanges for "western," or "northern" for "southwestern," as the newspapers indicate the various general localities, are constantly in progress.

It may be found, occasionally, that the owner in a western state will consider exchanging a more or less desirable property for something back east, but he does it on what he calls a "cash out" basis. Let us assume that the western property is an apartment house with a reasonable value of $50,000 with an encumbrance in the form of a first trust deed amounting to approximately $30,000. This leaves an equity of $20,000. This owner either directly or through an exchange broker contacts the man in Cleve land who has two houses worth $15,000 and an apartment worth $25,000. Both properties are clear and represent clear equities of $40,000. They perhaps will not sell for $40,000 but let it be assumed the equity is substantially that, nevertheless. At least they can be placed under a first mortgage for $24,000.

Here is a "natural" for the quick-witted Arizona trader. He promptly inflates his price to $70,000 and increases his equity to $40,000, which he proceeds to trade for an equity of a similar size in the Ohio property. What happens then? The fast working Arizona trader hastens back to Ohio, smacks a $24,000 mortgage on his new holdings, gets the cash and hurries back to his home, satisfied to forget any actual equity he may have in the Cleveland property or entirely willing to trade it for almost anything he can get for it or whatever it actually can be readily sold for above the $24,000 mortgage. If he cannot sell it he will, through nonresident management, proceed to "milk" it of income until such a time as the bank or mortgage company which holds the $24,000 encumbrance wakes up and finds that it actually owns the property by reason of foreclosure. In the meantime the Clevelander who has paid $70,000 for the property in Arizona which is reasonably worth $50,000 subject to a $30,000 mortgage finds that he has been bilked out of about $20,000 in the deal.

This is typical of some of the "fast pitching" which occasionally takes place in connection with long distance trading in real estate. The moral of this is, of course, to know what one is going about when making a trade. Investigate every fact and feature which comes up in connection with a trade deal. One of the best ways, if you contemplate making such an exchange, is to go to the trouble and expense of having a broker, preferably a member of the American Institute of Real Estate Appraisers, give you a detailed valuation of the property which you are agreeing to take over and have the appraisal made *before you assume any obligation of ownership.*

Let it not be assumed that all trade deals are fraudulent. There are so many opportunities for small irregularities to creep in, however, that great caution must be exercised in any exchange. There seems to be such abysmal ignorance about the subject of real estate values and how to ascertain them that extraordinary claims on one side or the other regarding such values must be challenged constantly until they are proven to be correct, or otherwise. Get corroborative evidence of value if it is possible to do so. Get a bank or a mortgage company to give you an appraisal and an indication of what it would be willing to lend on the property. Contact realty brokers in the neighborhood and inquire what they will be willing to list the property for if you buy and want immediately to sell it. In no event accept entirely your own judgment of value without further confirmation.

An exchange of properties to be logical and beneficial to both sides should be fairly equitable, and if each side does not benefit, the deal should not be consummated. Both parties should be satisfied, just as in the case where a regular sale takes place.

The most active period for exchanging properties, in all probability, is during times of recession. Owners, although unable to sell for cash, for one reason or another are anxious to get rid of what they have and take on something else. Sometimes an owner sees difficulty ahead with the mortgage holder. His equity seems to be constantly diminishing, and he is anxious to realize something on it before he is wiped out. He will trade for almost anything and may be willing to take on obligations that he perhaps hopes may never have to be met. He can be traded properties which brokers refer to as "cats and dogs." From this combination of circumstances an unusual deal may emanate.

One is reminded of the proposed trade deal between one man who owned a loft building, a marble yard with dock privileges, a factory site and a summer garden, all of which he was going to swap with another man who owned a flock of tenements, a small subdivision, an abandoned lime kiln and a farm.

"He assumes a $20,000 mortgage on the loft building," explained the first man to his wife, "and I take over a second mortgage on the subdivision. Understand?"

"I guess I do," responded his wife, wearily, "but what is holding up the deal?"

"Well," he said. "You see, I want $4 in cash!"

Trading techniques

There seems to be a fascination with trading techniques which enthralls certain operators so that they engage in it to the total exclusion of almost all other kinds of business. Once a confirmed trader gets that way he usually stays so until he either makes a lot of money or goes broke. And he is liable to do both quite often over a period of years!

Sometimes both sides to a trade deal will own cripples which may be used to make a satisfactory deal simply because they match up fairly well. Such properties in new ownerships may prosper and take on additional value. No money passes and the person to worry is the broker engaging in the transaction who may have to wait months to realize anything out of the deal.

The new and rather important property for trade which has just loomed up on the horizon is the delight of exchange brokers. After almost every vestige of equity has been wrung out of it, or it has become so plastered with liens of one sort of another that it can scarcely be traded again, it may fall into the possession of someone who understands its proper treatment and it may emerge later as a fairly good property. Likewise, it may become a candidate for total foreclosure and then be started on a new and hectic career not a great deal unlike what it has experienced in the past.

Sometimes a property may become hard to move, and a discouraged owner may trade it for a small and unimportant equity, just to become free. The new owner may go ahead with remodelling operations which may make a new property of the old one, converting a losing venture into a profitable one.

Trading flourishes in the larger cities particularly, although in small towns there are always exchanges of one kind or another in progress. There are few accepted rules to guide negotiations beyond the natural trading instincts of those engaged in the transactions. If the principals and the broker are proceeding honestly, good may result; if not, a transaction may get snarled up and nobody will benefit.

The successful broker seeks at the outset to ascertain just what motives prompt the owners of the properties concerned Usually these motives are quite proper, in which event a satisfactory deal will result. If one side is trying to seek an adventage over the other, the broker must be wary in his negotiations or they will collapse. The wise broker who makes a specialty of trading will insist that all the cards be placed upon the table, and that values of properties and the equities of the owners be honestly and definitely indicated and recognized. To do this the broker must clearly ascertain the motives of each party. For instance, one owner may have been "milking" a property and be in a position where the mortgage holder is about to take it away from him. The exact status of this must be made known to the party on the other side, otherwise difficulty may ensue at the time actual equities are compared and transferred.

Frequently, an urgent demand for ready cash is the cause for a trade. An owner of clear property which he can neither sell nor borrow money upon will readily agree to trade it for another property on which money may be raised. This can be frequently accomplished, especially if a property in another and perhaps far distant city is taken in trade and then mortgaged.

Another type of property that may be traded is groups of lots which in some way or other have come into the possession of a banking institution. These concerns know little of how to sell such property and will frequently agree to trade it for other types of real estate which may be more readily salable at the time. When banks foreclose on very expensive houses for which there is no demand because of heavy taxes and maintenance charges, they will sometimes agree to trade such houses, free of encumbrances, for almost any kind of property which they can dispose of by either selling it or trading into another deal by which they can get their money.

An important feature of the broker-trader's art is the proper listing of property. The broker should obtain every single fact about a property before he agrees to attempt a sale or trade. Here the honesty of the owner will be tested, for, due to various causes, he may seek to misrepresent the lot size, the mortgage or its duration, or income. These should be checked thoroughly and confirmed against the day the property may actually become part of a deal, because errors will arise and cause trouble unless infinite care has been taken to get all the data right at the time of listing. For this reason most trading brokers in giving out a statement on property have printed on such a statement a qualifying note that all information has been received from what are thought to be reliable sources and is believed to be correct but is not guaranteed by the broker

A broker engaging in exchanging properties, under rules of real estate board procedure, is entitled to two commissions in a trade deal, one from each side, on the very definite assumption that an equal service is being rendered each side. The only qualification is that the broker notify each party at the outset that if he negotiates a successful deal, he proposes to collect a full commission from both parties. It may be preferable, however, to have each side represented by its own broker.

Prices and values

A curious thing about trade deals is that in almost every instance each party insists on quoting inflated prices. This is done on the evident assumption that the other fellow is going to ask too much for his holding, therefore the price must be inflated to meet such a practice! Here the broker may be able to get the parties back on the ground, to a consideration of honest values. If he is not able to do so and is still able to make the deal, he benefits by reasons of the larger commissions he should collect on the values of properties involved. Remember—the commissions are not quoted on the equities of the various parties but upon the total values of the properties as represented in the deal.

As long as there are misfits in business and as long as buyers take over properties with which they later become dissatisfied, there will be real estate trading. A favorite type of exchange is turning in country property such as farms, ranches, orchards, and groves for equities in city properties. If the country property is productive of income and not too heavily encumbered, these deals are often quite successful.

Another productive source of trading material is with operative builders who erect new apartment or store properties establishing equities in such operations. If the new property lags and fails to sell readily, and carrying charges such as taxes begin to pile up, the builder is glad to trade himself out of the new property into one which is clear and on which he may raise cash, or a property which has a good equity and is earning a return in the form of rent. Later, the builder may trade such an equity for a vacant lot, get himself financed again for the total cost of a building, and proceed once more to erect another enterprise to again trade or sell if he can dispose of it that way.

A useful service is frequently performed by a broker engaged in trading properties in that he is able to get a property out of the hands of what is called a "turbulent" owner, into the hands of another owner who understands it and the way it should be handled, and makes it a profitable investment. A turbulent owner is one who fails to look after a property properly, neglects it, fails to take the trouble to select tenants carefully, and otherwise fails on the managerial side which is often so important in the final sale of such a holding. A disagreeable or discontented owner is a poor advertisement of both the property he owns and the real estate business of which he is actually a part. Investors are attracted by successfully operated enterprises, and when a property which has been mishandled gets into new and understanding hands, everybody is benefited.

Most persons who engage in trading properties prefer to deal in types which have incomes that pay definite returns and help to carry them. This does not mean that vacant properties are not frequently exchanged for one reason or another, the most obvious being that they are ripe for development and finally get into the hands of someone who has the enterprise to convert them from non-paying vacant land into useful building sites which readily earn their way and render an income to their owners.

The trade deals which *are not made* are those in which one side very patently attempts to inflate a property to a point where, if the deal went through, the other fellow would "lose his shirt," as the trader says. Traders have horse sense and usually know values, so deals of this type are seldom successfully made. If proper adjustments for value are made, and each party gets a property he can use and is satisfied with, such a trade is just as useful and proper as an outright sale, although not a dollar in cash may pass between the contracting parties. The one having the most difficulty is usually the broker, who must pry out his commission on the deal in some way so he can continue eating regularly. And much might be said of his splendid ability to do this!

During a real estate boom values soar, and large mortgages are imposed on properties with good incomes. Later a recession may come and incomes decline, and while mortgages may have been whittled down to some extent, they are still burdensome. Meanwhile too, an owner may have met with financial reverses and may be compelled to use his property as a meal ticket. This "milking" of the income cannot continue very long before such a property gets to be dangerously near the class of one *which must be discarded,* usually a trade of some sort being the logical way out. The owner begins to look around for relief, contacts a trading broker, and before long a deal is conceived. A new owner able to carry the property in question comes into the picture, and the holding which was perilously near foreclosure is revitalized and made whole again.

Owners seeking to trade their properties often have perfectly honest reasons for doing so, and one cannot say that a property offered for trade necessarily has secret defects. An actual sale may not have been possible, but a trade appears which interests the owner and he proceeds to improve his position by making such a deal. Many a person has obtained a property through a trade which later took on greatly added value, largely because of the turn in the real estate cycle and the ability of the new owner to properly manage the new holding. What may be a miserable failure in one owner's hands may become a prime income property under the management of another better qualified person.

Over three hundred years ago some Dutchmen traded with the Indians for Manhattan Island, paying them $30 and a few pounds of tobacco. Today Manhattan is worth billions of dollars and business frontages soar to $25,000 per foot front and more. Since then innumerable trades have been made and most of them have made money for the parties concerned.[1] If you own property which might bring you a readier and perhaps better return by trading it, don't hesitate to investigate the merits of such a transaction. It may make you some real money!

---

[1] For a further elaboration of this subject of exchanging real estate, see Richard R. Reno, *Profitable Real Estate Exchanging and Counseling* (Englewood Cliffs, N.J.: Prentice-Hall, Inc., 1965).

TWENTY-THREE

Speculating in Real Estate

During World War II real estate prices skyrocketed. Rentals in urban areas were almost impossible to find. During post-war years, monumental housing developments, much of it under government influence, made an attempt to bring the housing situation under control. Some progress was made to alleviate housing shortages during the 1950's, but the 1960's saw the war babies married and setting up homes by the millions. So the boom in housing has continued, although some specific areas have been depressed.

With the 1970's upon us, it seems that the matter of relocation of slum dwellers through urban renewal will be an important factor in real estate. Twenty-two million people need to be moved out of the slums, so the time is still ripe for speculation. The overall population continues to increase too.

Through all of this, would-be speculators have said with considerable chagrin, "If I had only bought back when prices were down, look where I would be today." On the other hand, speculators have not held back. They have not been dismayed just because prices were three times what they were twenty years ago. They have gone ahead and bought, *and look at where they are today.* For the most part speculators in real estate have done well, but many have gone broke too.

When prosperity comes and real estate starts to vie with stocks and bonds for popular investment favor, then speculators will direct their attention to buying and selling real estate on a speculative basis. This being so, the practice becomes a recognized part of the real estate business. It seems quite logical, then, that the subject of speculating should be considered in this book. A speculator in real estate is one who acquires property, whether vacant or improved, entirely with a view to resale or trade at a later time, thereby realizing a profit.

There are men throughout the country who have surplus funds for ready use, who frankly style themselves speculators, and justify their actions by pointing out that by the exercise of keen vision and definite knowledge, they are able to buy real estate, often develop it into property which produces a fine income, and then sell it at a substantial profit.

It is not intended here to enter into a discussion of the status or value of a speculator as such. It is apparent that many men and women do speculate in real estate, and others desire to join them, but don't know how to go about it.

Dangers to avoid

Here are a few things *not to do* in speculating:

1. Don't venture into speculating in real estate unless you can afford to take a chance on losing money. Become an investor instead, and buy only such real estate that you know has a well defined value, relatively unaffected by fluctuations of any kind.
2. Don't become a speculator unless you have studied the field in which you intend to operate. If you do not know your field and cannot visualize its future, you may lose money. Then you won't be even a speculator—you will be a dismal failure!
3. Don't speculate in real estate unless you are somewhat familiar with the underlying fundamentals of city growth.
4. Don't speculate in real estate in a new and untried manner. In all probability, you will lose all or most of your money. If the speculation offered you can be tested by comparison with similar operations previously engaged in by either yourself or someone else, you will have a basis on which to compute the possibilities of gain.
5. Don't speculate on a falling market. You may be burdened with carrying charges which will ruin you before the cycle turns upward again.

6. Don't speculate with anyone's money but your own. You may get into serious trouble. If it is your own money and you lose it, it isn't the business of anyone to criticize, except your wife.
7. Don't spread your speculations out too thinly. Speculate on the theory that conditions may become depressed, and you may have to carry the property through a slump.

Having indicated some of the things not to do when you venture into the speculative field, there may be considered some of the ways in which real estate speculation may be a profitable enterprise. After all is said and done, few real estate speculators, if they operate sanely, lose very much money. They may not make very much at times, it is true, but if they do lose their money it is because they have violated the ordinary rules of good business.

Opportunities in speculation

Granted that one is willing to assume the chances involved, where and how is the best way to enter the field of speculating in real estate?

Main outgoing thoroughfares, extending from the heart of a growing city to its circumference, offer opportunites for speculation as well as investment. It is amazing the manner in which outgoing radial thoroughfares develop and property values on these streets increase. Choose a street which leads from a main business district to a high-grade residential district, and then buy property on this artery linking the two. This is probably the safest and most profitable speculation the average community can offer. There may come a slump, but it is seldom, indeed, that such property recedes much in value. It may remain stationary in value for a time, but later it is almost certain to advance.

New business centers developing in outlying sections are fertile fields for speculation. One successful Chicago speculator maintains that active business districts spring up along main thoroughfares about two and one half miles apart. He goes to the edge of such a development, settles down upon one or more pieces of property, and waits for the steady flow of development to roll over him, increasing his values, and making his holdings worth more money as time passes.

Small towns close to large cities often offer opportunities for speculation. Of course under a program of this sort the entire territory must be experiencing general prosperity. Los Angeles has a score of small towns and cities clustering about its borders, in many of which excellent speculations in real estate have been encountered.

One successful speculator makes a practice of confining his operations to fields of this kind. He will survey a town which is close to a much larger city and ascertain that the city and towns are growing together by the impetus of each other's natural expansion. He will select a vacant property which is just outside of the high-priced district, and in a year or two he finds that the development of the town has enveloped him, his property has increased in value and is salable at a profit.

The tremendous increase in the use of automobiles has compelled the opening or widening of radial thoroughfares in many cities. These attract speculators in the early stages, because men have been keen-witted enough to realize that after an improvement of this sort has been completed, frontage values increase for business use. Before or just after the improvement is announced, a speculator with vision will be able to buy properties which owners sell at what they then think are high prices, not realizing the importance of the development which is to come. Later prices realized by speculators are much greater than the original owners ever contemplated, or they would not have sold. This faculty of visualizing the future is the one which permits the speculator to realize his profit.

One of the important things to be observed in speculating in real estate is to secure favorable terms of payment. Suppose that you have set your heart on buying a well-located vacant corner lot on a good business street and that the price asked is $60,000. An asking price is seldom an evidence of value. Owners have a habit of asking more than they expect to get, and buyers almost invariably offer less than they expect to give. Let it be assumed that the owner is persuaded, finally, to accept $50,000 for the corner lot, which cost him $35,000 two years previously. If a payment of $10,000 cash and a first mortgage to be carried by the owner for $40,000 can secure the lot, it doubtless will be a good buy, especially if the mortgage does not need to be amortized, and extends for several years. Let us assume that the lot is carried two years and sells for $70,000. On an original investment of $10,000, you have made $20,000 less carrying charges in two years' time as against $1200 you would have realized if you had invested your $10,000 in a six per cent mortgage, or other security for two years. Such an increase in a speculative real estate market is not unusual when conditions are right and times are prosperous. Remember that favorable terms are advantageous in every speculative deal, and the greater the actual burden the former owner of a property can be made to carry on a reasonable interest charge, the easier the carrying burden will be for you.

How can one determine if a property has speculative value? This is a revelation which will come only by a study of the elements of speculation as indicated in districts where there have been unusual rises in values. History repeats itself in real estate as in other lines, and if a similar situation arises which duplicates one in which there have been great increases in values, it is reasonable to suppose that a speculative market will follow, and there will be opportunities to buy and sell at a profit. A competent speculator is usually only a good guesser, who bases his guess on definite conclusions and conditions which indicate that growth will be steady and constant.

There is no recognized period of time which may elapse between buying and selling in a speculative market. In one instance, a turn of a property may be effected in a few months. In other cases, where the demand is less insistent, the time which may elapse may be years. No two speculative markets have exactly the same history. In the city of Los Angeles, there have been times when property could be turned at a substantial profit several times in a year, and nothing thought about it. In a more conservative eastern city, a speculator may have to hold a property two or three years before he realizes his profit, and even then the accomplishment may be looked upon as phenomenal.

Inherent elements of growth, such as the entrance into the territory of population, must accompany the most active type of real estate speculation. Thus, in boom towns where large numbers of people are coming in every month or season, there is nearly always an active speculative market. If the population of a town or city is not increasing rapidly, there is no incentive for rapid turnover in property, and the speculative element is always absent.

Factors to consider

Is real estate speculating dangerous to the operator who participates in it? If cautiously engaged in, and with an amount of money at hand necessary to carry the property if the market slumps, it carries with it no greater risk than the buying of any other commodity. Nearly every loss sustained comes through the inability of a speculator to meet payments in principal or interest. The "shoestring" speculator gets burned very often and has no one to blame but himself. The "shoestring" speculator is one with a comparatively small amount of money who assumes obligations which call for future cash payments and carrying charges, and who is unable to effect a sale of the property before payments come due. This sort of operating is inadvisable. Such a speculator, for the most part, is a gambler pure and simple. He bets on his chance of finding a buyer who will pay him a profit. If such a buyer fails to appear, the speculator loses his stake. He usually goes into the deal with that possibilty in view, and, if seasoned, he usually has less to say about his loss than others who learn of it.

Can speculation be recommended to those fortunate persons who have surplus funds drawing low rates of interest or tied up in securities, which render only moderate returns? If properly conducted and re-enforced with a liberal knowledge of how to judge property values and the elements of community growth, there seems to be no reason why anyone's money should not be placed in properly located tracts of real estate, the idea being to resell at some future time at a profit. Shrewd businessmen in all parts of the country have been doing this for years, and many have made money as a result. Some who have had neither enough money nor the necessary knowledge have lost money, but usually they have violated the important principle that the speculator must be ready to hold his property if a ready market is not at hand.

There is an essential difference between speculators in land and those who, for instance, manipulate food stuffs. No one suffers particularly because there is an active speculative realty market. Improvements usually follow, and the district builds up. When a food commodity is cornered, it may cause suffering among a great mass of poor people.

Real estate speculating is not to be recommended as a public benefit, neither is it to be condemned as a public evil. It resolves itself largely into the nature of a game; to play it one must be properly financed. Granting the game is played the way it should be, there is better than an average chance that the result will be the accumulation of profits.

In speculating in real estate, it is well, then, to observe these factors:

1. Have courage. When you buy a property, you may have to carry it a considerable time before realizing a profit. You take an unnecessary risk when you operate on borrowed capital, or are not able to carry on if the anticipated sale does not materialize.
2. Buy only on a rising market. Markets have a way of rising, remaining static for a time, and then falling. Learn by observation or from expert advice when the proper time is to buy.
3. Sell when you can realize a good profit. No one ever got into trouble taking a good profit on a deal, even if one does give the other fellow a chance to make some money.
4. Don't buy at the place where prices are at a peak, nor too far

out where the demand will not make itself felt for some time. Settle in between these points, and then wait for that magic element, increment, to get in its fine work.

5. To be a good lawyer, doctor, or minister, one engages in years of preparation. Don't expect to be a successful real estate speculator or operator unless you know the fundamentals of the real estate business. Become a student of real estate, read every book you can secure, and become familiar with movements in land and the growth of cities.

6. Take a loss, if you should encounter one, philosophically. Because one fish gets off your hook, it doesn't mean there are no more fish in the pond. By the same token, it is better not to put all your bait on the hook until you become a skilled and seasoned speculator. Even then it may be a dangerous practice.

7. It is usually wise to confine your speculations to one class of property. Learn all about its peculiarities, and don't venture rashly into new and untried fields, unless under competent direction of one who knows the new field.

8. Engage in speculation as a sideline. Don't expect to make it a regular occupation, for there are often months or years at a time when it is not a profitable venture.

9. Become a speculator with your eyes wide open, fully aware of the benefits and burdens of such a calling. If you fail, don't blame anyone else.

TWENTY-FOUR

Periods of Booms and Recessions

When times are good and a real estate boom is in progress, few believe that it ever will be followed by a recession. Likewise when a recession is in full swing, few owners can be convinced that it will ever end and that there may be happy days again. Everyone declines to believe that values may ever recover to their former levels and that the recession as such may disappear and be remembered only as a nightmare.

It is significant that a general business reversal always occurs some months in advance of a noticeable disruption of an active real estate market, the delay often extending from twelve to eighteen months. Likewise, when business recovers, real estate activity often lags several months behind.

Fortunes have been begun or built up during periods of real estate inflation. The United States is a comparatively new country and there is constantly abroad a spirit of investment adventure that prompts and fosters booms.

With the opening of new territory in this country during the last century or two, booms have taken place periodically while new towns were being established "at the end of steel," which was the term applied to the new settlements which sprung up at the temporary termini of railroads engaged in spreading out their tentacles into new territory.

It was the general experience that people passed by established districts served by railroads and hurried on to newer territories where land was cheap. Many people flocked into these sections hopeful that they could acquire land at low prices which would later materially increase in value with the coming of transportation. Then a boom ensued. Everything was infected with speculative mania. Money was plentiful, and business roared along with high prices prevailing. Good times were in evidence for a while, then the attention of many of the fortune hunters was diverted to new fields, and the boom gradually flattened out. Nearly every pioneer western town experienced its boom.

New railroads, discovery of oil and gold, opening of canals, and vast irrigation projects developed to completion have all been causes of real estate booms. Periods of prosperity following great wars likewise have prompted tremendous real estate activities in cities. Following a period of building repression, such as occurred in the United States during World War I, there followed in 1919 and 1920 booms in real estate in may sections. Nor was the land boom confined to cities alone. High prices procurable for farm products during the war caused a rush on the part of certain types of farmers and investors to corner farm land. The war ended, exporting of food products ceased, rural land prices fell, and the boom was later transferred into a depression.

Just as the business and real estate boom of the 1920's was probably the greatest on record, so was the depression which followed it. This was due first to the fact that up to that time there had never been a war of the magnitude of that fought between 1914 and 1918. Never had a war covered so much territory and affected so many millions of people. Furthermore, the advancement of all countries through invention, technological developments in science, medicine, sanitation, and general cultural gains which come to a civilized world, was at an all-time peak when the first world war broke out. With that war ended, there came a great wave of business activity in which an attempt was made to restore what had been lost or ruined. Excess followed excess and the boom advanced to its height in 1926. Then business started to skid and by the end of 1929, with the collapse of the American stock market, the house of cards which had been erected began to collapse, to be followed by the most severe depression in America's history, lasting over a decade.

Then came another world war, sprung by Germany upon a surprised and incredulous world in 1939. By 1941 the world became embroiled, and the real estate depression which started in 1931 ended. With billions being spent for armaments, this "shot in the economic arm" brought response in great building activity, higher rents, and another boom in real estate.

Business cycles

Many economists sincerely believe in the theory of cycles in business, claiming that depressions invariably follow booms in ceaseless procession— that they are as inevitable as the fact that night follows day.

Roger W. Babson, business analyst, has maintained that there are ten definite stages in the business cycle.

1. Period of increasing money rates.
2. Period of declining bond prices.
3. Period of declining stock prices.
4. Period of declining commodity prices.
5. Period of declining real estate values.
6. Period of low money rates.
7. Period of increasing bond prices.
8. Period of increasing stock prices.
9. Period of increasing commodity prices.
10. Period of increasing real estate values.

"It may be seen," said Mr. Babson, "that during a depression the decline in real estate prices comes after bonds, stocks, and commodities have declined, and that during a period of prosperity an advance in real estate values comes after the advance takes place in bonds, stocks, and commodity prices. While land values fluctuate to a certain degree with general business conditions in a growing country like ours, the general trend is upward."

The psychology of highly speculative movements of real estate during boom times is interesting and more or less mysterious in character.

"It can't last," says the banker as he sits on the side lines and sees increasing activity in real estate. Sales are being made in large volume, prices are rising overnight, huge profits are rolling up on individual deals, and the banker, being so close to the investment picture, cannot realize that it is real. Months afterwards, while the boom is still in progress, he perhaps berates himself that he was not wise enough to participate earlier. "When shall I quit?" is the problem the real estate operator worries about as he buys and sells in almost a frenzy during boom times.

"Times of unexampled prosperity," said Washington Irving, "are weather-breeders of trouble. Every now and then the world is visited by one of those delusive seasons when the 'credit system,' as it is called, expands to full luxuriance; everybody trusts everybody; a bad debt is a thing unheard of; the broad way to certain and sudden wealth lies plain and open; and men are tempted to dash forward boldly, from the facility of borrowing. Promissory notes interchanged between scheming individuals, are liberally disccunted at the banks, which become so many mints to coin words into ~ash, and as the supply of words is inexhaustible, it may be readily supposed that a vast amount of promissory capital is soon in circulation. Everyone now talks in thousands; nothing is heard but gigantic operations in trade; great purchases and sales of real property, and immense sums made at every transfer. All, to be sure, as yet exists in promise; but the believer in promises calculates the aggregate as solid capital and falls back in amazement at the amount of public wealth, for the 'unexampled state of public prosperity.' Now is the time for speculative and dreaming or designing men. They relate their dreams and projects to the ignorant and credulous, dazzle them with golden visions, and set them madding after shadows. The example of one stimulates another; speculation rises on speculation; bubble rises on bubble; everyone helps with his breath to swell the windy superstructure, and admires and wonders at the magnitude of the speculation he has contributed to produce. Could this delusion always last, life would indeed be a golden dream; but it is as short as it is brilliant. Let but a doubt enter, and the season of 'unexampled prosperity' is at an end. The coinage of words is suddenly curtailed; the promissory capital begins to vanish into smoke; a panic ensues and the whole superstructure, built upon credit and reared by speculation, crumbles to the ground, leaving scarce a wreck behind.

"When a man of business, therefore, hears on every side rumors of fortunes suddenly acquired; when he finds banks liberal and brokers busy; when he sees adventurers flush with paper capital and full of scheme and enterprise, when he perceives a greater disposition to buy than to sell; when trade overflows its accustomed channels and deluges the country; when he hears of new regions of commercial adventure, of distant marts and distant mines swallowing merchandise and disgorging gold; when he finds joint stock companies of all kinds forming; when he beholds the streets glittering with new equipages, palaces conjured up by the magic of each other in ostentatious expense; in a word, when he hears the whole community joining in the theme of 'unexampled prosperity,' let him look upon the whole as a weatherbreeder and prepare for the impending storm."

A good deal of advice has been given by some of the experts about "coming booms in real estate." Prophecy is an easy thing to indulge in; proving a prediction is quite another. Beginning with 1934 and annually for a number of years thereafter, prophets soberly predicted that the boom was "just around the corner." Doubtless many of these prophets were deep and sincere students of real estate economics and believed what they were depicting, yet the fact remained that the boom didn't come as scheduled. For that very evident reason it is not intended here to attempt to indicate when, where, or how real estate booms come into existence or when they may end. There are a few general observations about the whole subject that may be worthwhile considering, but even these must be adapted to each occasion.

Government safeguards

Time was when booms and recessions could be calculated to occur at regular intervals. In the political and economic atmosphere of this last third of the century, it is unlikely that the same type of cyclic pattern will continue to prevail. Some say that with the level of governmental control now being implemented, depressions of the type experienced in the 1930's are no longer necessary, indeed no longer possible.

It is true that there are a number of safeguards in the hands of the politicians who guard the nation's economy that heretofore did not prevail. The government is able to control such things as income taxes, interest rates, and even the crops that farmers may plant. With this degree of control and with a careful weather-eye always turned to the economic trends, astute economists can largely control business cycles.

This is certainly not to say that there will be no fluctuations whatever. The recent past has demonstrated that the politicians who have the possibility of controlling the economy do not always act with due deliberateness for one reason or another. For the most part, these reasons are political—few administrations would raise taxes just before election, for example. So we do continue to experience business recessions even though the spectre of a complete business collapse is no longer with us.

In this day and age, the real estate operator would do well not to key his thinking to an imminent recession on a nationwide basis. At the same time, there are certain types of business recessions that the smart operator must study constantly.

Local recessions

Recessions are more and more becoming local in nature. It doesn't matter so much that the state of the national economy is moving upward. More important is the blighting of the local economy in which the operator functions. The operator must study local trends even more closely, while not being oblivious to the national trends.

A large part of the possibility of localized recessions resides in the tendencies of the federal government to initiate programs of cut-backs on spending.

In many localities the government has quite suddenly closed facilities such as air bases and other military installations removing millions of dollars from the local economies annually. With such projects thousands of families are displaced from the local communities leaving behind thousands of homes to be sold on a glutted market.

For a given group of real estate investors, this type of situation is often worse than a complete nationwide depression. Communities thus deprived of huge payrolls often require decades to catch up from the loss; indeed, they may never recover.

Beyond the matter of localized recessions due to shutdowns of various types, the modern real estate operator must realize that even in periods of business acceleration, there may prevail a recession in the utility of certain types of properties. It is inevitable that various events will affect different types of properties variously.

A good example is observed these days in the resale of homes, even those no more than five or six years old. One of the factors operating here is the higher transiency of our population. People have left one community, placing their homes on the market for disposal, and have themselves elected to join the hordes of apartment dwellers because they know that in all likelihood they will be moving on again in a matter of only a few years. Thus, there are thousands of homes left with no buyers.

Another development affecting this type of property is the introduction of new materials which are at one and the same time more beautiful and functional as well as cheaper to install. This means that new houses are built with greatly improved features and modern design at prices compatible with the homes on the market which are five or six years old and somewhat behind the times in design. Thus, the boom market is for new homes, and there is a hard recession in used homes. The investor must know this or he will be burdened with properties he cannot sell.

Most metropolitan areas are overrun with homes that can be bought simply by the expediency of picking up the payments, thus dealing the original owners out of their equities. These original owners are often delighted just to get out from under. It is no bargain these days to be able to buy a house with no down payment by picking up the payments. Only a foolish operator would go heavily into this type of investment. So, for all practical purposes we do have a recession in this type of real estate market.

Don't be misled. Even though the governmental controls are able to keep the national economy on an even keel, recessions and even depressions of property values on the local level and with certain types of properties will always be with us.

Investors with little knowledge of real estate cannot make profits unless they are very lucky, or are *guided by experts*.

Rules for operators and investors

To avoid the losses that recessions of various types produce, you should observe the following rules:

1. Set aside a certain amount of money which you are ready to risk, even lose, if necessary, and operate with it. *Don't endanger your permanent capital.*
2. Don't go into operations which are beyond the scope of your capital. Invest in small and interesting properties which are likely to move readily.
3. In buying a property never assume too great an encumbrance. Be prepared, if necessary, to clear it at comparatively short notice. In other words *don't spread your speculations out too thin!*
4. If you can't afford to lose money in real estate, stop operating or investing when you perceive that a boom market is in progress. You may make a lot of money continuing, but, on the other hand, you may become hopelessly involved, and lose everything you own.

TWENTY-FIVE

Hints on Selling a Property

There comes a time when a property which has been carefully bought and skillfully handled so as to bring out its highest and best points must be offered to the public for sale. By such a transfer the owner stands to reap his profits, so it behooves him to give earnest thought to the manner in which he seeks to attract the favorable attention of a prospect able, willing, and ready to buy

Proper presentation of a property offered for sale will have much to do with its successful disposal at a price representing a profit to an owner.

Knowing how to analyze a property so that its good points may be presented logically and convincingly takes years to master and is developed by the successful real estate broker, who usually is best qualified to do this work.

Familiarity with property is essential

Complete familiarity with a property offered for sale is essential. Many a sale has been lost when a broker or owner has been unable to answer some pertinent question which a prospective buyer has suddenly asked. If the information is not known or easily available, complete frankness should be used in answering. It does little good to "stall" a customer who desires to know something and wants to know it at that particular time. Confidence will be undermined, and a sale may go glimmering if a question is ignored or answered in an evasive manner.

Either frankly confess that the question cannot be answered or definitely agree to secure the information and transmit it at a subsequent interview. Do not refuse to secure the information and do not ignore the question if the buyer really desires an answer. You may forget it, *but he will not!*

Carefully prepared typewritten statements are used by skillful brokers. These are prepared with infiinite care and usually contain every fact bearing on the value, size, condition, financing, and availability of the property in question. The greater the care taken in preparing and presenting such definite statements, the greater confidence the buyer will have in a transaction. If a seller has any respect for his word of honor and for future consequences, he will never, of course, make a false statement in presenting such a description to a prospective customer.

The physical appearance of a property will have a great deal to do with its salability. If a home, it should be shown in its best possible state. The house should be painted, windows cleaned, the grass cut, all litter removed from the premises and everything placed in a condition that will properly impress a person who wishes to acquire it. If a business property, the buildings should be painted, show windows washed, the sidewalks kept free of refuse, and the entire place made to appear as prosperous and attractive as possible. Tattered and disreputable real estate signs should not be countenanced, nor should there be more than one sign on the property. Nothing so arouses the distrust of a buyer as to see a number of "for sale" signs on a single property.

The discerning buyer of real estate will be properly impressed with a careful summary of income and expenses, which should by all means be included in the prepared statement to be presented to him. He will be interested in knowing the revenue to be derived, and he also will be eager to find out exactly how much he will have to pay out of the revenue in the way of expenses. The amount of gain each year should be stated plainly in dollars and cents, and a computation made as to the percentage of earnings each year on the capital invested. Nothing interests a buyer so much as a definite statement of the possible profits he will realize if he makes a purchase. If possible, always satisfy his curiosity in this respect if you hope to clinch a sale.

The stability of the investment may be pointed out with the greatest freedom, for no one gets offended when you show him how he is to be protected. Some investors prefer stability to a large percentage of earnings, and will question you keenly if the property promises to return a rate of interest above the average made on that particular class of real estate.

If the property is of a speculative character, care should be taken to point out the possible increases in value which will come to it during the next several years. Public improvements in the neighborhood may be pointed out, possible street openings referred to, and every fact presented which will convince the prospective purchaser that he is acquiring something that may increase in value with the coming the years. The speculative element in a property appeals to the natural gambling instinct which everyone possesses, and if authentic information can be given that will tend to show that speculative elements make a property worth purchasing, such facts should be presented clearly and honestly.

If it is a residence, all of the facts which increase and maintain values in such properties should be carefully reviewed. If the place has an exceptionally fine view, it should not be overlooked, for every purchaser of a home desires to have a view from his premises which will be pleasing and restful.

The growth of a neighborhood should be carefully analyzed, and the prospect shown that it is advancing in population and popularity, and that because of these facts there need be little decrease in values at some later time.

Dealing with prospective buyers

"Am I getting my money's worth?" is the question asked instinctively by everyone who is sold a piece of real estate. Lacking knowledge, the customer is anxious and eager to learn every possible fact as to why he should buy and pay the price asked. If this element of interest is satisfied, it will be found that a sale will be registered much more quickly than if the seller himself is ignorant of the advantages offered by the property concerned.

The character of a neighborhood, whether residential or business, should be pointed out. The better the character of the section, the greater the increment eventually will be, and that fact will greatly interest the buyer. All neighborhoods have character of high, medium or low degree, and the seller or broker should be able to translate into words a picture of the type of neighborhood in which the property is located. Close familiarity with the section will be gained only after an exhaustive survey has been made by the seller or broker, and all the facts connected with the locality should be presented in as truthful and forceful a manner as possible.

A knowledge of structural conditions and values will always be of benefit to a seller. If one is able to point out the kind of material, the type of workmanship, the fact that a building is decidedly modern, with all the latest improvements installed, the buyer will more readily be convinced of its merit. Little things which sometimes seem inconsequential are often the deciding factors in making a sale, especially if they point to a thoroughness of detail and construction used in the erection of a building about to be purchased.

If a business structure, attention may be directed to the manner in which it may be converted into new and better use.

"What is the matter with that building?" asked a broker of a prospective buyer of a business block. The building had a frontage of 100 feet, with two stores on the ground-level, suites and offices above, and presented an ordinary appearance.

"I don't know," was the answer. "What is the matter with it?"

"Well," continued the broker, "you see, that building is not being properly utilized. This neighborhood is filling up rapidly with comparatively small stores which are renting at constantly increasing prices. That building has only two stores, one with a frontage of forty feet, and the other with a frontage of sixty feet. Both are too large in size for the rent being obtained. That forty-foot store is rented for a poolroom. That is not a good class of occupancy, but fortunately there is no lease on it. That other store is used for a men's furnishing store, but due to the fact that a long lease was made some years ago, it is not producing a proper rental return. Its lease expires in eighteen months.

"Now, the thing to do is to cut that frontage up into five twenty-foot stores. The present rental can be more than doubled after eighteen months, and the building can be bought today on the basis of its having only two stores. You can afford to wait eighteen months for a time when you can increase the earning power of the ground floor 100 per cent."

That argument, made at the right time, clinched the sale, and subsequent events showed that the astuteness of the broker was the responsible factor for the later remodelling of the property, and its adaptation to a better class of occupancy.

With the coming into almost universal use of the automobile, and the restrictive policies as to its use being adopted so generally in towns and cities throughout the country, the questions of auto parking and garage facilities are important with almost all kinds of property. Big office buildings in cities are installing parking spaces in their basements. Some business concerns are leasing or buying adjoining lands for the purpose of furnishing facilities so their customers may park their cars. Factories are allotting considerable land near their plants for storage spaces for automobiles owned and operated by employees. Every house has its value enhanced by the presence of a garage. Apartments in cities are becoming difficult to rent if there is no place a tenant may keep his car. With this condition in effect, any information which may be given a prospective buyer of a property about the convenience afforded in taking care of automobiles may assist materially in making a sale.

Proximity to transportation lines, schools, libraries, playgrounds, churches, and stores has been the determining factor which has sold thousands of properties. Never fail to point out any special advantages concerning these features. They may seem to be self-evident facts to you, but a buyer may not know about them, and their revelation may be the point that makes a sale.

In the case of business properties, a recital of the improvements which have come recently to the neighborhood will prove of interest to a prospective buyer.

"That large building was completed just sixty days ago, and is forty-five per cent rented," explained one broker who was interested in selling a piece of downtown property. "Three of the four ground floor stores have been rented at new rental levels for this entire neighborhood. Over there is a three-story building occupied by a retail concern which came to this section recently, bringing with it a trade built up over a period of thirty-five years. Over there a large commercial building is to be erected shortly, which will change the character of the neighborhood beyond it as soon as the improvement is completed. Growth is coming this may, and this property I am offering you is bound to feel the influence of all this new development." The broker, through familiarity with what was going on, was able to tell an interesting and alluring tale. He made a deal because he had possession of the requisite knowledge required for that purpose.

"Knowledge is power," is an old adage which is only partly true. Knowledge is power only if directed into the channels where some proper use of it may be made. The seller or broker should be in possession of just as much knowledge about the property he is offering as it is humanly possible to obtain, and then he should present the facts in a way which will convince the prospective buyer that the property possesses all of the merits attributed to it.

Don't misstate or overstate the facts. You are likely to be tripped up by some quiet-appearing buyer who will refute a false statement instantly. Then the deal is off, for nothing will so undermine the confidence of a buyer as a misstatement knowingly made by one who is attempting to sell real estate.

Don't underestimate the knowledge of a buyer if he happens to open up and tell you a few things you don't know about the territory. Perhaps he knows a lot more about things in that neighborhood than you do.

Don't argue with a buyer. It is a tremendous temptation sometimes to tell a buyer that he is a blockhead and doesn't know what he is talking about, but you can't make a sale that way. Everybody talks too much, anyway, and many a deal has been talked to death. Present your facts as fully as possible, and if the buyer wants to make an oration let him do so. A sale certainly won't be made by clapping down the buyer's safety valve. He is then likely to explode, and all the seller or broker can do is to wander sadly home, minus a profit or a commission.

It is a good idea to set down in writing the general points you want to present when making a sale. It is not necessary to read them to the buyer. The fact that you took the time and care to set them down probably impresses and anchors them in your mind so they will come up for utterance at the proper time.

Nothing is needed so much in selling real estate as *good old-fashioned horse sense*. If a property has real merit, if the seller knows what he should about it, and if the person to whom it is shown is in a position to buy it, and it meets his requirements, there should be a sale recorded. If a sale does not follow, it is most frequently due to the fact that the seller did not present his subject in a sufficiently interesting and alluring manner.

"When is the time to sell?" inquires someone. A rather general statement of this may indicate that the best time to dispose of a property is when the demand exceeds the supply. As a matter of fact properties are sold all of the time. Business is known to revolve in cycles, with dull times succeeding prosperous times. The time to buy real estate is when the market is quiet, even dull. The time to sell it at the greatest profit is when there is a general period of business prosperity, and a spirit of investment or speculation is rife. This can be determined by reported transfers of property of a character similar to that of which you may desire to dispose.

TWENTY-SIX

Closing a Deal

Closing a deal for the sale of a piece of real estate seems to the average purchaser a simple matter, until he has gone through the experience and has overlooked details which should receive attention, with the result that every detail overlooked generally causes extra annoyance and expense.

In order to safeguard the interests of both the buyer and the seller, and have a true meeting of the minds, there should be a written agreement signed by both parties, accompanied by a deposit, called *earnest money*. The responsibility for the proper preparation of such a contract is imposed upon the broker who makes the deal, and, if he is a reliable broker, he will carefully look after all of the necessary details. However, it is well for the buyer or seller to check up on these details to see that they are all properly taken care of in the contract. Attention is therefore directed to a few of the essential elements of such a contract.

Elements of the contract

In the first place, there should be an adequate description of the property, either by legal lot number, or a sufficiently detailed description of frontage and depth in relation to adjoining property so that there can

207

be no mistake as to the exact property to be sold. A description by house number is not regarded as sufficient, although desirable, because people are not always particular about getting the house numbers correct from the city authorities, and there have been cases known where house numbers have been changed. The contract should clearly state the purchase price, how it is to be paid, whether in cash or by the assumption of mortgages, whether the property is being sold upon a land contract, or by warranty deed. If by the latter method the contract should provide that dower rights shall be released, and that the deed is be accompanied by an evidence of title in the form of either a certificate of title of some reputable abstract company, title insurance policy, or an opinion of title by someone competent to render such an opinion. This varies somewhat, according to locality. Such an opinion of title should state that the seller has a good title free and clear of all encumbrances, except restrictions of record and such other exceptions as are noted in the purchase contract.

If the property is subject to easements or involves a right of way over an adjoining property or properties, these should be carefully noted in the contract, with sufficient detail so that no misunderstanding can arise over them. This applies also to driveways in common with adjoining property owners, and other arrangements of a similar character.

The contract should provide for the prorating of interest on mortgages, rentals, water rentals, insurance premiums, and for the refunding of advance deposits made for water, gas, or electric light meters. One arrangement is to prorate such charges as of date of acceptance of the offer to purchase or, in other words, the date that any increase in value which may accrue to the property justly inures to the benefit of the purchaser, so that the only just and equitable method is that the interest, and all other charges, should begin to be paid by him on the same date. By having a fixed date for adjustments, a delay in securing title examination and recording papers will not work a hardship on either party in connection with such a settlement of fixed charges.

In distinct contrast with this method, another form of contract provides that all charges and proratings shall take effect as of the day of transfer of the property, it being claimed that ownership does not actually pass until that time and that each side should take care of his own affairs up until that critical time.

There should also be a provision made for the prorating of taxes and assessments, both general and special. The method of adjustment is entirely a matter of contract agreement, and should be thoroughly understood and decided upon at the time the contract is drawn up and before it is signed. There is no more fruitful source of misunderstanding and hard feeling than is found in the settling of matters of this kind.[1]

Where the property sold is bringing in rentals, a date of possession should be provided, and also a definite date for the adjusting of such rentals.

The actual examination of title and the making of adjustments should be entrusted to someone who is an acknowledged expert along these lines, and the buyer and seller should not object to paying reasonable fees for such expert assistance. It is usually money well spent, as expensive mistakes are thus guarded against. Where a broker is negotiating a deal, the contract should provide for the payment of his commission, and where an escrow agent is available, it should provide for placing the funds and papers necessary for closing the deal in his hands within a given number of days.

The contract should always provide that "time is of the essence of the contract," or, in other words, that the element of time is an essential part of the deal, the same as the payment of the purchase price, so that if either of the parties does not perform his share of the contract within a specified time, he has then broken the contract, giving the other party a legal right of action known as "specific performance."

When a written offer is made on a piece of property, the offer should contain a clause stating that it expires by limitation upon a certain date, so that in the event the contract is not returned to the prospective purchaser, it automatically becomes void at the expiration of the indicated time limit.

The escrow

Where a responsible escrow agent is available, the deal should be placed in his hands. Such an escrow agent will see that the following details have been carried out:

1. That no title search will be commenced until all of the deeds and mortgages involved in the transaction and the cash or other consideration have been deposited in his hands. Sometimes a seller goes to the expense of having a title examination made only to find that the purchaser has backed out of the deal and left him to pay the title company's bill.
2. That all deeds, mortgages, and mortgage notes have been properly

---

See Contract Form in the Appendix.

drawn and executed. This includes the checking of the description for inaccuracies, and seeing that the signatures to the deeds and mortgages are made before the proper number of witnesses, and acknowledged before a notary public in good standing.

3. That the proper number of revenue stamps are affixed to the deed.

4. That insurance premiums on the fire insurance policies have been paid, and that proper assignments of the insurance policies from the seller to the purchaser have been executed.

5. That a title search is made for liens against the seller and against the purchaser. Escrow instructions usually provide that when the title examination shows that the seller has a good title free of all encumbrances, except such encumbrances as are noted in the contract of sale, he is authorized to record the papers which have been placed in escrow and bring down the title examination, showing the property standing of good record in the name of the purchaser. If the escrow agent finds from the title examination any liens against the purchaser which might affect the title to the property if taken in the purchaser's name, he should notify the purchaser, as it might be advisable for the purchaser to take title in the name of someone else. The reason for this double search is that a pending suit against the purchaser might go to judgment after the purchaser has taken title to the property, and as the judgment would date back to the first day of the term of court, it might become a lien against the property being acquired.

6. That a detailed accounting of receipts and disbursements is made to each party involved in the escrow, showing exactly what distribution of funds has been made.

7. That a receipt from the county recorder's office for the recorded papers is furnished to the proper parties, or else the recorded instruments themselves returned.

8. That all defects of title are cleared up before the transfer of the property is made.

9 That the certificate of title, or the title insurance policy, is made on behalf of the purchaser, so that if the purchaser of the property later has any cause of action against the title company for damages for mistakes, he can bring an action himself. If the title examination has been made on behalf of the seller, then only the seller could bring action against the title company, and the purchaser would have to fall back on the seller instead of directly on the title company.

When a person has an attack of appendicitis and requires an operation, he generally calls in the best surgeon he can find, in order to take no more chances than are necessary. Do the same in closing real estate transactions. Go to an expert who is handling transactions of this kind as a part of his daily routine of business. He can give you much valuable information and save you an untold amount of grief. Instances are constantly occurring where people unfamiliar with these details attempt to handle their own transactions, and frequently acquire a defective title to property. Naturally these defects of title do not appear until they come to dispose of their holdings, possibly years later, when the chances of curing the defects and recovering damages are doubtful. In connection with closing a deal, thoroughly familiarize yourself with the contents of the next chapter, entitled "Escrowing Real Estate Deals."

TWENTY-SEVEN

Escrowing Real Estate Deals

Experience has shown that the escrowing of real estate transactions with a regularly organized department of a competent title company or bank is advantageous to the seller, the buyer, and the broker.

A bank or a savings and loan company which conducts a regular escrow department can act in the capacity of an escrow agent, and this often is a great convenience to principals and brokers in deals when such occur some distance from the downtown headquarters of the bigger title companies, which make a business of conducting escrow operations on a larger scale.

The custom of delivering a deed in escrow, and the law governing the practice, dates back to the early English law, and is aptly expressed by English law books as "a writing under seal delivered to a third person, to be conveyed by him to the person whom it purports to benefit, when certain conditions shall have been performed or satisfied; until which time it does not acquire the force of a deed."

What an escrow involves

The modern conception of an escrow has grown to mean considerably more than this, and the word "escrow" is applied, possibly incorrectly, to many transactions which involve a great deal more than the mere delivery of a deed and paying for the property.

There are transactions involving the refinancing of projects, the paying of liens, and a clearing of title objections, which can be done most advantageously through an escrow department. These are somewhat in the nature of a trust business.

The first essential of a delivery in escrow is that the one delivering the deed has entrusted it with a third party, and has put it beyond his power to withdraw the same, at least for a time, until certain conditions have been complied with by the grantee. When the grantee has complied with these conditions, the delivery of the deed to him then becomes absolute, as the actual delivery of the instrument is what governs, and not the recording of it.

In years past there was a greater possibility of the buyer and the seller knowing each other, and business was done on a basis of faith between parties to a transaction. The custom was for an abstract company or lawyer to make a search of the title to the premises, a deed would be prepared, the parties would go to an attorney's office, and the seller would transfer the deed and receive payment for the property.

A competent title company's evidence of title is accepted as a correct statement of the conditions of the title up to the time it ends its search, the date and hour of which is named in the evidence of title. By reason of the fact that the evidence of title must be written and compared and placed in a proper condition to deliver, a certain time necessarily elapses from the last date of the examination of the records to the time of actual delivery of the document to the customer.

In various offices of a city and country, there are many places where transactions affecting the title to real estate are proceeding daily, and a knowledge of which can be gained only by carefully examining the records themselves. Judgments and decrees are entered in various courts; deeds, mortgages, leases, mechanic's liens, agreements and numerous other papers are recorded; taxes and assessments are levied or reinstated on the county treasurer's books; public improvements are established, and levies and executions are issued, all of which vitally affect title to property. Furthermore a federal statute now makes a man's income tax a first lien on any property he may own, and this is true as to third parties when certified to the clerk of the United States District Court, if the tax is not paid.

It can be readily seen that from the date of the examination of the title by a title company to the time of actual transferring of the deed, under the old system, many things might intervene, which are not contemplated by either party to a transaction.

By transferring property in escrow, these risks are avoided. The seller deposits his deed with an escrow agent with written instructions. These instructions state definitely what the grantor is depositing, the amount of money or other consideration that he is to receive, the amount of taxes, interest, mortgages or other items which are to be paid off from funds due him, and also stipulates the kind of evidence of title which he agrees to furnish.

The grantee or purchaser deposits his funds with definite written instructions as to what he is to receive in return for his money, the contemplated condition of the title being definitely stated. All taxes or other liens which he is to assume are mentioned, and an agreement as to purchasing the fire insurance from the grantor, if the same is contemplated.

It then becomes the duty and responsibility of the escrow agent to comply with these instructions, and if any unforeseen matters arise in regard to the title, no papers are filed or funds paid until they are corrected, or new arrangements made in regard to them.

The real estate broker, after having brought the buyer and seller together and caused them to enter into a bona fide agreement for the sale of a piece of property, is thereby, according to law, entitled to his commission, but he naturally does not feel entirely relieved of the matter or satisfied until the transaction is closed, papers are on record, and the funds paid to the grantor, and last, but not least, that his commission is paid, as is done in escrow. After he has made a deal, he would like to forget it, as far as possible, and promptly turn his activities toward new business.

In most transactions placed in escrow, the escrow agent not only arranges to have the title to the property examined, but also arranges for preparation of the papers, which the broker may not care to take time to do. While an escrow officer is not acting in the capacity of an attorney, yet from his experience in handling complicated transactions, he is able to assist the real estate broker materially in many ways in correcting errors, in settling disputes among the parties as to minor details, in preparing affidavits to cure inconsistencies in title, and in other ways to keep the parties to the transaction in a pleasant frame of mind.

Fire insurance should be transferred immediately after a deed is recorded. In transactions not handled in escrow, two or three days may elapse after a deed is placed on record, before the fire insurance agent is actually notified of the change in ownership and the transfer made on his company records. When handled in escrow, the policies with proper assignments are deposited with the escrow agent, or if the policies are held at a bank with the mortgage, proper separate assignments are left with the escrow agent. He receives notice from the title examiner immediately after the deed is filed, and fire insurance assignments immediately are sent to the company representative, who effects the transfer on the insurance company's books, consents to the same, and attaches a mortgage clause to whomever is entitled to it. While reputable fire insurance companies would undoubtedly be willing to pay a loss if one occurred, to whomever was actually the owner of the property, even though not of record, yet there are many instances which could occur which would allow an insurance company to conscientiously refuse to pay a loss, or at least a full one, if the record owner was not the actual owner. One of these instances might occur in case the premium was in arrears. In this event the company would be entitled, and does not infrequently refuse to consent to the assignment.

In most cases where the grantor or seller has insurance, it is agreeable to the grantee or buyer to assume it, and the escrow agent, as one of his duties, adjusts insurance premiums and collects for the seller the pro rata amount due.

The advantage of promptly paying off mortgages or other encumbrances not assumed in the transaction, in order to stop the accumulation of interest, can be readily appreciated. The escrow agent, as soon as the papers are filed, immediately pays off such encumbrances, and secures their proper cancellation. If mortgages are assumed, the interest is adjusted as of the day of transfer, so that the grantee assumes the burden of interest only from the date on which he actually takes over the property.

There are some transactions which are difficult to close in any way, except through escrow. For example if a loan is being secured by a purchaser, the funds from it go to make up the amount due a seller. In such a case, the individual or bank making the loan will not allow funds to be paid over until the mortgage is on record as a first or second lien, as the case may be. Of course, the one selling the property will not allow his deeds to be transferred to buyer, until he receives the funds. Consequently a "melting pot" is necessary in such cases. The bank or individual making the loan gives the escrow agent written instructions that the funds are not to be used until there is a record of proper deed and mortgage; and immediately upon filing of the deed and mortgage, the funds are paid by the escrow agent to the seller.

The absolute necessity of an escrow is also apparent where a transaction involves a retransfer of property to a third party, the funds of the third party going eventually to the original seller. By placing such a transaction in escrow, it is possible for the broker to handle the deal without the original seller necessarily knowing that the property is being resold by a purchaser.

Frequently real estate investors or brokers have transactions involving the exchange of local real estate for property in another city or adjacent town. In trading property it is essential that deeds do not pass, or funds be paid until both titles are in the names of the respective purchasers, and all details completed, according to their contracts. The escrow agent in one city is able, through a correspondent in another, to place half of the transactions with him, and retain half himself, stipulating that deeds be filed concurrently. The practical way of doing this is that both title examiners make their searches up to the last possible moment; and then, conferring by telephone, advise each other at exactly what time to file papers.

There is another class of transactions which, according to the strict legal interpretation of the word, should not be called escrows. This concerns property which has become invoved in a lawsuit or a foreclosure, or on which liens have been filed, and where the property is not being sold, but is being refinanced, or by some other means various claims are being paid. Lien holders do not care to cancel their rights on record by a mere promise of payment, but are willing to deposit a proper evidence of their claims with an escrow agent who, when he has all liens properly satisfied, is able to record all satisfactions at one time, and pay them off.

If for any reason an escrow cannot be completed eventually and the parties desire to withdraw the papers, a broker does not lose a commission, because the contract between the original parties is not annulled. There is some legal question as to whether an escrow agreement supersedes a contract, but a careful escrow agent always inserts in the instructions a provision that the escrow agreement does not in any manner change any previous contract which the parties may have entered into between themselves.

Practical advantages

Practical advantages of escrow, therefore, are:

1. If the buyer is interested in knowing the conditions of the title up to the time he considers purchasing a property, then why not up to and including the time of filing the papers and the paying over of his money? Without an escrow, the buyer can only ascertain the condition of the title up to an approximate date, necessarily a day or more prior to the actual delivery of the deed; whereas, in escrow, he has named as a condition of using his money, that the title be in a certain condition, *in his name*. This is entirely fair to the seller because, if his title complies with the conditions of the escrow agreement and the deed is filed, he is at once paid the money by the escrow agent.

2. The buyer has the advantage of raising part of his purchase price by mortgaging the real estate and using the mortgagee's funds toward the purchase of the property, the mortgagee being willing to deposit funds with instructions that protect him.

3. The one lending money to the buyer of the real estate is protected since his funds are not used until his mortgage appears on record, as a first or second mortgage, as the case may be.

4. When the escrow agreement is signed, and the funds are deposited, the seller has the advantage and satisfaction of knowing that during the time the title is being examined he is certain that the transaction will be completed providing his title is as represented.

5. The seller also has an advantage in that he may instruct the escrow agent to use the funds, which become his upon the filing of the papers, to pay off present encumbrances and liens not assumed by the buyer. In this manner, the seller is not required to advance other money to close a transaction.

6. Both parties have the common advantage of knowing that all computations of interest, rents, fire insurance premiums, and so forth, will be made in an accurate, careful manner by individuals especially trained in such work, the parties to the transaction thereby being relieved of these burdensome details.

7. Fire insurance will be transferred and mortgage clauses attached promptly upon the filing of the papers, which is an important matter to all parties concerned.

8. A real estate broker who has negotiated a sale is, according to law, entitled to his commission without any further work. The broker wishing to give his client service, and to see that the transaction is eventually properly closed, may accomplish this by having the transaction placed in escrow.

The seller should be certain that the escrow agent covers the question of means in which the consideration is accounted for; the giving of a warranty deed, which in no way warrants inconsistent with the title; that the proper cancellation of liens against which he warrants is provided; the return to him of any land contract which may be outstanding; that definite understanding is made as to the date of possession to be given; and the rental the seller is to pay if he remains as a tenant in the property.

The buyer is interested in seeing that all taxes and rentals are prorated as of a date agreed upon; that the mortgages he has agreed to assume can be assumed; that the mortgages are not in default, and whether they can be paid on or before maturity; and, last but not least, that he is given a proper title opinion by a responsible company or attorney that the title is good in him, subject to the things he assumed.

Real estate brokers in most cities where adequate facilities are afforded now escrow practically all of their deals. In Los Angeles it is estimated that ninety-five per cent of all deals are closed in escrow. In eastern cities, the percentage is less, but is increasing from year to year.

The investor in real estate, to be thoroughly secure in many intricate matters of a highly technical nature, should insist that important transactions, at least, should go through escrow when they are being closed.

What to watch for

Things to watch closely in escrowing a real estate deal are:

1. If furniture or other personal property is involved, provide for delivery of a bill of sale as a deed conveys title only to real property. If seller is taking back a mortgage or deed of trust as part of the purchase price, he may want a chattel mortgage on any personal property being conveyed.
2. Be sure the buyer has signed instructions that fully approve all known encumbrances and unusual rights or easements.
3. If unpaid balance of encumbrance to be assumed by the buyer is uncertain, see that escrow instructions provide as follow:

   Should mortgagee's or beneficiary's statement show unpaid principal balance of encumbrance of record to be more or less than $_____, then you are to adjust the cash consideration through escrow so that the total purchase price will remain the same.

   Such a provision will eliminate the necessity of securing amended instructions from the parties.

4. Should a building on property being sold have been recently constructed or extensively repaired, be sure that all bills for labor and material have been paid because under certain circumstances, claims by laborers and material men become a lien on the property regardless of who ordered such work or material.

5. If it is anticipated that it will be difficult for any of the principals of an escrow to call at the office of the escrow agent, such principal may authorize any other named person to act for him in signing either the original instructions or any additional instructions required in the escrow. This procedure is frequently used when the husband does not wish to require his wife to call at the office of the escrow agent after the original papers and documents have been executed.

TWENTY-EIGHT

Evidences of Title

Since the value of real estate from a commercial point of view depends upon its marketability, it is essential that the investor in real estate know something about the different methods of evidencing title.

In the nature of things, there must be a difference between the methods of evidencing title to personal property and to real estate. Ordinarily, possession is the only evidence of title demanded of the seller of personal property, but since the possession of real estate is not necessarily evidence of ownership, it has been necessary to devise a system of tracing titles to real estate, based not upon possession, but upon a careful examination of the public records.

We are apt sometimes to smile in a superior sort of way at the primitive ideas of our ancestors; and those who may have read in Blackstone, or other books on the history of real estate law, of the quaint custom known as "livery of seizin" have doubtless had many a quiet chuckle at the expense of our ignorant forebears. And yet, this seemingly meaningless procedure had its inception in the fundamental distinction between land and personal property, and a recognition of the fact that the transfer of land cannot, of necessity, be as simple as the transfer of a chattel.

Briefly, the ceremony of "livery of seizin" was this: If "A" desired to sell his farm to "B," he called his neighbors; and in their presence as witnesses, he took a twig, branch, or piece of sod, and gave it to "B" as a symbol of the transfer of ownership. No deed was made and no record of the transaction was preserved, other than in the memory of the witnesses. Primitive as the method seems to us, it was the best that could be devised at a time when few could read and write, and at a time when land was rarely sold and ordinarily passed from one tenant to another only upon death.

In the course of time, deeds, as they are now known, came into general use, and the symbolic transfer of land by "livery of seizin" was supplanted by a written instrument as the evidence of title.

Since colonial time in America, it has been the custom to record all deeds, mortgages, encumbrances, wills, proceedings on the states of deceased persons—in short all matters that may affect titles—in some public office. In order, therefore, to determine whether or not the seller has a good title to the land intended to be conveyed, it is necessary that a careful search be made of the public records.

Formerly this work was done by attorneys, and in many smaller communities the attorneys are also abstracters of title for their clients, but in most places the work of preparing abstracts or histories of titles has become a specialized business carried on by professional abstracters and title companies, which maintain elaborate "plants" for this purpose.

How shall the purchaser know whether or not the seller has a good and marketable title to the land which he has contracted to sell? The answer to this question depends largely upon the custom of the community in which the land is located.

Generally speaking, there are four methods of evidencing title to land·

1. The abstract and attorney system.
2. The certificate of title system.
3. The title insurance system.
4. The Torrens system of title registration.

The abstract system

An abstract of title has been defined as a "short, methodically written history of the title to a designated parcel of land, containing a brief of each recorded instrument." The purpose of an abstract of title is to show the entire history or recorded evidence of title from its source to the present time, with the view of having such title passed upon by someone well versed in title law.

In communities where the abstract and attorney system is in use, it is the custom for the seller to furnish the abstract of title for examination by the attorney for the purchaser. If from his examination of the abstract, the purchaser's attorney finds the title marketable, he so advises his client. If not, he outlines his objections to the title, and it is the duty of the seller to clear up any substantial defects in the title before he can compel the purchaser to take the title.

It cannot be too strongly urged upon the purchaser that the abstract of title is merely the basis for his attorney's opinion, and that the abstract without an attorney's opinion is not an evidence of title upon which he can rely. His reliance is not upon the abstract, but upon his attorney's opinion.

Certificate of title system

Because of the fact that the question of what is a marketable title is often an intricate question of law, and because of the fact that attorneys' opinions as to what is a marketable title often differ, there has grown up in some communities, especially in many of the larger cities, a system of furnishing not an abstract of title for the examination of an attorney, but a "certificate of title," whereby the title company searches the records and furnishes an opinion upon the title, upon which the purchaser may rely without consulting an attorney.

The form of certificate varies in different localities, but substantially it is in the following form: "We have examined the title to the land described in the caption of this certificate and we find the title vested in John Smith subject to the following encumbrances." Here follows a list of the encumbrances and objections to the title.

The object of the certificate of title is to exhibit to the purchaser the true condition of the title without setting forth in detail all the recorded instruments in the chain of title from its source to the present time. In furnishing the evidence of title by means of a so-called "certificate," the title company combines the work of an abstracter of titles and an examining attorney, and the layman may, in most instances, determine whether or not the title is satisfactory without consultation with an attorney, although consultation is usually advisable.

Title insurance system

There has grown up a further development of the title business, known as title insurance. In discussing certificates of title, it was pointed out that a title company, in issuing so-called certificates of title, combines the work of abstracter and attorney. In title insurance the title company goes a step further and adds to the functions of abstracter and attorney the function of an insurer.

There are many defects in titles which are not disclosed by an abstract, defects for which neither an attorney examining an abstract, nor a title company issuing a certificate would be held responsible. There may be forged deeds in the chain of title; there may be insufficient evidence as to who are the heirs of persons who have died owning the land; there may have been deeds made by minors or insane persons, whose incapacity is not shown by the public records; there may be various real defects in title which an examination of the records does not disclose. But if the title company insures the title, it is responsible for these defects, even though the records do not disclose them. Of all the forms of private examination of title, title insurance is generally recognized to be the safest and best, although it is sometimes more expensive than other forms of evidencing title.

The Torrens system

In recent years there has grown up in various localities a form of public evidencing of title known as the Torrens system of title registration. The theory of the Torrens system is that the title to a parcel of land shall first be established by court decree and that this court decree shall be filed in the recorder's office as a certificate that John Smith owns the land subject to whatever encumbrances are laid down in the decree. When John Smith sells the land, the recorder cancels the original certificate and issues a new certificate in the name of the purchaser. Where land is registered under the Torrens system, it is always possible to go to the recorder's office and learn who is the owner of the land, and what the existing encumbrances are, without examining the chain of title from its source to the present time. Twenty-one states have adopted this system, but it is not widely used.

It is not intended herein to discuss the relative merits of the various forms of evidence of title. Whatever form of evidence of title is customary in the locality in which the land is situated is usually sufficient.

While it is true that in communities in which either certificates of title or title insurance are current, a lawyer's advice is not absolutely essential, yet it is also true that in so important a matter as the purchase of a valuable tract of real estate it is not safe to proceed without the aid of a lawyer.

Tracing the title

A question that often occurs to the layman is "How far back is it necessary to trace a title to show a good and marketable title in the vendor?" The answer to this question differs in different jurisdictions. The title must be traced to what is known as the "root of title." By the "root of title" is meant the title existing in someone at a time sufficiently remote to bar by force of the statute of limitations and by the lapse of time all persons under disability, namely minors, persons of unsound mind and persons imprisoned. In England this period has by custom been sixty years, but in comparatively recent times it was changed by statute to forty years.

In those parts of the United States where titles are derived from a government grant, it has been the custom to demand the titles be traced to the government patent no matter how remote that date may be. Most titles today are searched back to the year 1900.

Defects in title, which no search of the records would disclose, any one of which might cloud a title or render it unmarketable, but against which, by reason of lapse of time or other reason, a title company might be justified in issuing a policy of title insurance, are noted as follows: Old unsettled estates; lack of publication of notice by administrators and executors; no formal election by widow or widower to take under the will; ancient mortgages, either uncanceled or improperly canceled of record; imperfect, indefinite and ambiguous descriptions; tax titles, the validity of which depend upon the regularity of the proceeding upon which they are based; the regularity of judicial proceedings appearing in the chain of title; the rights of children born after the execution of a will; the question as to whether a will contains apt words to dispose of property acquired after its execution, and the validity of deeds executed under power of attorney.

While it is not the policy of any company to insure absolutely unmarketable titles, yet there are cases of temporarily unmarketable titles which may be insured—provided the company be indemnified by means of a bond, or the deposit of money or securities, during the process of perfecting title. Among these are: Estates in the process of administration;

pending suits for money only, in the few jurisdictions where judgment dates back to the first day of the term; disputed mechanics' liens; titles in the process of being quieted by suit.

In this connection the following quotation from the bulletin of the Texas Association of Title Men is relevant:

> When real estate is bought, the purchaser should be more interested in the title than in the land itself. The land only represents so much dirt that may be bought at a dollar a load. The title represents the right to occupy without molestation, and the right to sell, alienate and devise by will—in short, the right to possession and enjoyment.

The important element in real estate as a matter of investment is the marketability of title. No matter how otherwise desirable a parcel of real estate may be, it is of no value as a commercial asset unless it be marketable. And the essential element in marketability is the question of whether or not the title is good.

Do not buy real estate without a thorough investigation of the title. Things to watch for in obtaining evidences of title:

1. Determine what matters are covered by the title evidence offered; and then, be sure you are satisfied as to the matters not covered thereby.

2. As most forms of title evidence do not insure against adverse possession by a person holding an unrecorded deed, contract for sale, lease, and so forth, you should determine the rights of the parties in possession.

3. Ordinary title insurance does not insure against matters that are disclosed only by an inspection of the premises, such as the encroachment of adjoining buildings or overlap of buildings on to adjoining property, therefore a careful examination should be made of the premises. If buildings are close to lot lines a survey may be required.

4. If a Torrens certificate is offered as evidence of title, secure a separate report as to federal liens, current municipal taxes and any other matters not covered by the Torrens certificate issued by the state.

5. The state of delinquencies in taxes is never shown in title examination; neither are many types of liens imposed by municipalities and counties. Check at the City Hall and County Recorder for these items.

TWENTY-NINE

Increasing Realty Values by Building up Neighborhoods

Transportation within the urban areas of our country continues to be a major problem. Transcontinental travel via the SST (Supersonic Transport) which will move four or five hundred persons across the country at up to 2,000 miles per hour has been assured by recent government contracts issued for the building of these mammoth aircraft. But travel within urban environs is still a major problem.

Some cities have experimented with overhead monorail, most have developed extensive bus services, some are utilizing helicopter shuttles effectively, and the commuter trains around the New York area are still in use. Except in quaint old San Francisco, the street cars are all but gone. Through it all, the automobile has reigned supreme, and the concentration of effort has been on providing freeways over which auto traffic can quickly and safely make its way.

Shopping centers

With all these transportation developments, the outlying neighborhood shopping centers have become very much involved in the American

227

way of life. These little "business villages" are scattered all about the larger cities of the country. They have a distinct tendency to grow together along main arterial highways, at the junctions of which they first develop.

Potential wealth lingers around such busy neighborhood centers. It is amazing how, in some instances, property values develop from a few dollars per foot front for land to prices ranging to several thousands of dollars per foot front. These districts begin with the establishing of one or two stores at a crosstown motor highway, to be followed soon after by more stores, a theater, a lodge hall, a branch library, a fire or police station, a bank, a furniture store, a savings and loan office, more stores, a private market house with many small stalls, garages and automobile branch agencies, another theater, some more stores, and so on until the locality presents all of the appearances of a complete town in itself, surrounded by many streets lined with residences or apartment houses. Many of our modern shopping centers have not just grown from small beginnings at crossroads. The more recent trend is to establish these centers according to a well-developed plan. First, there is a great open field near a major traffic artery. A year later there is a multi-million dollar shopping center and a residential area in the making which will soon become a self-contained city within a city.

Community planning

To assist in the orderly development of such a neighborhood, which usually takes from five to fifteen years to accomplish fully, various plans have been used which will bear repetition in other small but steadily growing communities. By organized effort among property owners, who will reap their reward in increased increment for their land and growing rentals for their buildings, much can be done which will benefit such sections.

Neighborhood improvement associations, chambers of commerce, and property owners' leagues have been organized and operated with great success in many of these rapidly expanding centers. Unless some such medium is definitely created and merchants and property owners work together, many opportunities will be missed in bringing profits to the neighborhood. Festivals, banquets, parades, picnics, and contests of various sorts may be held under the auspices of such organizations. Old friendships will be cemented, and new ones created. Trade which formerly was attracted to the large downtown stores will remain at home in a larger degree, provided the merchants are alert to their opportunities, and let their customers know of their wares.

Effective service may be rendered by neighborhood associations in securing new pavements, and better caring for old ones. New "white way" street lighting systems can be planned and secured, changing dark, somber districts into areas as bright as day. Street cleaning can be made more effective. Objectionable and dangerous wires may be placed underground in conduits. Residential districts can be beautified by tree planting, and by a spirit of co-operation not only homes but also business buildings can be made to be brighter and more prosperous looking.

Effective help is often secured from neighborhood weekly publications which devote their entire attention to singing the praises of the sections from which they are securing their patronage. Successful merchants, who have become successful through their knowledge of the value of advertising, patronize these weekly mediums and often secure new and profitable business which would otherwise drift downtown to the large department stores.

The organization of a neighborhood real estate board is often helpful in the formulating of concerted plans for building up a territory. Los Angeles is perhaps one of the most conspicuous examples of this in the entire country. Like other large cities, it has annexed many towns and villages about its borders. One of the rules of the National Association of Real Estate Boards is that there shall be only one recognized board in each incorporated city. Realizing, however, that occasions might arise where neighboring towns would be absorbed, the National Association has an arrangement whereby divisional boards may become affiliated with the main board in a large city, functioning as neighborhood units, but receiving all of the benefits of membership in the larger organization. These groups of Realtors, working harmoniously together, are often able to effect many improvements in a neighborhood center, to the benefit of all property owners. Los Angeles has several such boards operating in conjunction with the main body of brokers.

Small banks often are organized in such centers, the officers of which have an intimate knowledge of the needs of the builders and merchants in the community, helping them as the occasion demands. Savings and loan companies, supported in their membership by residents in a district, are formed and help in the solving of home building problems.

Always alive to the best interest of a center, an association of merchants may inaugurate a contest for the best decorated show windows.

Attractively decorated and brilliantly lighted show windows do much to retain home trade. One live community made a great hit by buying a medium-priced automobile, dividing the cost into small trading checks which were given away with merchandise over a stated period, one of the contestants winning the prize. Later a large number of prizes was donated by a group of merchants, and interest was maintained in this way.

With the coming of weather-conditioned, enclosed malls around which shops are gathered, the attractions currently used to bring the customers are legion. If you go to shop at one of these malls, you may expect to see such things as trout fishing in portable tanks, auto shows, boat shows, dog shows, small carnivals with pony rides for the children—anything at all that will attract families to the air-conditioned mall.

The bringing of new public service facilities which do much to enhance property values can be stimulated by properly directed associations. These efforts, if conducted on an individual or political basis, might often fail.

The brightly illuminated movie theater, which comes to almost every business neighborhood as it begins to grow into importance, is always an important asset, much more so relatively than it would be in a downtown section of a city. Such institutions do most of their business in the evenings. It is significant that while the downtown areas of a city have few stores open at night, these shopping centers maintain many stores which keep open every evening, profiting from the traffic which patronizes the movie theater.

The main corners in a neighborhood center are nearly always monopolized by a drug store and a soda fountain, a confectionary store, and often a bank. These institutions, if properly patronized, can afford to pay high rentals; which reflect themselves in other store rentals in the neighborhood, and the owners of business property generally are benefited.

Churches, hospitals, fire and police stations, and schools which naturally develop with neighborhood centers are not classes of institutions which attract business. Instead of monopolizing busy corners, they should be located a block or two from the main thoroughfare, where it will be found that they will enjoy every advantage to be offered, yet will not detract from the usefulness of a business center.

However, such facilities should be planned from the beginning and space for them provided.

It is typical that motel areas spring up in close proximity to these shopping centers, and it is almost always true that apartment complexes and condominiums will locate nearby because the shopping center is a big attraction to those who dwell in apartments. With fewer and fewer people cooking and eating at home, cafeterias are flourishing in these shopping centers. Plush cafeterias seem to be the modern emphasis in eating establishments.

Gradual growth

Efforts to boom a budding business district, other than by thoroughly legitimate methods, seldom are successful. Growth is a gradual process which takes place over a period of years, and mere spectacular display and circus methods seldom prove effective.

One of the most potent methods of building up a growing district is the erection of artistically designed business blocks. These need not be a highly expensive character; indeed, it is a mistake to build beyond a neighborhood's requirements. Mere display in the form of five or six-story fireproof structures or other fancy building programs may be followed by the investors finding that they cannot collect an adequate return upon their investments. Good looking one- and two-story structures properly designed by capable architects, and honestly built, will lend a charm and air of prosperity to a neighborhood, which will soon reflect higher rentals, and the attracting of a better grade of buying power to a section than would come to one improved with small, one story, wooden shacks.

Time was when the "chain stores" were a nemesis to local merchants who fought them fiercely. Today the chain stores are definitely here to stay with the emphasis swinging to discount stores which through volume buying and selling are able to sell at reduced prices.

Local merchants are simply expanding, buying into or establishing multiple stores, and in general are developing skills of merchandising to place them as worthy competitors with the powerful chains. Few people bemoan the chain stores any more, and they are accepted as a desirable facet of life in America. Business has to learn the meaning of the old phrase "the survival of the fittest" where chain stores are considered.

In the larger cities it is found that intensively developed subcenters of business exist in many of the foreign neighborhoods where the residents do practically all of their buying in the stores of friends and acquaintances. Creditable business sections are maintained in many of these foreign communities, the community leaders in many instances being heavily interested in a financial way in the business properties where the best stores are maintained. High rentals are often obtained in such sections.

In smaller cities nearly everyone goes downtown to do their shopping. As a city's boundaries expand, however, it takes longer to make the trip to the principal business center, and enterprising merchants open small stores to meet the business demand. By careful development these centers grow and expand into definite commercial communities.

The fact that centers of this sort are almost certain to come into being at important crossroads at the edge of a large city is so well recognized that there are real estate investors who are ready to buy in such localities far in advance of the market. A wait of several years brings transportation facilities in most instances. Then come a school and a church, and the little city is in full swing growing just as rapidly as the general territory builds up with homes. Tremendous advances in outlying business property values have been noted again and again in cities all over the country, and the wise investor will not go far astray if he will make a careful analysis of prospective centers with the idea of getting in early and buying or leasing advantageously situated corners which later may teem with business life and become a modified type of a city's central business district.

Zoning laws which are being adopted in many cities have exerted a curious effect on business subcenters. A zoning law is designed to restrict the use of property for specific purposes, and to prevent encroachment of undesirable classes of business into residential areas. In adopting a zoning law, certain sections are usually set aside for retail business purposes. A certain quantity of land is thus given a monopolistic privilege to house business enterprises. There is just so much of it, and when it is all built up more may be added, but it will come slowly at best. It has been noted that within a few months after the passage of a zoning law these restricted business districts have often enjoyed a distinct boom, and that property values have increased rapidly. Having this condition in mind, a survey of the situation in advance or just after the passage of a zoning law may help an investor to gain possession of property, which within a year or two is almost certain to take on added value by reason of the intensive business purpose to which it may be put.

Developers of immense subdivisions make great capital of this principle. As the subdivision which perhaps covers five hundred acres or more is planned on paper, certain districts are set aside by the developers for business. Because they control so large an area, they know with certainty that these areas restricted for business can be depended upon to bring huge prices since there can be no competition in the immediate area. Cities virtually always accept the zoning plan of the large development planners just the way the planners project it.

Since 1959, FHA has operated a program wherein developers of these huge projects can obtain insured loans. The size of these projections is indicated in the fact that for a single such enterprise the ceiling for these land development loans has been placed at 25 million dollars. Such a system as this has resulted in vast, well-planned, and well-developed suburban centers.

THIRTY

Recapturing Value Through
Remodelling and Modernizing

Judicious remodelling of buildings
subject to out-of-dateness will be found to result in returns far in excess
of the costs involved.

Buildings, like automobiles and other *commodities,* wear out, despite
the fact that the average owner likes to think that his structure of fifteen
or twenty years of age is still worth what he paid for it. Appraisers contend that an average frame building has a normal economic life of about
thirty-five years while a brick building may be given a normal life of fifty
years. That does not mean that such building will not stand up physically
and give service for much longer periods. It does mean that they suffer
from obsolescence to a degree that, for all practical purposes, they must
be discounted as economic assets in such periods unless they are completely
overhauled and brought up to date through modernizing processes.

Remodelling from time to time is the best way in which to maintain
any building. A residence, for instance, should be rebuilt in some particular every ten or fifteen years. This may be done by the installation of
new plumbing or lighting fixtures, replacing the roof, re-siding exterior
walls, or by adding structural additions such as bedrooms, sunrooms, or
bathrooms. The things which become obsolete most quickly are the

plumbing fixtures, the tile work, the heating plant, the kitchen, the lighting fixtures, and the interior trim. New decorations help from time to time, but the application of mere paint and paper does not fully overcome the obsolescence which constantly creeps up on an old building.

Home builders and designers have caught onto the system used by the auto makers and manufacturers of women's apparel. They have found that by changing some significant features they may cause a five or six-year old house to appear up-to-date.

For instance, the installation of sliding glass doors will give a more modern appearance. Closet doors change in design from year to year, and if a home doesn't have louvered closet doors of the "glide and fold" type, the customer knows the house is at least six years old. Most of these "new" features are relatively insignificant so far as function is concerned; but in terms of salability, they can make a sale.

While there are well-established types of architecture in the United States, a great many dwellings from time to time may be improved with changes in their exteriors. Under clever treatment the architecture of a house can be modified, new windows added, roof lines changed, and new rooms provided, thus making the building over into a satisfactory dwelling that will continue to serve for another generation

Every city has business districts which are twenty or thirty years of age, where some of the structures are distinctly out of date and where extensive remodelling is needed. In most cities this changing-over process is going on, to some degree, almost all of the time. New store fronts are being installed, and in some cases upper stories are being entirely eliminated to allow, first, for the use of stairway space for ground floor store purposes and, second, to reduce taxes which are charged against second-floor space which is not needed and which is seldom productive of adequate revenue sufficient to pay a return on the investment.

Lifting the face of almost any kind of building can now be profitably engaged in by any owner who is wide awake enough to observe that rental returns are waning because his structure is becoming obsolete. It is no great task to finance such operations, and many owners are constantly realizing that it is profitable to engage in such operations.

Conditions requiring remodelling

There are a number of types of owners who find it advisable to remodel properties from time to time:

1. Individual house owners who occupy the premises or who rent them for income purposes.

2. Owners of income properties such as apartments, flats, and duplexes. Many tenants dislike living in out-moded properties, and rents sag very definitely when premises fall into such a class. In many instances the remodelling which must be done to this type of holding is not large but it is necessary nevertheless.

3. Proprietors of store properties in major or minor business locations. The buying public is critical of doing business in old shabby shops, and the average storekeeper knows the advantages of being up to date in his merchandising methods. Consequently store remodelling is almost constantly in progress. After a period of years, a building may call for a major operation and it may be necessary to rebuild extensively to meet current demands.

4. Mortgage companies and individuals holding liens on properties which have been foreclosed find it imperative to remodel to some extent before attempting to sell or rent them. The Home Owners Loan Corporation was a notable example of an institution which finally realized that if it were to resell thousands of dilapidated holdings, complete rehabilitation had to be proceeded with on every old house. Since 1965, the program under the Department of Housing and Urban Development has offered "rehabilitation loans" to homeowners.

5. Real estate investment companies, holding buildings as income investments, find it profitable from time to time to remodel their properties, thereby being able to increase rents and obtain better financial returns.

6. Owners of industrial properties find it necessary to rebuild, keeping up with the changing tempo of industrial and business life. Following a long and serious depression, there is always a considerable amount of factory and shop remodelling done, often accompanied by a considerable volume of new construction.

7. During boom days many banks and mortgage companies made large financial commitments which later went bad, following which many run-down premises were repossessed. With book charges at high figures and with incomes lagging much behind, the challenge was faced by such institutions to make their holdings produce more income. About the only way this could be done was to remodel them extensively. In many cases careful modernizing resulted in greatly increased prices being realized.

Why remodelling is profitable

There is no question but that remodelling is profitable. Five ways are mentioned by Kenneth Kingsley Stowell in his excellent book *Modernizing Buildings for Profits:*

1. Stops losses by creating more rental.
2. Attracts new tenants of higher grade.
3. Creates rentable space out of otherwise useless space.
4. Decreases operating costs in many instances.
5. Retains good will of old tenants.

In the matter of store fronts alone it has been found that with progress made in lighting equipment and the invention of new plastic materials, as well as the use of glass, mirrors, metals, and so forth, it has been necessary to rebuild the average store front every few years to keep it strictly up to date and in line with modern usage. This pays big dividends for it brightens up the merchant's place of business, permits him to do more business and often makes it possible to collect back in a short time the cost and something more from the tenant.

Sometimes campaigns are conducted by entire neighborhoods for the modernizing of their business frontages. An improvement association in many a city has organized a campaign for the complete rehabilitation of an entire district of old stores which were ready for treatment but which had gone neglected through the years until merchants threatened to move to newer sections. It has been found in most cities that high-grade business districts shift every fifteen or twenty years, sometimes more often. This can be overcome to quite a degree if landlords will face the problem and maintain their properties in good condition. It is a simple matter to summon property owners together, form an organization, call in a competent architect and have designs made for new fronts and other structural changes. Estimates of cost may thus be obtained, sketches will reveal how the remodelled premises will look, financing can be secured, and in most cases tenants are willing to pay the cost in additional rent over a period of time if given bright modern accommodations.

An old building made new by modernizing is usually in a better financial position than a new one for doubtless much of the old building's cost has already been written off, and even relatively low rentals may make it a better investment than a brand new one.

Many a canny real estate investor has observed an old building, soundly built and possessing many advantages from a structural standpoint but somewhat run down from lack of care. The investor, bearing down on the unfavorable condition of the structure, acquires it at a bargain price. The first thing he does is to give the tenant notice to move. Then he remodels the place, adding a fine new front, with attactive interior fixtures and appointments. The rent is then increased twenty-five per cent or more, a new satisfied tenant is signed up, and the property is sold at a handsome profit after remodelling costs are deducted from the total received. There are operators who are doing this sucessfully all of the time.

Obtaining professional services

Professional building modernizers operate in nearly all cities. These men leave standing orders with brokers for the purchase of old run-down properties, especially homes located in good neighborhoods. Buying at a bargain, the operator gets an architect to make new designs or prepares them himself. Workmen are called in. Sometimes the whole façade of a dwelling is changed, sometimes only a few new windows are added, an old porch removed, a front door relocated, a new bathroom provided, and a bedroom added. For every dollar spent the operator often collects a profit of two dollars or more when he resells the property. Many a place has been obtained at a price which was later matched with a similar amount from a mortgage company after a few hundred dollars had been spent in wise remodelling. There are plenty of instances where the newly obtained mortgage was even considerably more than the original cost of the old building.

Imitation is still the sincerest flattery in the matter of remodelling. In almost every city there are examples of good work done in this field that will serve as suggestions to other property owners as to what they may do. Even new buildings in a neighborhood may bring forth clever suggestions for the treatment of an old one nearby. In most cities there are architects or builders who specialize in this type of work, and conferences with such men will often be fruitful in the way of suggestions concerning specific cases ready for treatment.

There are a number of ways in which modernizing work may be done from a cost standpoint. With adequate plans available an owner can usually get estimates and bids on such work. Preliminary estimates may be furnished by an architect as a basis of the general expense involved but the test will come when the actual bids themselves are submitted by builders. This is a very difficult type of work to give definite bids upon because of the fact that unlooked-for conditions may be encountered, which may increase costs materially.

This element of uncertainty sometimes leads to the use of the cost plus contract type of financing. The builder will do the work, the owner paying for all materials and labor, and allow the contractor a fixed fee of say ten per cent upon the final cost involved. It may even be a higher percentage in involved cases or less in simple ones. When there is a fixed price a contractor naturally tries to do the work as economically as possible. When the cost plus plan is used he is under no obligation to hew his expenses close to the line for the more he spends the bigger his fee will be. By and large the use of competitive bidding is preferred. If the contract method is used great care must be observed to have complete specifications which will cover the entire work, otherwise the matter of extras is likely to enter into the picture and involve a good deal of unexpected expense.

While the architect is naturally relied upon to do the planning in any operation calling for extensive operations, a professional building manager is occasionally most helpful for he is acquainted with problems of use, operation, and maintenance, as well as the demand on the part of the public for certain types of space in larger buildings. With an architect working in close co-operation with a building manager and an owner, and with efficient workmanship on the part of a capable building contractor, any kind of remodelling operation has a good possibility of success.

The architect is required to provide detailed plans and specifications for the work to be undertaken and he also supervises the preparation of forms on which contractors make their actual bids. When the work gets under way it is conducted under his personal supervision and his word is law insofar as the builder is concerned. Of course the architect co-operates with the owner and any advisors, such as a building manager, and the resultant work coordinates the entire operation into a useful and successful one.

Fees for architects vary in different kinds of work from six to ten per cent of the total cost entailed. This includes not only the preparation of the plans but the complete supervision of operations from the day the building permit is taken out until the work is turned over in a finished condition to the owner. Sometimes an architect, for a pre-arranged fee will take the contract to do the work himself, hiring his labor and acting as contractor on the work. This will be in addition to the preparation of plans. This is known as the "lump sum" fee. Any extensive changes in plans call for additional remuneration.

At the outset there should be a definite understanding between an owner and an architect as to the routine to be followed, and it should be put in the form of a written contract so there may be no difficulties when the final settlement is reached.

Careful and cautious planning on the part of a capable architect and a conscientious owner will eliminate many "extras" on a job of remodelling, the bane of such work. Carelessness will lead to much additional cost unless great care is taken by everyone concerned.

Financing modernization work may be accomplished in various ways. Sometimes a lien holder is willing to advance additional money and incorporate it in his mortgage, feeling that the security is being made more valuable. Many banking institutions now have funds for this kind of work which they will advance on the note of the borrower, to be repaid regularly over a period of a few months. Banks and other leading institutions also may take advantage of the Federal Housing Administration's title which guarantees modernization loans when made by certified lending institutions. Occasionally contractors may be found who will do the work on deferred monthly payments. Likewise persons with good credit backgrounds may be able to obtain materials on long-term credits, simply having to pay labor expenses at the time the work is done.

Typical opportunities

In recent years a good deal of modernization work has been done on hotels and apartment houses of from twenty to thirty years of age which have become obsolete through lack of a sufficient number of bathrooms and modern kitchen facilities. Many old apartments had exceptionally large rooms with only one bath to a suite. This may be overcome by installing new bathrooms by cutting down the size of large rooms, and adding additional closet and hall facilities. Sometimes an apartment of from six to ten rooms can be cut up into two or three smaller units. With new modern equipment now available kitchens can be remodelled so they cannot be distinguished from those found in new buildings. Such work, while expensive, invariably attracts additional income and usually makes the investment well worthwhile.

In modernizing multiple dwelling units an architect starts with the foyer and works through from cellar to roof. New elevators are installed, lighting fixtures are replaced throughout. Kitchens are completely rebuilt, and where buildings contain furnished units it is often customary to scrap all of the old furniture and equip the place anew. A full length mirror adorns a door in at least one bedroom in every suite. Many new electrical units or outlets are furnished for floor lamps, and it is customary to equip every room with radio and TV connections. Mechanical equipment throughout is renewed and refrigerators of the latest type are installed in every unit. Practically every renovation includes year-round air conditioning.

Owners of old, out-of-date office buildings face the problem of maintaining the prestige of their structures which rapidly drift into third- and fourth-class establishments as compared to newer structures. If of good design the problems are not serious and may be met by a thorough overhauling and a repainting and decorating job. In some instances it will be found that old-style partitions must be replaced. New elevator installations must be provided. Sometimes entire floors must be redesigned as to room layouts. Careful attention must be paid to lighting fixtures which usually must be completely replaced. At the same time many additional electrical outlets are installed. Wainscotings in halls sometimes have to be completely replaced. Not infrequently the whole exterior of a large building must be changed either by chipping off old surfaces and applying a new cement coating or by completely refacing with brick or terra cotta.

The most typical face-lifting job for office buildings these days revolves around the plan of furnishing complete air conditioning, thereby eliminating the need for windows. The windows are sealed and new façades are provided out of huge slabs of prestressed concrete aggregate to the end that the old building is completely encased and is no longer even recognizable.

Given a valuable downtown site and a sound, well-designed structure, it pays to go thoroughly into the job of rebuilding such a structure, into a modern one. The architect starts with the heating system in the basement and either scraps or rebuilds it. From an old coal heating plant he will change to gas furnaces with refrigerated air units in conjunction. Then the architect follows through right up to the roof, rebuilding the project for another thirty years of use.

Downtown office buildings with banking quarters on the main floors offer exceptionally perplexing problems when it is found that the banking room is no longer needed. Here a major operation often becomes necessary. The exterior walls in many cases must be completely removed and the entire ground floor, and sometimes the second floor as well must be rebuilt. In place of the big cumbersome room where money and credit were traded, there come into being a number of sleek, modern shops that frequently rent at top figures. Sometimes entire floors must be leveled to the sidewalk. Occasionally great vaults, no longer needed, must be blasted out with pneumatic hammers and the space converted for retail use. All in all, the modernization of an old banking structure constitutes an important operation but is almost invariably worthwhile if the building is well located.

Nothing is quite so useless or lacking in profit possibilities as an old abandoned theater or church in a district which has been passed by for other and newer districts. Theaters and churches have been remodelled for a variety of purposes, including automobile garages, auction marts, storage warehouses, factories or retail stores with offices above. It is frequently necessary to gut the entire building and reconstruct everything except the outer walls. Many old antiquated theaters have been rebuilt into movie houses. Indeed, in New York City a theater was changed into a bank and later, when movies became popular, the bank was again shifted back to its old use as a theater. If a site is valuable it sometimes pays to wreck the old building completely and erect a new one in its stead.

The coming years will see a volume of modernizing work much greater than ever attempted heretofore. Methods for successfully rehabilitating buildings are more or less standardized in many cities as the technique becomes established among men engaging in such work. New materials are becoming available which readily lend themselves for remodelling use in the hands of capable artisans. Year by year buildings grow older and more out of date. Physically their shells have lives for long years extending into the future. As it doesn't pay to tear them down and construct new buildings, the only logical thing is to rebuild them into units which are practically as good as new, but at much less cost.

One thing must definitely be kept in mind, however. There is a limit to the amount of money which can be wisely spent on any given job, a point of vanishing return beyond which money may be wasted and upon which no adequate rental return can be realized. The skill with which the operator learns to know just how much work to do and how much expense to incur will measure the success of his operations. This may take time and involve costly mistakes, but through the experiences so gained will the operator continue successfully in this interesting field. The tendency is either to skimp and not do enough or to plunge and do more than the anticipated income will warrant. When one learns to strike the happy medium then the greatest profit may be realized.

THIRTY-ONE

Financing Real Estate

Skill exercised in the financing of transactions in which real estate is being bought, sold or exchanged frequently measures the success of the operator's activities. It has a direct relationship to almost every deal encountered and demonstrates the investor's ability to make money in this field.

Books have been written about this interesting but involved subject so necessarily only the highlights may be considered here. No opportunity should be lost in studying methods and examining practices whereby real estate operations may be financed to successful conclusions.

In some deals it will be found that financing arrangements have been set up in advance. This means that the transaction will be more easily consummated, and bespeaks the experience of an operator who seeks to make it *easy for a customer to buy,* without encountering perplexing problems. A clever owner will always seek out the best means by which a property that he hopes to sell can be adequately refinanced for a variety of buyers. Then it is only necessary to conduct selling negotiations, accept an offer, and close the deal in escrow, the entire transaction taking a comparatively short time. When involved financing arrangements must be made, interminable delay results.

The larger and more important transactions call for considerable ingenuity in the working out of details to the end that the financing may be advantageous and as ample as possible. Familiarity with methods and with the instruments used in assuming financial indebtedness is necessary to the successful investor. There follow brief references to some of the more important financing methods which may be considered in connection with ordinary transactions.

Financing methods

A *first mortgage* is used in many sales. It is an officially signed legal instrument, usually recorded at the county courthouse, and is given by a borrower, or mortgagor, to a lender, or mortgagee, by which the latter is delegated the right to take possession of the property described in the mortgage, in the event the borrower defaults in meeting the indebtedness for which the mortgage is given. A certain rate of interest is stipulated, and a time is definitely stated at which the entire loan falls due, or the loan is amortized and payments made monthly. Failure to pay interest or principal permits the lender to assume possession of the property, after due legal steps have been taken to declare the mortgage void. Mortgages in most states provide a term of twelve months in which a default may be made good and the position of the debtor made safe.

A *second mortgage,* sometimes called a junior mortgage, is one placed on a property which already is encumbered with first mortgage. It is assumed that the first mortgage covers a valuation of at least fifty per cent of the full worth of the property. It is seldom wise for a lender to take a second mortgage for an amount which brings the total indebtedness to more than seventy-five per cent of the full value of the property, although sometimes a larger mortgage may be justified on the basis of the character of the borrower. In most cities second mortgages have gone out of use. Some first mortgage holders prohibit the placing of second liens on the assumption that the debtor has all he can take care of in keeping the first mortgage in good shape. This is a rule of the FHA system.

A *trust deed* differs from a mortgage, in that it conveys title to property to a third person or trustee for the purpose of securing a debt or other obligation. The instrument empowers the trustee, in case of default, to repossess the property. Under the terms of a trust deed a designated period is allowed for redemption, when foreclosure may proceed. Then the trustee, usually a bank or a trust company, may file papers which sever the debtor from his holding. Actually a person acquiring property under a trust deed *never has title* to it and is largely in the position of a contract holder. In the case of a mortgage the property is actually conveyed to the owner and he does have title to it until such time as a period of redemption has expired, when the lien holder takes possession.

There are also what are known as *"third mortgages,"* which constitute an additional lien on a property on which first and second mortgages or trust deeds already exist. These are seldom encountered although in times of great real estate activity they are sometimes used to finance properties for short periods. They usually are used in connection with highly speculative deals and heavy bonuses must be paid for money thus employed. Their use is ordinarily not considered sound financial practice.

Individuals and groups of investors, the latter organized into incorporated companies or personally controlled syndicates which buy and sell properties, are constantly using mortgages, trust deeds, and similar financing instruments. These papers should be prepared by experts or at least approved standard forms should be used, for these instruments cover matters of importance and one cannot afford to have mistakes made in documents of this character. Unless thoroughly competent to do so, *never attempt* to prepare complicated legal papers but consult a real estate lawyer. Every lawyer does not necessarily have the experience to act in matters of this kind, and the pitfalls into which buyers and sellers may be plunged through incompetent representation are many.

During periods of real estate activity a favorite practice of investors is to form what are known as real estate *syndicates.* These are unincorporated groups of persons, usually comparatively few in number, who agree to operate under a syndicate agreement[1] for the purchase and sale of property. Funds are subscribed and pooled. Some syndicate members may invest more than others and profits, losses and maintenance charges are distributed pro rata. These syndicates are usually promoted by real estate brokers or operators, who assemble a group of investors, who agree to assume the ownership of a property. They divide the cost of acquiring it into shares which are assumed by individual members of the group. Syndicates are often incorporated into companies, though many simply operate under syndicate agreements, trusteeing the property in the name of one person. If the property maintains itself, the trustee manages it for the benefit of the group. If not self-sustaining, the various members of

---

[1] See Syndicating Agreement in the Appendix.

the syndicate are assessed from time to time for enough money to meet the obligations as they become due. Properties which are not self-sustaining may grow in increment, and can be sold or leased at a profit after being held several years.

Land contracts are extensively used in real estage transactions, especially where relatively small-sized payments are being made and the seller does not feel justified in giving a deed to the new buyer until a substantial portion of a purchase price has been paid. A land contract is an agreement between the seller and the buyer whereby the former agrees to sell and the latter agrees to buy the premises described. The statute of frauds, in effect in most states, was enacted centuries ago in Engand, and was designed to prevent fraud in land transactions by providing that contracts relating thereto be put in writing. There are two kinds of land contracts. The first is a temporary type, setting forth in writing all of the terms of a contemplated deal, to stand until a deed, evidence of title, and other papers can be prepared. The other is of a more permanent character, establishing the *present sale* and providing for *the future transfer of the title*. The seller is usually designated as the vendor and the buyer as the vendee.

The seller, under such a contract, agrees to sell the property and to transfer satisfactory title upon the performance of certain conditions by the buyer; and the latter, in his part of the contract, so agrees to do. It is not necessary that the property which the vendor agrees to sell be free and clear of encumbrances at the time the instrument is signed .

Land contracts are extensively used by subdividers in the selling of lots in new developments. Where the buyer pays a very small down payment, he then proceeds over the months to whittle down the encumbrance until the debt is at least half paid when, usually, a deed is given and a mortgage goes back to the seller from the buyer for the balance due, although many times a full payment is required before the deed is given.

Where an involved land contract is encountered and the buyer has little experience in the matter, he should submit it to his attorney for examination. Strange things sometimes are found in such instruments. For instance there have been cases where, in the fine print of the land contract, the vendee has given the vendor, or some third party controlled by the vendor, the right to waive priority of the land contract in favor of any mortgage put on the land *after the execution of the land contract itself!* In such a case the vendor may put a mortgage on the property equal to sixty or seventy per cent of its value although the vendee may have a paid up eighty per cent equity in the property he has purchased. For this and other reasons land contracts must be very carefully examined when presented for signature.

During periods of real estate activity in the past, when land was selling at high prices and money was flowing freely, there were a number of ways in which real estate was financed which have, for the most part, been discarded. One was the *bond issue* method of financing important holdings. Title to property was conveyed to a trustee who proceeded to issue bonds of various denominations to the full extent of its value. These were sold at par to investors to yield five, six, or eight per cent interest annually. Apartment houses, business enterprises, even subdivisions were so bonded. Many paid out successfully, many got into trouble and defaulted and bondholders eventually lost millions. Not a great deal unlike such bond issues were land trust certificates or certificates of equitable ownership, which also proved unsuccessful in many instances and caused much loss.

Another ingenious method used for financing purposes during the boom time was the promotion of *co-operative* apartments. These multiple dwellings were developed in the larger cities where tenants were sold individual apartments in more or less pretentious buildings. These units the buyers were to own outright but subject to certain charges for upkeep. Part or all of the cost of each apartment was paid before the structure was erected. If enough money was not available a mortgage was placed on the property to be retired as the apartment owners paid in their funds. Unfortunately many of these enterprises collapsed financially before the buildings were finally paid for, and huge losses were sustained by all concerned. Modern condominiums are huge successes, however.

Financing a subdivision has alway been a difficult thing to do. Banks do not look with favor on them nor do mortgage or insurance companies. In most cases the most satisfactory way to finance a subdivision is for the real estate operator who expects to market the lots to pay down a substantial amount in cash and then get the seller of the land to take back a blanket mortgage with waiver clauses, agreeing to release lots as they are sold and paid for. Unless something occurs to interfere with the selling out of the property, such an arrangement is usually a satisfactory way to finance such enterprises.

Farms are difficult properties to finance. Insurance companies and banks have sunk many millions of dollars in farm mortgages, only to find many of the properties back on their hands. This led to the formation of Farm Land Banks under federal jurisdiction which have worked out plans for long-term mortgage commitments, with low interest rates and many years to pay back the principal on the debt. This has done much to stabilize the financing of farm properties in recent years.

Difficulties are nearly always encountered in connection with the financing of industrial properties. Banks are loath to assume such indebtedness, unless for nationally known concerns which usually can sell their own securities for puposes of expansion. Smaller organizations usually have to pay much of the cost of new improvements out of capital funds as they are brought into existence. Often a seller of an industrial property will take back a substantial mortgage, payable over a term of years at current interest rates. Many companies start their industrial lives in a small way, gradually expand, and pay for plant additions as they are made.

Major sources of financing

Funds for financing real estate projects are available from a number of sources. There are individuals who have money for investment; banking institutions of all kinds; mortgage companies formed for the express purpose of using funds in such transactions; insurance companies that find real estate a profitable field in which to invest surplus funds; building and loan associations formed for the express purpose of lending on new house construction as well as refinancing older properties, and even business and industrial concerns which have surpluses they are willing to lend on interest-bearing accounts. Wealthy estates also enter the market from time to time for the purpose of putting extra funds to work.

The *individual investor,* unlike organized institutions which lend money, seldom works under as strict a code of procedure in his loaning activities. One man may be ultraconservative and willing to accept a modest rate of interest. Another may be quite willing to take a greater risk but wants to be paid for it. The latter will always demand a higher rate of interest and may even want a bonus when he makes a favorable commitment. The individual lender of money may be much more difficult to negotiate with than the bank or mortgage company which maintains an appraisal department and has an established routine of procedure. The institution may want ample amortization of the loan, but the individual may desire to keep his money actively at work and may grant so-called "straight loans" in which no repayments are required. For this a higher rate of interest is sometimes demanded.

The individual investor may be somewhat erratic regarding the value he may place upon property. In most cases he is inexperienced as to the scientific manner in which real estate is appraised. He works on "hunches," and general impressions he receives of a property and the neighborhood in which it is located are likely to guide his judgment as to the amount of money he will lend and the terms of the contract as to expiration and amortization of the debt.

Banking institutions, of course, have been lending money for years on what they regard as one of their best types of security for loans. Many banks have well-educated appraising departments to guide them. Likewise they have extensive experience concerning changing conditions in different districts in which they operate. Banks are more conservative, and the percentage of the loan to the appraised value of the premises is established by law. Banks do much to help real estate development and give special care to the needs of their own customers. They usually lend sixty to eighty per cent of appraised value, as the merits of the case dictate and state and national banking laws allow. They usually demand ample amortization of the debt in monthly payments, at the rate of from five to fifteen per cent annually, in addition to the payment of the agreed interest. Loans are now made for periods of from five to twenty-five years. Formerly they were for three years and then extended year by year upon payment of a bonus. This rather vicious practice has given way to straight terms at stated interest and amortization rates.

During active business periods there come into existence many *mortgage companies,* formed by selling stock on which good rates of interest are paid and even guaranteed. Some of these mortgage companies will take very large loans and issue them to the public for general subscription in the form of bond issues, with mortgage bonds in units of $100, $500, $1,000, and upwards. These bonds are also amortized by repayments on the principal at stipulated periods ranging from ten to fifteen years.

Life insurance companies lend from one quarter to one third of their surplus funds on real estate as a rule. While they have expert appraisal departments at their home offices, they usually operate through local agents who co-operate with expert appraisers in fixing values. Borrowing from such companies is advantageous when a long-term loan is required as the companies favor sizable loans at relatively low interest rates amortized over the periods agreed upon. When operating through local agents in the smaller communities the borrower pays up to four and one-half per cent for securing the loan, servicing, etc.

Most communities have *saving and loan associations* which maintain reservoirs of funds for new home building operations. These organizations confine their activity largely to this field, although occasionally they help in the refinancing of dwellings already in existence. These concerns charge up to six and one-half per cent interest and make loans for periods of from ten to thirty years in duration. Some homes are built with funds from this source, and then after the buildings are completed, the loans are transferred to banks or insurance companies as many such institutions do not always care to assume the bother of making construction loans.

A movement which revolutionized the financing of certain types of real estate, particularly dwellings, came into being when the congress of the United States created the *Federal Housing Administration,* its purpose being to "stimulate real estate and construction industries." The act originally was approved on June 27, 1934, and it has been amended over a period of years wherein its scope and authority has been greatly widened. In 1965, FHA became a part of the Department of Housing and Urban Development.

It must be understood at the outset that the Federal Housing Administration *does not lend money on real estate.* It simply *guarantees or insures loans.* There must always be an approved financial institution which will accept the application for the loan, make it when approved by FHA and carry through until the loan is paid off or defaults. It is only when it does default that FHA actually pays out money, at which time it takes over the property, wipes out whatever is left of the obligation held by the lending institution, and proceeds to sell the property at the best figure obtainable. This, in brief, is the theory under which the government has lent its credit in the real estate financing field.

Much has been said for and against the movement. Those who do not approve of the government entering this field charge that it is a form of state socialism; that it interferes with private initiative; that it is paternalistic in character; that it has ruined the sale of old houses because most persons want brand new homes and not used ones, and that it places in the hands of many persons properties in which they have very little financial interest and which they will turn back to Uncle Sam the minute they lose their jobs or meet with financial reverses. Those who favor the movement contend that most buyers eventually make good; that the government will not have any extensive amounts to pay out in guarantees; that it stimulates the erection of many thousands of small homes, produces work and creates a vast market for materials and labor that would not otherwise be called for.

The activities of the Federal Housing Administration are as follows:

FHA LOANS BY TITLES AND SECTIONS[1]

PROPERTY IMPROVEMENT LOANS
Title I, Section 2 .. .. Max. loan—$3,500

HOMES
Title II
Section 203(b)
1- to 4-family homes .... Max. loan—$30,000 single family
Section 203(h)
Disaster homes .... Max. loan—$12,000
Section 203(i)
Low-cost homes .... Max. loan—$12,500
Section 203(k)
Home improvement loans .. Max. loan—$10,000 single family
Section 213
Sales of individual cooperative housing units
.... Max. loan—not specified
Section 220
Urban renewal homes ...... Max. loan—$30,000 single family
Section 220(h)
Home improvement loans in urban renewal areas
.... Max. loan—$10,000 single family
Section 221(d)(2)
Low-cost homes for families displaced by urban renewal, etc.
.... Max. loan—$12,500 single family
Section 222
Servicemen's homes .... Max. loan—$30,000 single family
Section 233
Experimental housing ... .. Max. loan—not specified
Section 234(c)
Sales of individual condominium housing units
.... Max. loan—$30,000 each occupant
Title VIII
Section 809
Homes for civilian personnel of military bases, etc.
.... Max. loan—$30,000 single family

---

[1] Adapted from the FHA booklet, *Digest of Insurable Loans*. Courtesy of the Federal Housing Administration.

MULTIFAMILY
Title II
Section 207
Rental project housing ..... Max.   loan—$20,000,000   private
.... mortgagor
Section 207
Mobile-home courts .... Max. loan—$500,000
Section 213
Cooperative housing .... Max.   loan—$20,000,000   private
.... mortgagor
Section 220
Urban renewal housing .... Max.   loan—$30,000,000   private
.... mortgagor
Section 220(h)
Rental project housing improvement loans in urban renewal areas
.... Max. loan—$10,000 per family unit
Section 231
Housing for elderly .... Max. loan—$19,250
Section 232
Nursing homes .... Max. loan—$12,500,000
Section 233
Experimental housing ...... Max. loan not specified
Section 234(d)
Condominium housing ..... Max.   loan—$20,000,000   private
.... mortgagor
Title VII
Section 701
Investment yield insurance .. Max. insurable—90% of outstand-
.... ing investment
Title VIII
Section 810(f)
Rental housing for military or civilian personnel of military
bases, etc................ Max. loan—$5,000,000
Section 810(g)
Housing for sale to military or civilian personnel of military
bases, etc................ Max. loan—$5,000,000

LAND DEVELOPMENT AND NEW COMMUNITIES
Title X
Purchase and development of land
.... Max. loan—$25,000,000

Insurance in every instance is confined to first mortgages and these *may not be followed by second mortgages,* it being the contention that the risk might thereby be affected. Inasmuch as a borrower often starts with only a three per cent equity in a property, it may be seen that this is doubtless a wise provision.

Most of the loans granted under this system are under Title I, which covers remodelling and modernization loans for buildings already in existence and under Title II which provides money for newly constructed properties.

Applying for a loan

Some persons abhor debt and decline to acquire real estate unless they can pay cash in full for it. This, of course, is probably fine theory but poor practice. While a land owner is paying five or six per cent interest annually on borrowed money, the land which he controls may be increasing ten per cent in value during the same period if strategically located. By having equities of fifty per cent in each of several properties, he increases greatly his opportunity of reaping increment from all. In American cities most properties are mortgaged, many of them to the full extent that their values permit. The successful operator in real estate is usually the one who knows when to borrow wisely and wait for the increase that comes to well-located holdings.

Mortgages may be assigned, so if you have purchased a property and arranged a new mortgage in your own name, you can readily sell the property, and in most instances have the obligation assumed by the buyer. Occasionally the lender requires the original borrower to remain on the paper. The property itself is usually the security for the loan.

In planning to secure a mortgage be frank with a bank, institution or individual with whom you are doing business. Do not attempt to deceive, for if you are caught in any such deception, there will be small chance of continuing your financing arrangements through that channel.

In securing a mortgage a "waiver" may sometimes be advantageously used. This is particularly true when the property is a large piece of vacant land which may be sold in smaller parcels. The mortgage can be so written that certain parcels can be released upon the payment of specified amounts in cash, which will reduce the mortgage in the proportion that the amount of the land sold bears to the entire area held under the general mortgage agreement

In applying for a loan of any kind an investor or prospective buyer should study carefully the manner in which the application is made. Most lending agencies have regular forms in which questions are asked. There is always a space for "remarks," and the borrower naturally should adequately point out the advantages of the property which he wishes to pledge as security for a loan. Care and skill in doing this may result in a more liberal loan than otherwise.

There is a considerable latitude in the amounts different agencies will loan on fair appraised values of real estate. Banks are usually conservative and loan from sixty to eighty per cent of the reasonable market value as arrived at through their own appraisal methods. Savings and loan companies in most states are permitted to loan up to ninety per cent of the value of a property. Mortgage companies, by demanding higher rates of interest and sometimes a cash bonus, may even loan eighty or ninety per cent of the value of a property on a first mortgage. Individual investors seldom desire to loan more than seventy-five per cent on their idea of the market value of a property. Instances have been known, however, where a speculator has secured a first mortgage of seventy-five per cent and a second mortgage of more than sufficient size to buy the property outright and still have some borrowed money remaining. This, of course, is dangerous business, particularly if the lender has any consideration for the security of the funds at his disposal.

A borrower usually reserves the right, in making a mortgage, to pay back the principal *on or before* a given date. If he finds it desirable to refinance, he can do so under such an arrangement. Some individuals and institutions will permit this only upon the borrower agreeing to pay a small penalty if the loan is taken up sooner than its term indicates. This is done because of a desire to regulate the lender's business so that recurring expenses for cancelling loans and reinvesting the money will not be frequently encountered.

Ingenuity in financing real estate transactions has made many a man rich. It has also sent many an apparently clever individual to the penitentiary when his manipulations got beyond bounds, and he resorted to brazen trickery. Financing transactions should be keenly scrutinized, not merely for mistakes which may be made, but for any evidences of fraud. By handling real estate deals through escrow with a responsible company, the risk is minimized because an escrow officer is trained to detect and expose tricks of all kinds in financing realty operations. While it is not a part of his duty to insure against such irregularities, nevertheless, by his very training and familiarity with the transfer of property, he is able to do much to protect an innocent purchaser. If there is a broker in the transaction, he will, of course, be in duty bound to protect either side, should evidences of trickery appear.

In former days, some persons who had money to lend at interest, particularly widows and others dependent upon funds left in their care for proper investment, placed their entire assets in hands of lawyers for them to invest as they saw fit. The majority of lawyers are honest, yet there are some who have not overlooked opportunities to misuse their client's money. The better way, in such cases, is to establish a trust fund estate at a thoroughly reliable savings bank or trust company, and proceed to invest under the direction of a responsible officer of such an institution.

"Vigilante salus—in vigilance, safety!" is the motto upon the family crest of the author of this volume. It is an excellent motto to be guided by in real estate financial transactions. Your own common sense will in most instances tell you what to do, and what not do do. By all means take a direct personal interest in the details of your financial arrangements. Do not leave their investigation entirely in the hands of others. There are plenty of means available by the use of which you may avoid financial troubles in connection with real estate transactions.

THIRTY-TWO

Loaning on Real Estate

The conservative investor, who does not care to bother with the problems of acquiring real estate and managing it, is attracted by opportunities for securing an adequate yet safe return through the medium of lending on mortgages or trust deeds on properly appraised properties, in well-selected neighborhoods in forward looking communities.

Almost from the earliest times when real estate began to shift into private ownership, the practice of loaning upon it has been in effect. The Old Testament contains many references to mortgages and practices in connection with making them. Through all the ages they have been considered wise and safe investments when their selection has been surrounded by proper safeguards. The person, therefore, who seeks to earn a safe return on funds at his disposal is readily attracted to this field.

There are many ways to loan money on real estate. There are organized mortgage companies which make a business of it and sell to investors their own securities based on the return on funds placed in mortgages.

259

Such mortgage companies, as well as banks and other institutions, will often execute mortgages and then sell them to private investors, sometimes guaranteeing them as to return of principal.

Persons with substantial funds to invest enter the field, study the problems of appraising properties, and loan funds directly to owners at current rates. Experience over long periods of time has shown that when conservative appraisals have been made and other conditions properly investigated, comparatively small loss has ever been sustained even as the result of depressions. Such loss, when it has occurred, has been substantially less than that sustained in connection with the ownership of stocks and bonds.

Who borrows on mortgages? There are two main types of persons who find it necessary to finance their properties through this means. There are loans to be made owners of existing properties whose loans are coming due and for some reason are not being renewed. There are loans to be made to builders in connection with the erection of new structures of all kinds. Frequently this last type of loan is made for a brief term and then taken up by someone as an investment at a slightly lower rate of interest. When construction loans are made by banks, mortgage and insurance companies, they often extend for long terms of years at relatively low rates of interest.

Private investors seldom care to make what are known as building construction loans, that is, loans on structures to be erected. There is considerable specialized knowledge needed to follow through with such loans and these, for the most part, are left to institutions which specialize in them. Properties which are fully completed and, preferably, somewhat seasoned, present the best type of security for the average private investor.

Advantages to the lender

The advantages to the lender making a mortgage loan on property may be stated as follows:

1. The security is adequate, almost always less than two-thirds of the full appraised value of the property encumbered. Safety of mortgage loans has always been their strongest recommendation.
2 The interest rate is always somewhat above the returns paid by stocks and bonds.
3. They offer less troublesome details of ownership than most other forms of investments.
4. The history of losses sustained indicates that the percentage is much lower than in most other fields.

From the lender's standpoint, the disadvantages may be stated as follows.

1. Mortgages are not liquid securities, such as are stocks and bonds and cannot be as readily realized upon in case of emergency. Banks will usually accept them as security on short-term loans, however.

2. Occasionally it may be found that trouble is caused by inability to collect interest promptly.

3. It is necessary, if conducted in a businesslike way, to check annually to ascertain whether taxes and assessments have been fully paid, for these are always liens prior to a mortgage loan. Larger cities have companies engaged in this work, furnished on a fee basis.

4. Mortgage loans are of relatively short duration as compared to federal, state or municipal bonds or securities of railroads and similar institutions, and thus necessitate reinvestment of funds. In recent years, however, the terms for most mortgages have been extended from three and five years to ten or fifteen years. It. is seldom wise, however, for the private investor to loan for a period of more than a single decade.

Problems the lender should consider

The investor, at the outset, is confronted with these problems:

1. What interest rate shall be charged? This is largely subject to conditions existing in the locality where the loan is made. If a risk is taken, a higher interest rate may be demanded. If prime security and an exceptionally strong person signs the note, the interest rate may be lower.

2. What is the value of the property? This is the most puzzling problem and of paramount importance to the lender.

3. Is the title good? Are all of the papers properly drawn and, finally, have the necessary papers been properly recorded with the public authorities?

On the fixing of the valuation of the property on which money is to be loaned through the medium of a mortgage, is centered the most important part of the entire transaction. Determination of value is an involved process which few private investors ever fully master. If a thorough working knowledge of appraisal technique is not possessed by an investor, he would do well to engage a professional appraiser, preferably a member of the American Institute of Real Estate Appraisers, to make the valuations.

Among the chief considerations in fixing value may be named the following:

1. Study of the neighborhood to ascertain whether it is likely to improve, to remain static, or decline. Neighborhood influences on individual pieces of real estate are very important, especially when a loan is for a relatively long time. When it is considered that whole business districts will shift from one point to another in a matter of fifteen or twenty years, it may be seen that even ten years may witness a decided change in any single district.

2. A study must be made of the individual lot involved. Its size, topography, suitability for the improvements, public service facilities available and many other factors must be investigated.

3. A careful scrutiny must be made of the building on the property or to be placed there. Is it suitable for that locality? Does it meet fully the purposes for which it has been erected? Is the construction of a high grade? Are there dry rot or termites? What is the cost per square or cubic foot for reconstruction new and then, properly depreciating it for age, what is its value from a physical standpoint? These and many other factors must be investigated under this heading.

4. What capacity for the return of rental has the property? Some improvements are worth less than their actual cost the day they are completed, from the standpoint of the rental that may be obtained for them in that neighborhood. When there are flats or apartments concerned, as well as stores, the investigation of the rental return a property may be expected to bring is most important.

5. What is the value of the property from a comparative standpoint? Can an equally good improvement be obtained nearby or in a neighborhood relatively as good for less money?

6. What about the person or persons who wish to acquire this loan? Are they good credit risks? Are they stable residents of proven reputation?

Check the three fundamentals of value against each other. They are: (1) the cost of reproduction new, less depreciation, (2) the capitalization of rentals to obtain a net income which, capitalized at a satisfactory rate of interest, will indicate the investment's economic return, (3) comparative analysis, that is, comparing the property with others of a like kind in a district as good.

A problem which presents itself in connection with almost every loan is the margin of security—what percentage of full value shall the lender adhere to in fixing the amount of the loan? Banks, building and loan associations, mortgage concerns and insurance companies are all subject to legislative control as to percentages they may loan. Banks are usually allowed to make up to 75 per cent loans, building and loan associations, loaning for the most part on residential security, are permitted to loan up to 90 per cent. Mortgage companies may often do the same. Insurance companies vary from 60 to 85 per cent of total appraised value.

The private investor can loan as little or as much as his judgment dictates, having first obtained a sound value for the property which is to serve as security. The lender may consider the personal background and integrity of the borrower and be more liberal than if he realizes that the property alone must stand as security for the loan. Frequently loans which represent less than 50 per cent of value may be asked by persons who do not require more money than that. Even these, however, should be most carefully appraised and given a complete review, for the property may be depreciating more rapidly than appears upon the surface.

In many cities there are mortgage brokers who make a business of obtaining mortgage funds for clients. They usually charge a fee of two or three per cent upon the amount loaned. This is paid as an extra consideration by the borrower at the time the loan is negotiated. The agent submits his appraisal of the property but it may be reinforced by another appraisal by a thoroughly disinterested but competent valuator. In that way the lender avoids personal negotiations with the borrower, although it is usually wise for the principals to meet and study each other and their modes of operation. The private investor will do well to investigate the possibilities of working in conjunction with such brokers as he may be able to place substantial blocks of funds through them. It may be stated, however, that almost every kind of borrower who has been turned down by regular lending agencies usually winds up in the office of the mortgage broker, who finally negotiates a loan.

In times of real estate booms there spring into existence the practices of making second mortgages on real estate. Provided a first mortgage represents not more than 50 per cent of value, on a conservative appraisal a careful lender may be able to see his way clear to loaning on a second mortgage up to a seventy-five per cent appraisal. For this he will secure a substantial bonus or an inflated interest rate.

It is important for the lender to know that some states have laws that make second mortgages very poor risks. A number of states will permit second mortgages to be collectible by law only if such mortgages were given as "purchase money mortgages" at the time the property was acquired. Thus, in those states a mortgage taken on property which had been paid down (a sizeable equity accumulated by the owner) would largely be the same as a personal note against the owner in favor of the lender.

Unless a lender is thoroughly familiar with the execution of legal instruments he will be wise to have all papers in a mortgage transaction executed by a lawyer, a mortgage company, an escrow agent, or some well-qualified person who is thoroughly familiar with such procedure. Having the papers completed, he should see to it that the instruments are properly recorded and all fees are paid in full.

Professional mortgage lenders, both of an individual and institutional character, should be close students of current real estate conditions and should watch the trends of expansion and contraction which occur from time to time. Information of an interesting character may include the following:

1. Number of deeds and mortgages recorded—obtained at recorder's office.
2. Number of marriage licenses issued—from the county clerk.
3. Number of building permits—from local inspector's permit office.
4. Population data—from newspapers and census bureau.
5. Status of rentals and vacancies—usually obtainable from local real estate board.
6. Number of foreclosures—from the sheriff's office.

The individual who would invest funds wisely in real estate mortgages must naturally be a student of city growth. He must be familiar with what has taken place in the past as to changing business and residential districts and possess sufficient foresight to be able to judge future trends of development, for on these will the security of future loans be largely predicted.

There is much of a legal nature which pertains to the loaning of money on real estate, and the institutions which engage in this type of endeavor naturally have men properly trained in the law to advise them. That is the reason that the investor who loans his own funds directly on property should tie in with some institution or person who is qualified to guide him. Ordinary first mortgages on dwellings or income and business property are not very involved, and after a little experience the investor will feel at home. His greatest problem will be the establishing of evidences of value on which the basis of the amount of the mortgage will be determined.

The moral hazard is extremely important in the lending of money on real estate. If the borrower is honest, thrifty, of good repute in his business life, and a man of unblemished reputation, it may be just as safe to make him a 70 per cent loan as a 50 per cent one. This does not mean that the physical security should be inadequate nor that it should not be sufficient to carry the loan whatever size it may be. It should, indeed, be the chief security unless the lender of funds is willing to take a risk on the personality of the borrower as such.

The entrance of the Federal Housing Administration into the field of real estate development in the middle 30's changed, to some extent, many of the practices in connection with the loaning of money on real estate. This governmental agency does not actually loan money on real estate but simply insures or guarantees loans made by others. It has its own efficient appraisal system and rates the borrower just as keenly as it does the property itself. Its activities have resulted in lengthening the terms of years for which mortgages are made.

The United States government through its Federal Home Loan Banks has in the past several decades loaned vast sums to farmers of the United States. Despite this fact depressions see large volumes of farm mortgages foreclosed by the insurance companies and banks. Individuals who loan in this field should know what they are doing and should be very conservative. Many who loan on this type of security consider the value of the land alone and disregard the improvements. Land cannot be moved away or destroyed and there will always be a market for it.

The past few years has witnessed a great change made in the matter of repayments of funds loaned on mortgage. Formerly all mortgages were made for short terms such as three to five years, when they became due. It was a general practice for most lenders to renew upon payment of a bonus of from three to five per cent. No periodic repayments were required on such loans. Then came into existence the practice of amortizing loans, certain sums being repaid on the principal at the same time interest payments were made. Some institutions amortize loans at the rate of one per cent a month including interest and principal. Other concerns, including insurance and mortgage companies, will accept as low as on.-fourth of one per cent monthly. In this way mortgages may run for twenty-five or even thirty years, and be practically repaid in full in that time

There have been set forth but a few brief principles for the loaning of money on real estate by the individual investor. Little attempt has been made to cover the subject in relation to practices followed by institutions or banks. Such data is available in many places and the individual, if interested, can make himself familiar with some of the broad principles involved. To the investor who seeks safety of principal with a minimum of effort and bother, the loaning of funds through carefully selected mortgages on properly appraised properties will always prove attractive.

THIRTY-THREE

Property Management

Management plays a tremendously important part in the development and ownership of all types of real estate, whether such management be exercised directly by owners or through professional managers, whose number and efficiency increase yearly. Management is the technique through which income is extracted from real property, and the quantity and quality of the income is usually measured by the character of management applied.

Until a few years ago expert management was to be found only in connection with larger properties, such as office buildings, large warehouse enterprises, apartments conducted on an extensive scale, and hotels. It was entirely efficient as far as it went. Little was known about the subject generally and the experience a manager obtained was through solving the intimate problems with which he came in contact.

Professional managers

There then came into existence, under the auspices of the National Association of Real Estate Boards an organization known as the Institute of Real Estate Management, its membership composed of hundreds of professional managers from every city in the land. By frequent conferences and through study of the complex problems involved, this institute has established the management of real estate on a higher and more practical plane, to the very definite advantage of owners everywhere. The institute, after qualifying courses, bestows upon its members the title of C.P.M., Certified Property Manager, and this title is sufficient to distinguish one who is permitted to use it as being well qualified to handle property management problems of all kinds.

Not all properties require special or expert management. The average owner of a small apartment or store building is probably as well qualified as anyone to look after it. Quite frequently an apartment of some size may be handled by a resident manager in the person of a man or a woman who is furnished an apartment rent free and a monthly salary. Such a manager resides on the property most of the time, relieved when necessary, if the enterprise can afford it, by an assistant. Day and night clerks and help of different kinds come under the personal direction of such a manager who reports regularly to the owner the manner in which the property is being operated.

When an investor goes into real estate in a big way, when he owns a property some distance from his headquarters, or when he does not care to bother with the worrisome details of management he usually employs a C.P.M. to look after his interests, the compensation being either on a stated monthly salary basis or a commission.

Management, being a highly specialized field, requires a great deal of study together with experience, before one becomes qualified to pass muster as a capable candidate for the title of C.P.M. The wise investor who owns a property which requires expert management will do well to select a capable person and place him in full charge. Such a manager will at the very outset prepare a detailed program for each property assumed. A study will be proceeded with and an analysis of the neighborhood and site will be made covering such problems as:[1]

1. Market analysis and interpretation
2. Analysis of the financial structure of the property.
3. Rent schedules.
4. Budgeting.
5. Remodelling and rehabilitation.
6. Calendar of repairs and replacements.

---

[1] Suggested in an address by Harry Grant Atkinson, former director of the Institute of Real Estate Management.

7. Calendar of building maintenance.
8. Calendar of maintenance of grounds.
9. Calendar of purchases and specifications.
10. Plans for building a stable tenancy.
11. Personnel.
12. Collections.
13. Periodic reappraisements.
14. Many other things related to the preservation of the investment, net return and features which appeal to tenants.

It seems quite apparent that the coming years will see a tremendous increase in the rehabilitation of old property and in the complete remodelling of many building enterprises. Structures that have arrived at an age of twenty-five, thirty, or thirty-five years will be found to have become obsolete in many respects, although favorably situated as to location. Much of the physical value of such property remains, but it fails to earn adequate rentals because it requires expert attention. It is in this field that experienced management now available will function in the coming years.

Management contracts may be obtained from many sources, among which may be noted the following: Individual owners; savings banks; commercial banks and trust companies; building and loan associations; insurance companies; trustees and attorneys; estates; chain store concerns; receivers; the many local and non-resident owners who are not in a position to look after their properties. A good time to sign up management contracts is during periods of recession when properties are being foreclosed and new ideas must be injected both as to their rehabilitation and management.

To the owner of property who desires to do his own managing there are technical services available which will prove useful, including the ones quoted in the foregoing paragraph. There are also books on the subject which give detailed forms of many kinds which are useful in connection with the handling of managerial problems.

If the position of property manager seems to be an easy one, consider an analysis which has been made under the auspices of the Institute of Real Estate Management, as follows:

The Functions and Duties of the Property Manager

I. Administrative Policies
   A. Owner's primary objectives
      1. Preservation of capital
      2. Greatest net return

    3. Enhancement of value

    4. Prestige of ownership

  B. Tenant's primary objectives

    1. Safety and security

    2. Privacy and peace

    3. Comfort, convenience

    4. Standard of living

II. Executive Control

  A. Developing income

    1. Preparations for renting

      a. Neighborhood analysis

        (1) Population factors (2) Status and trends in land uses (3) Costs

      b. Property analysis

        (1) Inventory of improvements (2) Analysis of physical condition (3) Costs

      c. Highest and best use

        (1) Location factors (2) Character of demand (3) Functional conformity (4) Costs

      d. Market analysis

        (1) Supply and demand factors (a) Present (b) Potential (2) Unit supply comparison (3) How the property fits the market (4) Type and character of tenancy (5) Costs

      e. Ownership analysis

        (1) Income requirements (2) Cash status (3) Alternate possibilities (a) Maintenance as is (b) Rehabilitation (c) Modernization

      f. The rent schedule and budget

        (1) Schedule under perfect conditions (2) Best schedule attainable (3) Preliminary budget (4) Costs

    2. Sales

      a. Contracting prospects

        (1) Number and location of prospects (2) How to reach the prospects (a) Advertising (b) personal canvas (c) Inquiries at office and building (d) Costs

      b. Qualifying prospects

        (1) Social conformity (2) Economic status (3) Credit standing (4) Costs

    3. Maintaining income

      Preserving the utility and desirability of the physical property

      a. Control of depreciation

        (1) Deterioration (a) Curable (b) Incurable (2) Func-

tional obsolescence (a) Curable (b) Incurable (3) Economic obsolescence (4) Capital additions (5) Costs
  b. Maintenance
     (1) Grounds (2) Building exterior (3) Building interior (4) Equipment (5) Furnishings (6) Costs
  B. Services to tenants
    a. Utilities
       (1) Heat (2) Water (3) Light and power (4) Telephone (5) Gas (6) Costs
    b. Furnishings
       (1) Selection (2) Repairs (3) Replacements (4) Costs
    c. Building personnel
       (1) Janitors (2) Engineers (3) Doormen (4) Maids (5) Costs
    d. Extra services
    e. Resales
  4. Services to the owner
    a. Management agreement
    b. Fixed charges (a) Insurance (b) Fees (c) Taxes
    c. Collections
    d. Records
    e. Reports (a) Physical condition (b) Financial
    f. Consultation

In new enterprises it is often necessary to establish a schedule of rentals, and an owner is frequently at a loss when he comes to do this. The following formula is suggested:

1. Total all operating and fixed charges on the property;
2. Divide the amount by one of the following:
   (a) The number of square feet of rentable area (which will give the delivery cost per square foot) ; or, (b) The number of apartments if the apartments are all of the same size (which will give the delivery cost per apartment).

In estimating this cost, take into consideration the fact that normally space is not 100 per cent occupied and that therefore the cost is somewhat higher per square foot, room or apartment than if there is complete occupancy. This is illustrated with some very simple figures. Suppose there are 10 apartments of equal size. Operating and fixed charges amount to $5,400 per year. On the basis of a 100 per cent occupancy the delivery cost is $540 per apartment. However, normally only 9 apartments are rented. So, divide the charges not by ten, which is the total number of apartments available, but by 9, which is the number of apartments normally occupied. On this basis the delivery costs appear as $600 per apartment.

Now carry the example one step further and assume that the apartments are of different values. Set up on a rent schedule basis, the apartments appear as follows:

> 3 apts. at 120 per cent of base rate
> 4 apts. at 100 per cent of base rate
> 3 apts. at 80 per cent of base rate

The average delivery cost per apartment is $600. Therefore, 3 apartments will have a delivery cost of 120 per cent of this amount or $720 each. Four apartments at 100 per cent of the base rate can be delivered at $600 each. The remaining 3, which rent at 80 per cent of the base rate, will deliver at $480 apiece.

The problem of how much to spend for advertising often appears. In many buildings, such as apartments, a neat sign displayed will bring available tenants in sufficient numbers when neighborhood vacancies are few. When there are many local vacancies an owner must resort to advertising in the local papers, which seem to be one of the best mediums for obtaining tenants. Some managers recommend that from two to five per cent of the rental value of the space advertised be allowed for such a purpose or that from $25 to $50 be allocated to each vacant unit. This seems a large amount to spend for such a purpose and can probably be adjusted on a lower level. It must be remembered that vacant units soon drain the profits away from any rental enterprise. Where office buildings are concerned rental managers sometimes allocate for advertising a sum equal to from five to ten cents per square foot of the area advertised.

With tax and insurance costs mounting, a close scrutiny must be kept of these items. Insurance should be scrutinized from year to year and values adjusted to where they belong. Improvements in types of coverage are coming into existence and sometimes a shifting of insurance policies will save an owner money.

An owner, in selecting a manager to care for his property, may engage one of experience or he may train one for his own particular enterprise. If experienced, the candidate should have a reasonable amount of executive ability, be familiar with rental and real estate conditions, possess a reasonable knowledge of tax, insurance and mortgage matters, have organizing ability, possess diplomacy, exhibit salesmanship, and be able to master the multitude of details which will come to his attention. If the prospect is inexperienced he should be required to study all the services and books available on the subject and fit himself through experience as well as theory to master the problems involved. He must necessarily have a good reputation and have followed a calling which will be helpful in fitting him for his new work.

Preparatory to placing a new building on the market for occupancy as well as in considering the purchase of a structure, it might be well to conduct a survey to ascertain the condition of vacancies in the neighborhood and what rents are available. This latter should also have been done before the building was ever erected. A survey of buildings in the neighborhood and city should be made to establish the current rate of vacancies and what rentals are being obtained by managers in comparable properties. If special terms or concessions are being made by other owners these should be revealed at the outset as they may definitely affect the rentability of space. The question of what other building managers are doing in the making of allowances for alterations and repairs should also be closely investigated.

A capable manager will always get along pleasantly with his tenants. An owner may even live in his own apartment house or hotel if he is fair-minded and is willing to meet his tenants half way. A manager or an owner must be absolutely fair and deal with complaints in just the same way that he would wish his own to be treated. Courteous attention must always be paid to complaints, which should be promptly taken care of if of a legitimate character.

Tenants should not be encouraged to rent more or too expensive space than they need or can pay for. A little later that tenant will get into debt and trouble will ensue. Great care should be taken in selecting tenants and in most cases written applications for space should be required, following which an intensive investigation of the tenant's past record should be made before approval is given to his entering a building.

Standards of conduct

It will be found that in connection with most of the larger buildings, managers or companies which specialize in such work will be employed to look after them. For the most part these are entirely responsible firms, many of whom belong to their national management organization. For the purpose of standardizing conditions under which such managers operate, the Institute of Real Estate Management of the National Association of Real Estate Boards has established the following mandatory standards of professional conduct for their members, which should apply to all managers in this field.

These mandatory standards follow:

1. The client's funds shall be segregated from monies belonging to the management firm and shall be kept in a separate bank or bank account under some special designation as "Owner's Trust Fund" so that it is apparent that the monies in this fund do not belong to the agent.

2. The segregated account or accounts of clients shall, at all times, contain 100 per cent of all funds belonging to the client or clients.

3. The client's funds shall not be handled nor accounted for by an officer or employee who is not bonded.

4. Unless the client instructs otherwise, in writing, the agent shall, within the first ten days of each month send him a check covering in full the balance in his account on the last day of the preceding month, together with a complete itemized statement of receipts and disbursements.

5. The managing agent shall have a specific understanding with each client as to fees and commissions for managing, renting, and other services, and these charges shall be shown clearly on the client's monthly statements as items paid to the agent.

6. The agent shall accept no commissions, rebates, discounts, nor other benefits from the management of a client's property other than those specifically agreed upon.

7. When the agent deducts cash discounts from bills or purchases, his statement to the owner concerned shall show only the disbursement of the net amount actually paid.

8. The agent shall not use advertising which is inaccurate in any material particular or which misrepresents the agent's services, the client's property, or is otherwise misleading.

In addition to the following mandatory standards the association furthermore recommends adherence to the following policies under which managers operate:

1. Before making any lease, written or verbal, a detailed application from the prospective tenant should be required and written references secured.

2. A management agent should purchase materials and supplies, contract for labor and material, and assume other obligations on behalf of a client in the client's name and not in his own name.

3. All bills for disbursements of owner's funds should be approved by an officer or principal of the management agency.

4. Whether the relationship of the manager to the client is that of manager or contractor, the manager should be protected by Workmen's Compensation, Public Liability, and/or other insurance at the cost of the client.

5. If a client requires a Fidelity Bond, the cost thereof should be borne by the client.

6. Unless otherwise agreed, the client should pay for all of the advertising of his property.

7. Services rendered by management agencies in connection with tax objections and reductions should be compensated for in addition to the regular management fee.

8. The manager should distinguish between business and legal advice and should not assume the responsibility of attempting to give the client legal advice.

9. No member should advertise premises for rent with concessions or free rent.

10. No management agent should induce, or attempt to induce, the breach of an existing oral or written contract between a competitor and his client.

THIRTY-FOUR

What an Investor Should Know About Various Kinds of Insurance

Insurance, considered by some a necessary evil, is in reality a blessing in disguise.

No investor should attempt to own improved real estate without having buildings properly insured. As a matter of fact, most buildings that have any value are so covered, some not only by fire insurance, but often by other forms as well. The insurance business is now conducted on a high grade basis by unusually capable men, who seek to give real service to their clients. An insurance broker will cover your improvements with fire insurance, if you telephone, write or call and see him, and give him a proper description of the property. He maintains carefully prepared maps of the entire city or town in which you live, and can refer to the type, material and size of every building in the entire community.

Insurance is a voluntary tax, but it is an obligation well worthwhile. Fires and similar catastrophes are likely to occur without warning, and unless proper protection is carried, a partial or total loss may result, which may be of an embarrassing and wasteful character.

277

Fire insurance

There are a number of different kinds of insurance, but the ones applying most particularly to real property are fire, tornado, liability for accidents about a building, explosions and riot, whether from labor or other troubles, breakage of plate and other kinds of glass, damage caused by boiler explosions, rental and leasehold value insurance. The principal risk insured against, of course, is that of fire, damage to the extent of many millions being done each year throughout the country.

Some investors do not comprehend just what is meant by "co-insurance." This permits a property owner to determine the amount of protection he desires to carry. The nearer the amount of insurance taken approaches the actual reproduction value of the premises, the less the rate paid by the insured.

Insurance rates vary slightly from state to state, but we may logically quote some figures deemed to be the general average. Let us suppose that you own a $1,000,000 high-grade fireproof building. If you insured such a structure for $1,000,000, it would cost you at the rate of approximately 40 cents per $100 per year. If you insured it for 80 per cent of its value, the cost would be 45 cents per $100. If insured for 50 per cent of its value, the cost would be 60 cents per $100. Outlying property rates are naturally higher as are those of other classes than high-grade fireproof structures.

Failure to pay insurance premiums results usually in the cancellation of policies. If you are known to the agent as a good credit risk, he may carry you at his own expense for a period of thirty days. Substantial losses sometimes are suffered through failure to maintain fire insurance policies in force.

Extreme care should be taken in connection with the buying and selling of improved property to see that policies are promptly and properly assigned or renewed immediately after a new deed is filed for record, for this announces to the world the beginning of a new ownership. Contrary to the usual conception, insurance does not necessarily protect actual property, but actually covers the insured against loss. If a fire follows shortly after a property changes hands, and the insurance company has not been notified of the fact, the insurance really is held by the former owner, who cannot sustain a loss, having disposed of the property. The new owner cannot collect as the insurance company has not agreed to accept him as a risk. Difficulty of this kind usually occurs in connection with the sale of residential property, as business property is usually transferred through competent hands, and the transfer of the insurance is taken care of. More complete reference is made to this particular problem in Chapter 27 entitled "Escrowing Real Estate Deals."

Some owners of property do not understand why in giving a mortgage in return for money loaned them on real estate they are required to turn over all insurance policies to the lender of the money. This has become a universal custom and is quite fair as the holder of a mortgage has a first lien on the property, and if a fire loss ensues, his interests may be materially reduced if he is unable to collect the insurance paid. The careful property owner usually protects himself by stipulating in the fire insurance policy that payments for fire losses shall be made jointly to himself and the mortgage or lender. Neither the owner nor the person loaning money in this way can collect any funds paid for a fire loss without the interests of each being properly protected.

The most expensive and dangerous mistakes in connection with fire insurance are made in connection with the following matters:

1. Descriptions of property which are improperly given sometimes result in voiding a policy. It is the owner's duty to furnish a correct description, and the company's privilege to check it.

2. Owners or lessees sometimes fail to state definitely the particular interest they have in a property. A fee simple ownership is best, but there are also life estates, long-term leases under which an occupant holds possession, land contracts which give a tenant a certain interest in a property, and sometimes even a person owning such an interest as a mortgage insures the property for his own protection. An insurance company is entitled to all the facts, and these should be given correctly, carefully, and honestly.

3. The property should be used for the purpose stated in the policy. Usually the purpose is well defined, but if a building is devoted to stores on the ground floor, it is usually stated that it is being used for mercantile purposes. If changed in character of use, the insurance company should be promptly notified.

4. If you take out a co-insurance policy, stipulating 80 per cent as the interest involved, you should keep it at that percentage. If the value of the property increases, you should increase your insurance as the fluctuation occurs. For instance, if your building is worth $50,000, and you insure it for 80 per cent of its value, you would be entitled to a claim of $40,000, if it were entirely destroyed. If, however, it has doubled in value, and is worth $100,000, and a fire occurred before you had increased your insurance, you would receive only one-half of the loss. Let it be assumed that there is a loss of $10,000. Under the former set of

circumstances you would collect your loss in full as you have complied with the 80 per cent co-insurance requirement. However, under the second set of circumstances where the building value has increased and the amount of insurance remains at $40,000, you would collect only $5,000 because you have violated the co-insurance agreement of your policy.

5. You may be taking quite a risk when you change tenants in rental properties without notifying the fire insurance company, because your policy may become invalid upon such failure. The reason is that the risk changes with change in tenants as does the costs of premiums. Suppose you had a building leased to a photo shop. The rate would be $1.39 per $100. If these tenants moved out, and you replaced them with a furniture upholstery shop the rate would rise to $2.29 per $100, and your policy would become invalid unless you notified the company and increased your payment of premiums.

Liability insurance

Many property owners carry liability insurance to protect them against real or fanciful claims for damages in connection with accidents which occur in and around business properties, theaters, markets, parks, hotels, and apartment houses. The cost of liability insurance is not high, and is well worthwhile There are many unavoidable accidents that occur for which a property owner is liable under the law. Having the property at stake, the landlord is a ready mark for scheming lawyers who take personal injury cases on a percentage basis. Even if a claim is not awarded against the owner, the cost of defending such a suit is expensive and annoying. When a claim is made where a liability policy exists, the company issuing the policy sets its own lawyers to work, defends the property owner in court, and pays the loss up to the amount stipulated in the policy covering the property.

Among the kinds of claims covered by liability insurance are those where people fall off back porches of apartment houses, are hurt by swinging doors, injured by breaking or spraining a limb in a defective sidewalk or coal holes, being struck by falling signs or displaced coping from buildings, and a variety of other accidents. Even owners of vacant lots which are not fenced in sometimes carry such insurance, for if a person is hurt by a falling sign board or injured while crossing the lot, a claim for damages may be filed and expense caused whether or not the claim is confirmed by the court.

Liability insurance also applies to elevators. The average yearly cost per elevator of the push-button type is about $70.00 which carries with it a careful inspection service maintained by the insurance companies to ascertain that elevators are safe and in proper working order.

Most insurance policies are now being written with "extended coverage," which includes in addition to fire such things as tornado, damage from falling aircraft, and sundry other items. Most lien holders require this "extended coverage" on the policies protecting the properties on which they have advanced loans. The exact inclusions under "extended coverage" varies from one part of the country to the other dependent upon the nature of the disaster threats. In the southern and midwestern states over 95 per cent of the policies written include tornado coverage, for instance.

Rent insurance

It is not generally known that rent insurance is becoming quite common in some of the larger cities throughout the country. Many investors depend for their incomes upon the receipt of certain rentals. When these are suddenly cut off through fire, tornado, or other disaster, they are without income, which ceases wholly or partially until the property is restored to its earning capacity, which may be months later. It is now possible to secure insurance, so that if rentals cease or decline, the insurance company assumes the load, and proceeds to pay you your full rentals until the property is again in position to produce revenue to its normal capacity.

Rent insurance is usually made for a term of one year, as it is assumed that any ordinary damage can be repaired in that time. The cost is not prohibitive to those who insist on full and complete protection. Provided the rate on property damage by fire is about $1 per $100, the rent insurance rate would be 20 cents per $100. Frequently, policies are issued for less than a year, the assumption being that any property loss can be repaired in less than that time.

There are now several large companies which insure rental returns. There are two general types of policies, one called Rent Insurance and the other Rental Value Insurance. *Rent* is defined as the amount of money paid by a tenant to an owner for the use of certain premises. *Rental value* is the term used when an owner occupies a building, and it represents the sum for which he could rent it, or the amount he would have to pay for a building of similar location and advantages. Rent Insurance protects the owner from loss by failure of a tenant to pay rent. Rental Value Insurance compensates an owner when a building which he occupies becomes untenantable, through fire or a similar cause.

Companies in this field now write two types of policies for Rent and Rental Value Insurance as follows:

1. To cover the entire annual rental income. This gives the most complete protection to the owner, and is particularly recommended in severe climates, where cold delays construction work; or where the size of the building, or the materials or workmanship employed therein would require an unusually long time to replace if destroyed.

2. To cover rental income for only the actual period estimated by the owner to restore the building. This is adapted to milder climates, where weather conditions seldom delay building operations.

These two forms are divided into five types for convenience of making contracts, as follows:

1. The company is liable for rent, whether the building is rented or vacant at the time a fire occurs and is based on the rent for the time it takes to rebuild or restore the building to a tenantable condition.

2. The company is liable for the rent of only the occupied portions of the building, and is based upon the rent for the time it takes to rebuild or restore the building to a tenantable condition.

3. The company is liable for the rent whether the building is rented or vacant, and is based upon the full annual rental value.

4. The company is liable for the rent of only the occupied portions of the building, and is based upon the full annual rent of such portions.

5. Rental for season risk. The company's liability is limited to the actual loss of rent or rental value sustained for a certain definite period in the year. This form is particularly applicable for summer or winter cottages.

Leasehold insurance

Did you ever hear of leasehold insurance? Various companies have entered the field, guaranteeing to insure holders of leases against loss due to the failure of the leased property to pay them a return, or due to their inability to enjoy the use of the property themselves in connection with their own businesses.

Ninety-nine year leases usually contain a provision that a lease cannot be voided because of a fire, even if the improvements are completely destroyed. The lessee must wait until the insurance money is paid and the property is rebuilt or rehabilitated. Insurance companies will now agree to stand ready to insure lessees against loss on leases of ten, fifteen or twenty years, and sometimes for longer periods.

A lessee on a twenty-year lease, for instance, has the option of subletting the premises he holds under lease at a higher rental than he pays, and pocketing the profits. If the property is made untenantable through fire, cyclone, or other disaster, the rental ceases, but the property owner, in his lease, has probably stipulated that the lessee is not released if the premises can be rebuilt within a specified time. If the lessee does not sublet, he may occupy the leased premises for his own use. Perhaps he has a very advantageous lease at a low rental, and it will be a real hardship to be dispossessed of the use of the property during rebuilding operations. In either case, insurance can now be secured to cover the loss. The former is called Leasehold Profit Insurance, and the latter is termed Leasehold Value Insurance.

Insurance experts consider that as far as they are concerned, the best form of leasehold insurance is that in which the conditions of the lease call for a total destruction of a building before the lease can be voided, and the least desirable form is the lease which permits the owner the option of canceling the lease in case of only moderate damage. They claim that if the rental is low, due to the generosity of a landlord, through substantial improvements which have come to a neighborhood, or because of good times, and if only slight damage is done to the property, the landlord will be eager to cancel the lease, and re-rent the premises at a higher figure. If the lease is canceled, and is insured, the lessee collects, and the insurance company is subject to a loss. A lease considered profitable to a lessee is regarded as a good risk, one less profitable may be a fair risk, while a lease which has no elements of profit to a lessee is not considered insurable.

Under ninety-nine year leases, insurance policies are usually deposited with a bank or similar trustee with full power to disburse under the definitely stipulated provisions of the lease, even if the lessor, or land owner, is absent in another country. Insurance funds due on losses are paid out on an architect's estimates as a new building proceeds, or a damaged one is repaired and made habitable.

Demolition insurance

Another type of insurance coverage is what is known as "demolition" insurance. In many cities there are ordinances that restrict and control the manner in which buildings may be erected and maintained. Should a fire occur and an attempt be made to reconstruct a building to its former state it is sometimes found that city ordinances prohibit such action, and the owner is compelled to expend considerable money on the structure to repair it in a manner acceptable to the authorities. Demolition insurance is intended to protect an owner in this respect, and an owner should know if a structure he controls may be subject to such restrictions should a loss occur and he be prevented from restoring the premises to their former condition.

Homeowner's insurance

One of the latest innovations in the field of insurance is the "home-owner's policy." This policy is an extreme form of extended coverage which includes practically every conceivable risk the homeowner may face including especially liability insurance in case a visitor should be injured while on the premises. It also includes theft of personal valuables, glass breakage, etc. Most of these policies are written with $100 deductible clauses, which means the policy holder must pay the first $100 damages, and the insurance company pays the balance within the face value of the policy. This insurance is naturally more expensive costing about $1.72 per hundred on a brick veneer home, for example.

Due to the property values involved, every investor should give care ful attention to insurance matters and see that policies are kept properly in force and that premiums are paid regularly.

THIRTY-FIVE

How the Real Estate Broker
Can Save You Money

A real estate broker is one who engages himself, for a commission consideration, to represent sellers and buyers in the transfer from the former to the latter of property in which the broker has no financial interest.

If it were not for the trained brokers of this country most of the real estate deals that take place would never come into being.

Services performed

Through knowledge of property values, experience in negotiating transactions of all kinds, and a readiness to act as fair-minded agents between buyers and sellers, brokers actually create most of the real estate business that transpires from day to day.

Buyers would have a hopeless task searching about for properties which meet their requirements, while owners would be at a loss to find purchasers, and having found them, to present properties in the best light, and then follow through with the complicated problems which surround almost every real estate transaction.

The broker is the investor's best friend when dealing in real estate, just as the doctor's ministrations are appreciated when one is ill. Instead of ignoring brokers when desiring to buy or sell real estate, it is the wisest plan to develop the friendship of one in whom you can feel full confidence, and then deal through him whenever possible. If he appreciates his calling, and really senses the duties of a broker, he will save you money in buying a property, and secure a better price when selling one.

Furthermore, when you are dealing through a Realtor—a broker who is an active member of the National Association of Real Estate Boards—he is required to observe the high ethical standards set forth in the Association's Code of Ethics. The Code is shown in its entirety on pages 288 to 291. The first ten articles of the Code pertain to his relations with the public.

A real estate broker, as such, has nothing to sell but service, although he may have many listings and facilities which will be used as the medium for the exercise of complete service.

There are few businesses which are, after all, more complicated than the selling of real estate on a brokerage basis. The wise broker realizes that the more he learns about real estate, the less he actually knows about the great, wide field which he is constantly studying and exploring.

A broker, above all other things, must have infinite patience. He must handle those persons with whom he comes in contact, whether clients or customers, with the greatest diplomacy, tact, and consideration. He must know much about many phases of real estate, and must be ready instantly to furnish solutions to the perplexing problems which are constantly projecting themselves into his business life. If he doesn't know, offhand, every fact necessary, he must have means of finding out.

The broker must be prepared to accept many disappointments. Deals which look rosy may be destroyed over matters that seem trifling and unimportant. Details or complications suddenly project themselves into a situation which results in one or the other party to a transaction becoming disgruntled, dissatisfied or merely uninterested. Sellers frequently are avaricious and greedy for undeserved profits, while buyers are sometimes niggardly and refuse to pay fair prices for property.

Few persons possessing practical common sense attempt to buy or sell stocks or bonds except through a duly accredited stock broker, one who usually is a member of his local stock exchange. Stocks and bonds, however, are usually bought in much smaller units than the consideration represented in the average real estate deal, yet, sometimes a person who always buys his stocks and bonds that way blandly believes that he can go into a complex real estate market, select a property, and buy it without expert advice of any kind. The fact that real estate is inherently safe as an investment is perhaps the only thing that saves many such adventurers from suffering loss.

How much better it is, then, to be guided in real estate activities by a broker who can point out the pitfalls to avoid and smooth the way in negotiations which have a way of getting hopelessly snarled when buyer and seller come together directly.

There is a psychology about operating through a real estate broker that manifests itself at some point in almost every deal. Through intimate knowledge a broker can point out the advantages or demerits of a property, he can keep the contracting parties off the rocks of personal arguments, and by skillful presentation of facts and figures he can bring to fruition many a deal that otherwise would end in an expenditure of useless effort.

There seems to be a popular notion that a real estate broker can be called on for information and advice, without any monetary consideration being given for such service. A lawyer or a doctor, of course, will render a bill for such service. With the broker, however, the idea still prevails that he should be a good fellow, and give everyone the benefit of his experience without any consideration. This, of course, is grossly unfair, and gradually this condition is being changed, and dealing in real estate is being placed on a higher business plane than ever before in the history of this country

It is interesting to know that many real estate brokers when buying or selling on their own account, almost invariably operate through othei brokers whom they engage to represent them. A broker who is constantly in touch with the business knows that to operate through an associate is good business, and that he makes more money in that way. This is not done for the same professional reason that doctors do not treat themselves or their immediate relatives, but because the broker who is buying or selling on his own account realizes that he can deal with a buyer or seller through a third party more advantageously than he can directly.

The average investor knows comparatively little about the fundamentals which underlie the purchase and development of real estate. He ordinarily does not know the time to buy, and knows little or nothing about the mechanics of negotiating or closing a real estate transaction. He learns, perchance, that there is an active market in some section because a friend bought a tract of land there, and sold it at a substantial profit. He often does not realize that the time to buy may have passed,

CODE OF ETHICS

NATIONAL ASSOCIATION OF REAL ESTATE BOARDS

Preamble

UNDER all is the land. Upon its wise utilization and widely allocated ownership depend the survival and growth of free institutions and of our civilization. The Realtor is the instrumentality through which the land resource of the nation reaches its highest use and through which land ownership attains its widest distribution. He is a creator of homes, a builder of cities, a developer of industries and productive farms.

Such functions impose obligations beyond those of ordinary commerce. They impose grave social responsibility and a patriotic duty to which the Realtor should dedicate himself, and for which he should be diligent in preparing himself. The Realtor, therefore, is zealous to maintain and improve the standards of his calling and shares with his fellow-Realtors a common responsibility for its integrity and honor.

In the interpretation of his obligations, he can take no safer guide than that which has been handed down through twenty centuries, embodied in the Golden Rule:

"Whatsoever ye would that men should do to you, do ye even so to them."

Accepting this standard as his own, every Realtor pledges himself to observe its spirit in all his activities and to conduct his business in accordance with the following Code of Ethics:

* Courtesy National Association of Real Estate Boards, Chicago, Ill.

Part I

Relations to the Public

ARTICLE 1.

The Realtor should keep himself informed as to movements affecting real estate in his community, state, and the nation, so that he may be able to contribute to public thinking on matters of taxation, legislation, land use, city planning, and other questions affecting property interests.

ARTICLE 2.

It is the duty of the Realtor to be well informed on current market conditions in order to be in a position to advise his clients as to the fair market price.

ARTICLE 3.

It is the duty of the Realtor to protect the public against fraud, misrepresentation or unethical practices in the real estate field.

He should endeavor to eliminate in his community any practices which could be damaging to the public or to the dignity and integrity of the real estate profession. The Realtor should assist the board or commission charged with regulating the practices of brokers and salesmen in his state.

ARTICLE 4.

The Realtor should ascertain all pertinent facts concerning every property for which he accepts the agency, so that he may fulfill his obligation to avoid error, exaggeration, misrepresentation, or concealment of pertinent facts.

ARTICLE 5.

The Realtor should not be instrumental in introducing into a neighborhood a character of property or use which will clearly be detrimental to property values in that neighborhood.

ARTICLE 6.

The Realtor should not be a party to the naming of a false consideration in any document, unless it be the naming of an obviously nominal consideration.

ARTICLE 7.

The Realtor should not engage in activities that constitute the practice of law and should recommend that title be examined and legal counsel be obtained when the interest of either party requires it.

ARTICLE 8.

The Realtor should keep in a special bank account, separated from his own funds, monies coming into his possession in trust for other persons, such as escrows, trust funds, client's monies and other like items.

ARTICLE 9.

The Realtor in his advertising should be especially careful to present a true picture and should neither advertise without disclosing his name, nor permit his salesmen to use individual names or telephone numbers, unless the salesman's connection with the Realtor is obvious in the advertisement.

ARTICLE 10.

The Realtor, for the protection of all parties with whom he deals, should see that financial obligations and commitments regarding real estate transactions are in writing, expressing the exact agreement of the parties; and that copies of such agreements, at the time they are executed, are placed in the hands of all parties involved.

Part II

Relations to the Client

ARTICLE 11.

In accepting employment as an agent, the Realtor pledges himself to protect and promote the interests of the client. This obligation of absolute fidelity to the client's interest is primary, but it does not relieve the Realtor from the obligation of dealing fairly with all parties to the transaction.

ARTICLE 12.

In justice to those who place their interests in his care, the Realtor should endeavor always to be in-

Part III

Relations to His Fellow-Realtor

ARTICLE 21.

The Realtor should seek no unfair advantage over his fellow-Realtors and should willingly share with them the lessons of his experience and study.

ARTICLE 22.

The Realtor should so conduct his business as to avoid controversies with his fellow-Realtors. In the event of a controversy between Realtors who are members of the same local board, such controversy should be arbitrated in accordance with regulations of their board rather than litigated.

ARTICLE 23.

Controversies between Realtors who are not members of the same local board should be submitted to an arbitration board consisting of one arbitrator chosen by each Realtor from the real estate board to which he belongs or chosen in accordance with the regulations of the respective boards. One other member, or a sufficient number of members to make an odd number, should be selected by the arbitrators thus chosen.

ARTICLE 24.

When the Realtor is charged with unethical practice, he should place all pertinent facts before the proper tribunal of the member board of which he is a member, for investigation and judgment.

ARTICLE 25.

The Realtor should not voluntarily disparage the business practice of a competitor, nor volunteer an opinion of a competitor's transaction. If his opinion is sought it should be rendered with strict professional integrity and courtesy.

formed regarding laws, proposed legislation, governmental orders, and other essential information and public policies which affect those interests.

ARTICLE 13.

Since the Realtor is representing one or another party to a transaction, he should not accept compensation from more than one party without the full knowledge of all parties to the transaction.

ARTICLE 14.

The Realtor should not acquire an interest in or buy for himself, any member of his immediate family, his firm or any member thereof, or any entity in which he has a substantial ownership interest, property listed with him, or his firm, without making the true position known to the listing owner, and in selling property owned by him, or in which he has such interest, the facts should be revealed to the purchaser.

ARTICLE 15.

The exclusive listing of property should be urged and practiced by the Realtor as a means of preventing dissension and misunderstanding and of assuring better service to the owner.

ARTICLE 16.

When acting as agent in the management of property, the Realtor should not accept any commission, rebate or profit on expenditures made for an owner, without the owner's knowledge and consent.

ARTICLE 17.

The Realtor should not undertake to make an appraisal that is outside the field of his experience unless he obtains the assistance of an authority on such types of property, or unless the facts are fully disclosed to the client. In such circumstances the authority so engaged should be so identified and his contribution to the assignment should be clearly set forth.

ARTICLE 18.

When asked to make a formal appraisal of real property, the Realtor should not render an opinion without careful and thorough analysis and interpretation of all factors affecting the value of the property. His counsel constitutes a professional service.

The Realtor should not undertake to make an appraisal or render an opinion of value on any property where he has a present or contemplated interest unless such interest is specifically disclosed in the appraisal report. Under no circumstances should he undertake to make a formal appraisal when his employment or fee is contingent upon the amount of his appraisal.

ARTICLE 19.

The Realtor should not submit or advertise property without authority, and in any offering, the price quoted should not be other than that agreed upon with the owners as the offering price.

ARTICLE 20.

In the event that more than one formal written offer on a specific property is made before the owner has accepted an offer, any other formal written offer presented to the Realtor, whether by a prospective purchaser or another broker, should be transmitted to the owner for his decision.

The agency of a Realtor who holds an exclusive listing should be respected. A Realtor cooperating with a listing broker should not invite the cooperation of a third broker without the consent of the listing broker.

ARTICLE 27.

The Realtor should cooperate with other brokers on property listed by him exclusively whenever it is in the interest of the client, sharing commissions on a previously agreed basis. Negotiations concerning property listed exclusively with one broker should be carried on with the listing broker, not with the owner, except with the consent of the listing broker.

ARTICLE 28.

The Realtor should not solicit the services of an employee or salesman in the organization of a fellow-Realtor without the knowledge of the employer.

ARTICLE 29.

Signs giving notice of property for sale, rent, lease or exchange should not be placed on any property by more than one Realtor, and then only if authorized by the owner, except as the property is listed with and authorization given to more than one Realtor.

ARTICLE 30.

In the best interest of society, of his associates and of his own business, the Realtor should be loyal to the real estate board of his community and active in its work.

CONCLUSION

The term *Realtor* has come to connote competence, fair dealing and high integrity resulting from adherence to a lofty ideal of moral conduct in business relations. No inducement of profit and no instructions from clients ever can justify departure from this ideal, or from the injunctions of this Code.

The Code of Ethics was adopted in 1913. Amended at the Annual Convention in 1924, 1928, 1950, 1951, 1952, 1955, 1956, 1961, and 1962.

but rushes in and purchases recklessly just because others have done so. It is the broker's business to know what is going on in his own particular field. He knows where to look for good investments or speculations, and having once assisted a client in acquiring a likely property he knows when and how to offer it for sale so the largest profit may be realized. He is the doctor and lawyer of real estate, all in one, and if he is worth his salt he can make himself invaluable to any investor whose confidence he holds.

The fact that you are operating through a broker does not mean that you must blindly accept every statement or fact he may bring to your attention. If he is experienced, he can prove his case through his superior knowedge of the field in which he operates. You are at perfect liberty to exercise your own judgment in conjunction with his, and if he does not render the service you seek, you are under no obligation to continue your relations with him. In the maze of technicalities which surround the real estate business, however, you are certain to fare better if you have a capable guide.

There is an interesting psychological change that comes over an owner of a property when a buyer goes to him directly to purchase a property.

"Aha!" chuckles the owner to himself. "This party wants to buy my property. There must be somthing about it that he especially likes. Here he comes running after me, asking me to sell to him. Here is my chance to realize a fat profit," and the owner immediately boosts his price to such a point that the buyer suffers under the handicap of getting the seller down to a normal level before matters may progress. In all probability, if the owner assumes this attitude then the buyer labors patiently for a time, then gets angry or disgusted, and the deal is declared off. If there had been a capable broker in the transaction, he probably would have gotten the parties together on a fair basis, and a sale would have been recorded.

The moment a buyer evinces direct interest in a property, it is a signal to the owner to begin angling for the highest possible price he can obtain, regardless of the value of the parcel involved. Constantly there are instances coming to light which indicate that buyers when dealing directly with owners pay higher prices than those listed in real estate offices in the same community.

A broker, however, approaches the owner who is not able to bluff the broker as to value. An owner, in any fair-minded broker's opinion, is fully entitled to a fair profit but not an exorbitant one. If the owner wishes to sell, the broker is able through his knowledge of prevailing conditions, to ascertain whether the price is fair. If it isn't a fair price, no self-respecting broker will bother further with the listing unless a reasonable price is finally quoted. If it is fair the broker can often obtain for a buyer the best price and terms on which the property can be acquired. Witness the presence in every community of able, conscientious, successful brokers who are performing real service for their clients from day to day.

"Next to religion there is no subject a certain type of man thinks he knows more about than buying and selling real estate," said an old, experienced broker recently. "We brokers come in contact with this class of men constantly. It is amusing, and often pitiful, to see the difficulties such persons get themselves into, whereas by dealing through an authority on real estate, they might save themselves trouble and money."

It is a broker's duty to himself to create a clientele. Either through himself or his salesmen he should be in touch with owners and investors, bringing them together for the purpose of making transfers of real estate. Owners, especially those who are not compelled through circumstances to sell their properties, are often unreasonable as to prices, believing they own the choicest parcels of land, worth more than all others in the neighborhood. An owner must be shown what the market values are in his territory, and the fact plainly pointed out that if a deal can be hoped for, the price he quotes must compare within reason to those being paid for similar properties. Buyers, on the other hand, sometimes have a queer notion that there are many "bargains" in real estate. This is a more or less foolish idea, as cities where real estate is advancing in a way to make it an attractive investment seldom have many properties which can be purchased below market value. There are what brokers term "good buys," which will, with a reasonable amount of time allowed to transpire, show a fine profit. In knowing the tone and temper of the real estate market in various sections, the real estate broker is in his own element, and able to give competent advice.

Relations with the broker

A few things in dealing with brokers which a real estate investor should consider are:

1. A broker is worthy of his hire. He has expert knowledge to place at your disposal which will save or make money in buying or selling.

2. Do not deal with anyone other than an accredited broker, preferably a certified Realtor. You are running a risk if you deal with unqualified or irresponsible persons.

3. Give your broker your full confidence. Do not compel him to work in the dark regarding your intentions. Rely on his good judgment to negotiate a profitable transaction for you. Be frank and honest with him.

4. Do not attempt to play one broker against another. In all probability, you will be the chief sufferer if you follow such a policy.

5. Do not haggle over paying commissions which have been honestly earned. Nothing is so discouraging to a broker who is trying to serve you faithfully. If he is self-respecting, you will lose his services thereafter.

6. Remember that you engage a broker to represent you because he knows more about the business than you do. Make him prove to you that his advice is sound. Don't repudiate it and do something different.

7. Treat your broker, if you have full confidence in him, as an ally, and he will bring to you the choicest offerings he has, often giving you the first opportunity to make substantial profits in your dealings with him. The successful broker thrives on "repeat orders."

8. If you are a new investor in the real estate field, and do not know a broker handling the kind of property you seek, ask your real estate board to recommend a broker with whom you can discuss your problems.

9. If you desire to buy property at some distant point, and need assistance, deal through your local broker, who, through his board affiliations, can establish proper contact by getting in touch with a reputable agent in that field to look up the kind of property you want, and submit locations, prices, and terms. Such intercity relations are carried on constantly between real estate brokers, and confidence is established by following this procedure.

10. Do not accept your banker's or your lawyer's advice on real estate matters in preference to your real estate broker's opinion. He, through training and experience, is more competent to serve effectively.

THIRTY-SIX

Publicity and Advertising

Publicity, which is one way of advertising, is a dominant force in business life. The skillful use of publicity has done much to make money for men engaged in all lines of business, and it can be advantageously used in the buying and selling of real estate.

The selling of real estate by organized companies is always stimulated by the careful and consistent use of publicity. Advertising is only a branch of the wide field of publicity, and consideration will be given first to news stories and the lessons they teach.

Newspaper publicity

Many an investor has made money by the intelligent interpretation of a paragraph in a newspaper. For instance, a little item appears some morning in the news columns to the following effect:

> City Engineer Smith has completed plans and estimates for the widening and extending of Ninth Avenue from a point where it now ends at Center Street, for a distance of two miles out through a district already built up extensively with homes and crossing Sixteenth and Twenty-Fourth Streets, two main

crosstown thoroughfares. The new street will be one hundred feet wide, with ten feet utilized for sidewalks on each side. Action will be taken by city council at its next session to confirm plans to proceed with the work, which probably will begin next spring, and be hurried to completion.

To many readers that little story means nothing, except a little more convenience in getting to a section of the city somewhat inaccessible heretofore. But to some keen real estate investor it means a lot more. He climbs into his car and goes to the city hall, and has a look at the plans for the new highway. He carefully notes where the new street will intersect with Sixteenth and Twenty-Fourth Streets, main thoroughfares, and then he secures the names of persons who own lots which later are to become corners on the new intersections. He goes quietly to the proposed intersections and looks things over, finding a scattering of houses in each district, surrounded by new subdivisions whose promoters are perhaps having a rather hard time selling lots. Gazing placidly on the scene, the investor visualizes exactly what is going to happen several years later, so he rides downtown, and drops into the office of a real estate broker in whom he has confidence.

"I've got a little job for you," he explains to the broker. He shows the broker the newspaper clipping, reviews his notes taken at the city hall, turns over the names of owners of property which will be on corners, and then gets down to business.

"Those corners are going to be ready for business in a couple of years Go buy them. Get them as resonably as you can, and buy them on the *best terms you can secure.*"

The broker proceeds to the territory, interviews the owners, and after some difficulty, perhaps, gets exclusive sales contracts or options as the case may be. A day or two later the broker again calls on the owners, and the properties are bought. Probably those owners never took the trouble to find out anything about where the new street was coming through. Perhaps they did know they were going to be on corners, but rather resented their privacy being interfered with. Even realizing they were becoming possessors of corner property in a neighborhood which was going into business, they probably did not realize the values which would come after improvements were installed, and business began to grow there. It is in this way that some operators in real estate make money They scan the newspapers regularly, and try to analyze every piece of news which may reflect a changing condition in some section of a city.

In large cities announcements that subways are to be built start a quiet investigation on the part of investors to discover where subway stations are to be located. When this is known the corners affected become prizes for which investors will bid.

Watch the news! Interpret it in its relation to real estate expansion. Newspapers are broadcasting valuable information almost every day. If you desire to invest in real estate learn to know what the announcements portend, and then have courage enough to go ahead and get in "on the ground floor."

Investors quite frequently learn of "good buys" from ads inserted by brokers or owners. They make a business of watching the papers closely for these. Announcements of deals sometimes indicate to the wise investor a trend of growth which may later develop into a boom. When several properties in a locality have changed hands, it is wise to ascertain the reason for the activity which is represented by such sales. Unusual activity, followed by numerous sales, is due to definite causes. The newspapers sometimes will be found to be directories as to these causes.

Premature publication of news stories concerning real estate transactions sometimes does great damage to the plans of brokers, investors, and real estate speculators, who are anxious to get control quietly of several pieces of property. Announcement in the newspapers, for instance, that most of the land in a city block has been acquired for the erection of a large department store will start a buying fever in the entire neighborhood, for certain classes of non-advertising concerns like to snuggle down near such large enterprises, and enjoy the reflected trade which heavy advertising nearly always brings. If, before all the property is securely acquired by the brokers or owners of the new store, a news story is printed that the establishment is to be placed there, it will be found practically impossible to buy the remaining holdings at anything like reasonable prices. Many large stores have found it impossible to buy small corners, and in cities throughout the country are to be found examples of adjoining owners holding up the promoters of new improvements by asking unreasonable prices.

It is a good plan, if possible, to gain the acquaintance and confidence of the real estate editors of the daily papers in a city where you are operating. Treat these men fairly and squarely and they will not betray a confidence. Such reporters sometimes carry stories around in their heads for weeks before publishing them, patiently waiting for some detail to be closed which will permit an announcement of profit to everyone.

"Double cross" a reporter covering the real estate field, and you may look for trouble. At some time or other he will learn of some operation you are interested in, and he will almost certainly make some reference to it that will cause you trouble, if the property concerned has not been fully secured before the reference appears in the press.

Favorable publicity in newspapers is most useful at times in working out real estate transactions. This is particularly true of the operations of brokers who are continually buying and selling. They appreciate having their accomplishments presented to the public in as attractive a light as possible.

If you have an announcement to make concerning a deal, write out your own copy in as complete detail as possible, giving every possible fact and figure you can remember. Then call in the real estate editor, and hand it to him, permitting him to ask further questions as he desires. If he learns that you always play square with him, he will give you liberal space, usually using your story in as complete a form as possible.

If a reporter discovers you have a deal under way, do not bluster around and deny it. Explain to him its details, and convince him that premature publication will probably ruin it. With scarcely an exception, he can be relied upon to maintain it in confidence until it is ready for publication. If another reporter from a rival paper does not come to you, do not attempt to convey the news to such a rival, for the reporter is entitled to his "scoop," particularly if he has not, at your request, published the news. There are certain ethics newspapermen observe. If you act fairly with them, they will not violate a confidence or betray you.

Newspaper advertising

In selling a property, the best single advertising medium usually will be one daily newspaper in your community which specializes in real estate advertising. There usually is one paper which predominates in its appeal to readers seeking information about real estate. Buyers who are acquiring investments usually scan this paper regularly for what it has to offer. An advertisement inserted in its columns will usually bring prompt response. In many instances you may be wiser if you place the sale of the property in the hands of a broker. He will earn his commission by securing you a better price and relieve you of many annoying details.

Tell the truth in advertising. The word "bargain" has been worn threadbare in real estate advertisements when no bargains exist. Discount an advertisement in which you see the word appear. If the market is active, there will be no bargains. State the merits of your property clearly, and if possible use an illustration. Pictures in real estate advertisements help to sell property as nothing else will do.

Other media

A great deal of money is wasted in non-productive real estate advertising. The advertiser is being continually pestered to use such media as theater programs, street cars, billboards, school publications, and the like. These media may be useful for certain kinds of advertising, but under normal circumstances they do not sell real estate of an investment character, and money spent in such media is usually thrown away as far as any practical return is concerned.

In selling a specific property direct mail advertising is sometimes effective. By selecting a well-chosen list of several hundred persons who may be interested in such a property, and able to buy it if it appeals, and then sending such a list with personal letters, or attractively designed and properly illustrated circulars, some excellent prospects may be obtained.

Newspapers frequently will carry news stories concerning the plans of corporations or individuals who intend to expand their businesses. This information often is useful in securing a buyer for a particular property which an investor may have for sale, and which he considers well adapted for use. Almost daily "tips" of importance will be gained by a close reading of the news and advertising sections of newspapers.

There will be, doubtless, one daily or weekly publication which will give a list of the real estate transfers which are passing through the recorder's office. A close scrutiny of such transfers, if one has the time to do so, will often reveal interesting development in different parts of a city. This knowledge frequently may be put to good use.

News about building operations, and the volume of permits being issued for new buildings is frequently indicative of active movements in central or suburban real estate, and it is well worthwhile to keep in contact with such operations. From time to time interesting bits of news appear which may be weather vanes of a city's development.

Undesirable publicity

Bad effects of undesirable publicity may be seen at times. An ill-considered reference by some newspaper to a locality as being a "high crime district" will place a curse on the territory which may be hard to erase or overcome for years. Because of such a stigma, property values may be visibly affected within a short time. Newspaper stories about raids on bootleggers, gamblers, narcotic addicts or other undesirable characters may have a similar effect. A riot, murder or some other unpleasant incident, may blacken the name of a street or district to a degree that real estate may be directly affected. On the other hand, favorable publicity about a section may prove helpful in boosting it, so the attention will be given it by investors and others. Neighborhood associations sometimes help their cause by advertising and publicity campaigns.

Publicity of a questionable character given to a person who has been a prominent or successful investor may cause such a person irreparable damage, and almost immediately eliminate him from the market. Businessmen generally will avoid him, banks will refuse loans, public confidence will be disturbed, or entirely lost, and there is little left for such a victim to do but to move to new pastures. Even in the new locality his sin may find him out, unless he operates secretly through brokers.

Publicity is a mighty weapon which may make or break a person towards whom it is directed. Favorable publicity may help an investor make money, and undesirable publicity may interfere greatly with his work. Care should be taken, therefore, not to do anything which may invite unfavorable publicity towards an individual or an operation in which he may be interested.

THIRTY-SEVEN

Helpful Hints About Real
Estate Law

All real estate activity is surrounded
and fortified by laws which have been enacted for the protection of those
who buy and sell. A knowledge of some of the more important legal matters connected with the buying and selling of real estate, while not absolutely necessary, is very useful to the investor, who during the course of
his operations picks up a smattering of law which he tries to amplify from
time to time, as the opportunity presents.[1]

Contracts

Negotiations for the selling or purchasing of real estate are usually
culminated by the preparation and signing of agreements or contracts.
Any contract with reference to the transfer of any interest in land must
be in writing to be legally enforceable. The kind of estate to be transferred
is immaterial.

A contract for the sale of the entire ownership or one for the lease

---

[1] Legal references in this chapter are general and do not necessarily apply to
the state in which the reader lives. Familiarize yourself with the laws in your own
state as differences are to be found in various localities and states.

of a house for a month are alike unenforceable, if such contract is an oral one. There is a prevalent opinion that a part payment of the purchase price or of the rent is sufficient to make the contract good, but such is not the case.

While it is necessary for the contract to sell real estate to be in writing, a principal may authorize his broker to enter into such a contract of sale in his behalf, although such authorization be by word of month only. In this connection, it is well for the real estate broker to remember that when the principal places property in his broker's hands for sale, he does not thereby authorize the broker to enter into a contract binding the principal to make a conveyance. Authority to make such a contract must be specially given, and will not be implied from a mere authority to sell. The principal has a right to refuse to sell to the purchaser presented by the broker to whom he has given no express authority to contract, even though it may well be that the broker has earned his commission by procuring a purchaser ready and willing to perform.

A third reason why the writing is so important is because of a rule of evidence to the effect that the contents of a document may not be contradicted, altered, added to, or varied by oral evidence. It is obvious that there would be little security in written instruments if a party to a writing could at any time show that the actual oral agreement differed from the writing. In the absence of fraud or mistake, therefore, the courts will enforce the rule of evidence mentioned. It is accordingly essential that the agreement or conveyance state exactly what the parties agree to do.

The matter of possession is worthy of consideration. Originally even the fee simple was transferred merely by a delivery of possession. The grantor or seller made what was called livery of seizin, or delivery of possession. He merely went on the land and there delivered to the grantee or buyer a twig or clod as a symbol, and thereby invested grantee or buyer with the ownership. Now that an instrument in writing is required to convey the ownership, great emphasis is still placed upon the matter of possession. For example, the grantee, as a general rule, is charged with notice of the rights of the person in actual possession, to the extent that he could, by reasonable inquiry, have ascertained the nature of such rights. It will not avail the grantee that he has an abstract which indicates a perfect title in his grantor, if there is in possession a person with equities superior to the grantor. The purchaser should always ascertain the rights of the man in possession.

Every state has a so-called Statute of Limitations, and one aspect of this Statute concerns the matter of adverse possessions or "title by prescription." Most states will award this title to the possessor who has held land under use (usually fencing is required) for twenty years.

It is clear that because of this "title of prescription," the buyer needs to become fully aware of the past use to which the land has been put and by whom. It is further clear that a title may be defective because of such adverse possession and the fault would not be revealed by examination of the abstract.

Possession is of great importance in taking an oral agreement out of the statute of frauds. Suppose Smith orally agrees to sell Jones a house for $10,000. Jones may pay down any or all of the purchase price, but Smith may refuse to convey because the contract was not in writing. Suppose, however, Smith permits Jones to take possession under the contract. Then the contract becomes enforceable by either party. It is on this principle that most persons rely in the taking of leases without a writing. Although such a lease is unenforceable until the lessee assumes possession, after the lessee does assume possession, he may enforce his oral contract, which has now been taken out of the statute.

Estates

A real estate investor should know about the estates which may be created in land, especially estates of inheritance. There are two estates of inheritance, fee simple and fee tail. The former estate is of indefinite duration, and if not alienated by deed or will, passes to the heirs of the holder lineally or collaterally. In the fee tail estate, the land only descends lineally. If land is given to John Brown and the heirs of his body, so far as the duration is concerned, John Brown has only a life estate, and at his death the land is bound to go to the lineal descendants of Brown, or to revert to the grantor. The estate in Brown is said to be entailed, and at one time in England such estates remained entailed for generations. In some states an estate may be entailed for only one generation, and in the case suggested the lineal descendants of Brown would take a fee simple. One cannot convey to another a fee simple in such states, and then restrain the alienation thereof, such a stipulation being deemed in operation as contrary to the nature of the estate conveyed.

Real estate titles easily become somewhat complicated. Consider a simple case which arises very frequently. Suppose William Brown purchases a home, and places it in his and his wife Mary's name. Later Brown dies without leaving a will, and surviving him are his wife and a minor child aged ten. Often the wife will go to a lawyer and expect him to arrange the matter so that she can dispose of the property at any time. As a matter of fact, she has a title that cannot be conveyed without litigation until the minor reaches majority. Mary Brown has an undivided one-half in fee simple, and she also has her dower, which is a life interest in one-third of the half interest owned by her husband. The minor owns an undivided one-half, subject to the dower interest. The minor, of course, cannot alienate, and the child's interest can be transferred only on a judicial sale. William Brown would probably have made a will, and devised his one-half to his wife, had he realized just what would be the situation upon his decease.

Building restrictions

The matter of building restrictions is becoming increasingly important, especially in cities. A deed is usually construed most strongly against the grantor or seller, and if, therefore, he wishes to restrict the grantee or buyer, he must make the restriction clear and explicit. If the grantor stipulates that the grantee is to use the property for residential purposes only, the grantor cannot complain if the court refuses to enjoin the erection of a duplex apartment. Naturally the court views the restriction as merely prohibiting the erection of a building to be used for business purposes, and says that the grantor should have restricted the property to a single residence by clear words, if he intended such a restriction.

Building restrictions are enforced in equity because fair dealing requires one who buys with a knowledge of a restriction to live up to the agreement to which he has impliedly assented. If the grantee has no knowledge of the restriction, either actually or by the record, he is not bound thereby. The usual system of recording gives notice of restrictions incorporated in any conveyance. Restrictions not appearing in any instrument may be binding on those who have assented thereto, and have notice thereof, but such restrictions are not binding on subsequent purchasers without notice.

Since building restrictions are enforced because of elements of fairness, the court will not enforce a restriction when it would be inequitable to do so. If one wishes to prevent the violation of a restriction by an injunction, he should act quickly as soon as a structure, in violation of the restriction, is commenced. If the one entitled to take advantage of a restriction delays and gives the impression that he is not expecting to insist on the enforcement of the restrictive covenant, he will usually be defeated in later efforts to obtain an injunction. If a section changes from a residential district to a business one, the court will usually refuse to enforce a covenant not to use certain property for business purposes, since it would be unfair to insist that one having property in what is now a business district shall not put his property to a use for which it is entirely appropriate.

Puzzling questions arise frequently with references to fixtures, articles which formerly were personalty, but which by reason of annexation to the realty have become a part thereof. Courts usually consider the nature of the annexation, and seek to determine the intention with which the annexation was made. What would be revocable if annexed by a tenant is often deemed a part of the realty which might be claimed by a grantee. Usually the tenant may remove any trade or domestic fixtures because by annexing them he does not intend to dedicate them to his landlord. The same articles, if annexed by the owner of the freehold, might be held to pass with the realty to nis grantee. It is well in case of any doubt to expressly stipulate as to shades, screens, lighting fixtures, and similar appurtenances.

Real property

What actually constitutes real estate, as contrasted to what is known as personal property? The following is a partial list of property legally defined as real estate, for taxation puposes, as outlined in the *Illinois Real Estate Appraisal Manual,* by the Illinois Tax Commission:

Land, buildings, structures, and improvements, and "other permanent fixtures"; interstate toll bridges; trees growing on land; mines, quarries, gas and oil wells; rights pertaining to mining, oil, or gas production; leasehold estates; buildings on leased ground; fixtures in a building which cannot be removed without physical injury either to the building or to the fixtures (Cross v. Weare Commission Co., 153 Ill. 499); fixtures in a building which can be removed without substantial injury but which are attached to the building by screws, nails, and so forth, are real estate if owned by the owner of the building (Fifield v. Farmers Nat. Bank, 148 Ill. 163); fixtures in a building that can be removed without substantial injury to the building but which are attached to the building by screws, nails, and so forth, are real estate even if owned by the tenant, if the lease provides that such fixtures shall remain with the building (Fifield v. Farmers Nat. Bank, 148 Ill. 163; Baker v. McClurg, 198 Ill. 28). The following shows the classification of borderline items:

Personal Property	Real Estate
Air conditioning units (portable)[1]	Air conditioning systems[1]
Boilers	Cases and cabinets (built in)
Carpets	Cottages or houses on leased land
Cranes[1]	Craneways and supports[1]
Curtains, other than steel or asbestos[1]	Curtains, steel or asbestos[1]
Draperies	Dams
Engines (steam, gas, etc.)	Doors
Fans (portable or removable)[1]	Elevators (grain)
Filling station equipment	Furnaces
Machinery	Incinerators (built in)
Mains laid in streets	Kilns (brick, etc.)
Motion picture projectors and sound equipment	Lighting fixtures (electric, gas, etc, built in)[1]
Partitions (stock, uninstalled)[1]	Ovens (bakers', built in)
Pipe lines (oil)[1]	Partitions (in place)[1]
Pumps (gas or other)	Pipe organs (built in)
Refrigerators (individual units)[2]	Piping (built in, for plumbing, heating, refrigerating, etc.)[1]
Scales (wagon or other)	Refrigeration (built in)[1]
Screens (motion picture)	Stage equipment (built in)
Seats (theater and auditorium)[2]	Stoves (gas, built in, as in apartment buildings)[1]
Signs (electric or other)[2]	Trees, including growing nursery stock
Stoves[2]	Vaults (bank, safety deposit, etc.)
Tanks, storage (steel or concrete)	Wiring (built in)[1]

[1] See related item or items in other column.
[2] If permanently installed and under the same ownership as the building, this item may be assessed as real estate.

Delivery

There are two kinds of delivery, the ordinary manual or personal delivery, and the delivery in escrow. Title passes upon the delivery, whether the instrument is recorded or not. A redelivery of the instrument to the grantor, or a destruction of the instrument does not revest title in the grantor, even when the parties so intend. In a case in Ohio, a husband delivered to his wife a deed of a certain tract of land, which she agreed to take in lieu of dower in his property. Later the wife redelivered the deed to her husband. At the death of the husband the question arose as to the rights of the wife. It was held that the wife had title to the land covered by the deed, which had once been delivered to her. It was also held that since the conveyance had been made to her during the marriage, she might repudiate her contract and take dower in all her husband's property, instead of the land conveyed to her, if she wished to do so.

Delivery in escrow is a delivery to a third person to be delivered to the grantee upon the performance of certain conditions. A deed cannot be delivered to a grantee in an escrow, and it is not a valid escrow, if a grantor reserves the right to recall the instrument at will. If the condition is performed, usually the title relates back to the time of the first delivery. If, therefore, the grantor should die before performance of the condition, the grantee upon performance would be entitled to a delivery, although death would revoke any ordinary agency. A delivery contrary to instructions passes no title to the grantee, and it is usually held that a grantee who has obtained the instrument without performance of the conditions cannot pass title even to an innocent purchaser.

In some states a deed which is not recorded is deemed fraudulent against an innocent purchaser. An unrecorded deed passes title, however, and one who knows of an unrecorded deed could take no advantage of the fact that the instrument was not filed for record. The rule should be the same in the case of mortgages, since the purpose of the record is to give notice. Except as between the immediate parties, a mortgage takes effect from the time it is filed for record. The first mortgage filed is, therefore, the first lien. One may lose his priority by failure to record his mortgage, even in a case in which the later mortgagee, who recorded his mortgage first, had full knowledge that there was outstanding a prior unrecorded mortgage.

It is contended by many lawyers that the Torrens system of land registration would greatly help to make land a liquid asset. Without some such system, no one is now absolutely insured against loss without title insurance. The Torrens system is not perfect, but its general adoption would be of tremendous advantage when the matter is viewed in the proper perspective. No class, it is contended, would be more directly benefited by the adoption of the Torrens system than real estate brokers and investors.

Finally, if in doubt or in trouble about your real estate affairs, don't try to be your own lawyer! See an attorney *who knows real estate law,* and you will save money. Furthermore, do not accept titles on which there are reasonable questions. Even if you should be told on good authority that the law is on your side, you almost never do well to buy into a law suit.

THIRTY-EIGHT

Real Estate as a Career

Recognition of the business of dealing in real estate as a constructive, profitable, and honorable calling has become an accomplished fact during the past few years.

Up to 1875 a real estate man, such as we know today, was almost unheard of. True, there were "traders" in real estate, who bought a property or two, selling from time to time, filling in the rest of their time "swapping" their holdings as best they could. They were often not regarded as very solid citizens, were looked at somewhat askance, and classed in about the same business category as horse traders. Maintaining a high-grade office for the buying and selling of real estate on a brokerage basis was unheard of, and practically no effort was made to conduct modern high-grade subdivision activities as we know them today. A few acres would be cut into building lots, and sold intermittently as the demand appeared. No regular sales campaigns were attempted, and the business was in no way standardized as it is today.

By the year 1964, 218 colleges and universities were offering courses in real estate, 66 of these were offering bachelors degrees with majors in real estate, and 15 of them were offering graduate study in real estate. In addition, there are hundreds of courses offered by local real estate boards, many in conjunction with YMCA educational departments.

When it is remembered that real estate is the underlying security in connection with all commercial and industrial activities, it does not seem strange that the business of dealing in it has become an important one, and that attempts to standardize the calling and place it on a high ethical basis have been successful.

Official recognition has been given to the business in all 50 states, the District of Columbia, and five provinces of Canada, by the passing of license laws which govern the character of the men and women who may deal in real estate. It will be only a matter of a very few years when every state will take similar steps to single out the proper type of persons who shall be legally in charge of this important occupation.

Qualifications

"Am I qualified to serve?" is the question which naturally presents itself to the aspirant who would take up real estate buying and selling as a business. What are the qualifications of one who may enter this business, and expect to make a success of it? A few of these qualifications may be noted as follows:

1. Natural intelligence, supplemented with an adequate education, which will permit one to understand and master the problems involved in the many branches which constitute the business as a whole.

2. A willingness to work hard by applying oneself to study, and then doing capably the things which naturally present themselves. It needs no great genius to succeed in real estate. *It does call for real work.*

3. Natural honesty and a disposition to be absolutely fair are requisite. The day when the man of crooked tendencies can succeed in real estate has long since passed. The world is altogether too small, with its telephone, telegraph, radio, mail, air, rail, and water transportation, for anyone to last long by trying to succeed by living by his "wits." The life of the real estate transgressor is especially hard, and his career is soon nipped in the bud. Dishonesty does not pay in this field any more so than in other fields. It is promptly rewarded with what it deserves.

4. To be a successful operator or broker one must have more than a

mere working knowledge of business conditions; he must comprehend mathematics; he must know something about legal matters; he must have sales ability; he must be a student of human nature, able to detect the subtle currents of thought which are stirred up incessantly in the buying and selling of real estate.

5. One must especially have an open mind, ready and willing at all times to learn from the experiences of others who have sought and found the solutions to problems which are constantly appearing. The more one finds out about real estate, the more he realizes how little he really knows.

A bricklayer, carpenter, or machinist will spend many years learning a trade. Physicians, dentists, and lawyers spend years in preparatory work, yet many persons believe they can go into the real estate "game" as they call it, and start making big commissions or profits in a few weeks or months. This idea, of course, is nonsense. One must qualify for the business, if one intends to follow it as a calling, working up as ability demonstrates itself and occasions offer advancement.

Incidentally, the real estate business has ceased being a "game." It is an active, serious, scientific, intricate occupation, which brings ample rewards to those who are willing to fit themselves for service. It is attracting a class of men who through education, experience, and an adherence to a high ethical standard are on a par with any other calling in America today.

Real estate attracts from time to time some of the ablest men in the professions of law and engineering, training in each of which is useful in many ways. Bankers naturally gravitate into real estate operating as a side line for the investment of their own private funds. Coming closely in touch with realty activities constantly, they realize the profits which are to be made in operating. Businessmen in almost every walk of life, who have surplus funds at their command, often become attracted by experience in a single deal, and become confirmed operators.

Preparation

Failure to become successful in the real estate business is usually traceable to lack of proper preparation. Anyone who is willing to study diligently the problems which present themselves, following with actual work in the real estate field, plus a willingness to work hard is likely to win. Men of even mediocre ability have won substantial success through a determination to apply themselves and master details.

Real estate as a career not only offers an honorable calling to which some of the best business talent of the country is attracted, but it also offers fine opportunities for the making of money in sums commensurate with the native ability shown in individual operation. Physicians, dentists, lawyers, bankers, and merchants often operate their businesses for the purpose largely of accumulating enough money to enter the real estate operating field for investment purposes. Every city in the country has men of this character, some of whom you know, and in most cases envy.

The real estate business is no longer a haven for the failures and derelicts in other lines. There was a time when any man who was unsuccessful as a merchant, a politician, a teacher, or a minister, entered the real estate business. For a time friends covertly smiled at the effort, and when such a man miserably failed once more, they smiled shyly and exclaimed: "I told you so." Real estate men must be of the caliber that will be successful in any business. It is a sphere in which the opportunities are practically unlimited, providing one proceeds to qualify himself to meet the exacting requirements.

That big business has come to a recognition in recent years that special training is needed in real estate is evidenced by the fact that nearly every important corporation in this country now has a trained expert real estate man in charge of a separate department, where liberal salaries are paid. No step is taken in connection with a company's realty activities unless the advice of this department controls. The larger cities of the country, instead of buying and selling real estate holdings through politicians, as in former days, now maintain property departments. The same may be said of school boards in many cities, which annually expend huge sums for educational projects.

There are over 1500 real estate boards in the United States and Canada. Those operating in the larger cities are sponsoring courses in real estate education, either conducting them under their own auspices or in conjunction with YMCA and other adult educational courses. The men who are responsible for the YMCA's educational work have realized for a number of years that the study of real estate is quite as important as engineering, accounting, and similar branches, which are now a part of the curriculum.

Real estate does offer a career which cannot be equalled when its scope and importance are considered. It needs men of intelligence, vision and integrity and it is attracting such men to its ranks. Never before has the broker been held in such high esteem. With the recruiting of new men to the ranks from the colleges, within the next decade the general mental and moral level of the men in the real estate profession will be on a cultural par with any profession or occupation in the country.

To be successful, then, in accepting the challenge to take up a career in real estate, there are three things to be kept definitely in mind: Qualify yourself for your high calling; apply yourself diligently to your chosen work, and then direct your operations in a way that will receive the commendation of those best able to judge your success!

THIRTY-NINE

Women in Real Estate

In 1964 the Women's Bureau of the Department of Labor reported that the number of women employed as real estate agents and brokers more than doubled from 20,339 to 46,108 during the decade 1950 through 1960. This significant increase gives proof to the statement coined by Edwin L. Stoll, Director of Public Relations of the National Association of Real Estate Boards, that "Women's place it in the home—selling it!"[1]

Opportunities for women

In many cities women have been active in a sales capacity with some of the larger real estate firms. They usually enjoy selling houses, as they are familiar with the problems of home maintenance, and often are able to present properties in an attractive light. In the operation of all large real estate offices women are invaluable in the accounting and stenographic departments, and sometimes ascend into more important branches of the business as their terms of service grow in extent.

---

[1] From an article which appeared in the December, 1952 issue of *Lifetime Living*.

Many women get their start in real estate selling through joining subdivision sales forces where many succeed from the start. When times are prosperous and there is considerable real estate expansion in the form of new subdivisions, special sales crews consisting entirely of women are formed. These deal solely with women prospects. As they have a single type of property to sell and can soon be trained to extol its advantages they often roll up considerable volumes of sales. Later many women who get their start this way join regular sales forces, selling houses and minor investment properties.

Another way in which some women enter the real estate business is through the rental department of some established office. Being a real estate "rental lady" keeps one on the jump, for she must not only handle her prospects—she must get out and line up her listings as well, and follow up her submissions to see whether her prospects have closed a deal when she hasn't been around.

In some cities, at different times, women have succeeded as apartment house builders, some even on quite a large scale. Structures have been erected and disposed of to satisfied buyers, who have recognized the fact that often women seem to sense those things that make an apartment livable and those refinements which make them sell readily.

Women have specialized, in some communities, in building attractive homes, furnishing them tastefully and artistically, and then selling them, at a profit, to newcomers. They engage in only one or two operations a year, and often move into and occupy their newly-created properties until they are sold. They thus realize profits in addition to having a home in which to live.

Women, for some reason or other, have seldom been conspicuously successful in the brokerage of business properties. They do not seem to be as greatly interested in that branch of the business as they are in homes. Men, indeed, may still decline to be told how to invest their funds in income properties by a woman broker. There are, of course, exceptions to this, as there are to all rules.

There are many women who are interested at times in investing their own funds in real estate. Nowadays many women earn good salaries, and are able to build up extensive savings, which they desire to place in real estate investments. They are able to make substantial down payments, and to supply funds regularly to the liquidation of debts they assume. If properly directed, such operations often result in the building up of good-sized estates in the course of a few years.

Women probably are a little less discriminating than men as to the kind of real estate they buy, and the sentimental features of the offering sometimes appeal more strongly than do its actual investment possibilities. There are always some classes of real estate salesmen who are more eager to collect commissions than to serve intelligently and faithfully. It is impossible to furnish any buyer with the judgment which must be exercised in making a purchase of real estate. Women must study the fundamental factors of investments in real property, and decide for themselves what they ought to buy, and whether it may be depended upon to furnish the profits which a salesman may claim for it.

In the case of buying a house or a business property it is safest to first thoroughly investigate the character of the broker or salesman involved. If he is a certified Realtor, the customer will have redress, for if she feels that she has not been fairly treated, she can always appeal to the local real estate board. Probably the number of women who are victimized in real estate is no greater in actual proportion than the number of men, yet it is a fact that a handsome, but persuasive salesman will sometimes get a demure little woman as a customer, and through the force of his personal attractiveness and magnetism persuade her that he is the one person in the world who can make her rich in real estate.

Beware of the philanderer type!

Buy real estate on the basis of reason, not sentiment.

Frequently widows come into possession of substantial funds from life insurance or by inheritence. They have always heard that real estate is a safe and profitable investment, and they often wonder why some eager salesman has not looked them up, and offered them some fine opportunity to make a fortune by investing a few thousand dollars in some real estate proposition. There are a few real estate men who make a practice of following up death announcements in newspapers, notices of wills having been probated, and similar "leads," which bring them to the doors of the recently afflicted widows who have money at their disposal. To such women the best advice is to consult a thoroughly reliable broker before spending a cent. Explain your circumstances, submit the proposition, and ask for advice. It will be given freely and honestly if you have picked out the right broker. If you are uncertain as to whom you should approach, and there is a real estate board, consult the president or secretary of that organization, and you will get honest and competent advice without expense. Probably the proposition which has been submitted is entirely all right. If so advised, you are at liberty to act. If there seems to be some question as to the facts, better pass the golden opportunity by, and deal with someone in whom you can feel full confidence.

Women find opportunities in the cities throughout the country in leasing houses or apartments for terms of years, furnishing them properly, building up a renting clientele, and then selling their leases and furniture at a profit. Carried on as a regular business, this often provides good profits. In California, particularly in Los Angeles, bungalow courts are handled in a similar manner, leases usually being for a term of several years. The individual units are attractively furnished, and are eagerly sought by visiting tourists. Even large hotels are handled by more ambitiously inclined women who have acquired the business experience necessary for the promotion of such ventures.

Rights of dower

Many women do not understand the rights existing under the law of dower. At the moment a married man takes title to a piece of real estate, his wife, in most states, immediately becomes possessed of a one-third interest in the property for the period of her lifetime. Likewise, when a married woman assumes ownership of real estate, the husband, by virtue of the same law of dower, becomes a lifetime owner to the extent of a one-third interest. A woman cannot bequeath a dower interest, as it is simply a life estate, the interest ceasing at the time of her death. Not until her husband dies may she assume actual control of her one-third interest. The life estate created by law covers all of the time the marriage relation is effective, or as the law terms it, coverture. While both husband and wife are living, the wife's interest is termed inchoate dower. Of course, dower interest does not come into actual existence until a husband or wife dies.

Remember these interesting facts in connection with dower:

1. A husband can by no act diminish in any way a wife's interest.
2. A judgment recovered against a husband, followed by a sale by the sheriff of a husband's interests does not affect the wife's dower interest, which remains intact.
3. The laws of the 50 states vary a good deal concerning the matter of community property laws. It is always advisable to require the wife to sign papers transferring title along with her husband, although most states actually require her to do so only when the property involved is a homestead.

4. A mortgage given by a husband cannot cut off a wife's dower interest unless she consents to the release of her rights in the property by joining with him in signing the mortgage.

There has been an agitation in recent years to clarify the dower law by extending a wife's life interest into a one-third direct ownership in property acquired by married couples. *Ascertain the exact dower laws in operation in the state in which you live.*

Advice to women who want to invest

Some pertinent advice to women who seek to make money in real estate:

1. Study the subject of realty investing. Read as many good books on this question as you can obtain.
2. Deal through a reliable broker. He will save you money in your purchases and sales, and direct your course aright.
3. In buying or selling a property insist that the deal be put in escrow with a reliable company. Your rights in the transfer will be zealously guarded by a concern which works merely for a fee, and is not interested in getting a cent of your money beyond that fee.
4. Avoid extraordinary opportunities to "get rich quick" in real estate. If the scheme is so wonderful that it offers remarkable opportunities, there may be something radically wrong with it, and you should know all about it, and secure competent advice concerning it before proceeding.
5. Be satisfied in taking a good profit on a deal. No one ever lost money in taking a reasonable profit, and reinvesting funds in another good proposition.
6. Don't be inveigled by some "friend" to go blindly into a transaction without proper advice from a disinterested party competent to advise you.
7. Don't go into a real estate deal without knowing the extent of the obligations you are agreeing to assume. Too many persons are constantly "land poor" without your joining the throng.
8. "I didn't know what I was signing" is no defense in a court of law. Only place your name on a document when you fully understand its import.
9. Do not buy real estate without actually seeing it, and knowing of what you are becoming the owner.
10. If your dealings with a broker result in your having full confi-

dence in his judgment and good intentions, patronize him exclusively. Don't shop around from office to office, for you may fall into unfriendly hands.

11 If you get into legal difficulties over a real estate transaction, don't depend upon your friends for advice. Consult a lawyer familiar with real estate operations who has been properly recommended to you. He will keep you from getting into further trouble, and will probably extricate you from your difficulties.

12. Do not, under any circumstances, assume ownership of property unless it has a thoroughly good title. You may have grave difficulties in disposing of it at a later date.

Have confidence in yourself that you can make money in real estate. It is a fertile field, and there is as much reason for your success as for that of thousands of others who have built up good incomes, or made substantial profits from deals.

FORTY

How Famous Men Have
Regarded Real Estate
as an Investment

Disinterested opinions on the part of many noted men concerning the subject of real estate should certainly be of interest to investors generally. The viewpoints expressed are, in many cases, from the actual experiences of the men quoted. Brisbane, famous columnist, was enthusiastic in his brief in real estate. He personally made a fortune in buying and holding it. Many of the vast fortunes represented by the men whose names appear on the following pages were founded and maintained on real estate Some, like John Jacob Astor, indicate how they went about the business of making money in real estate. All of them were deeply sincere in their appreciation of its investment merits.

Read what some noted men have said:

Chopin:
Home is the summary of all other institutions.
R. B. Armstrong, economist and author:
Real estate men sell civilization as much as land.
John Jacob Astor:
Buy on the fringe and wait. *Buy land near a growing city!* Buy real estate when other people want to sell. *HOLD WHAT YOU BUY!*

321

Elbert H. Gary:
Land—real estate—is the basis and foundation of wealth and security.

William Stanley Jevons:
Someone will say that he is beyond question rich who owns a great deal of land.

Southey:
Home—there is magic in that word—it is a mystic circle that surrounds comforts and virtues never known beyond its hallowed limits.

Ralph Waldo Emerson:
The first farmer was the first man, and all historic nobility rests on possession and use of land.

Marshall Field:
Buying real estate is not only the best way, the quickest way, and the safest way, *but the only way to become wealthy.*

James Anthony Froude, historian, in his great work on Caesar:
No form of property gives as much consequence to its owners as land. This is true of the past, the present and the future.

Hetty Green:
I advise women to invest in real estate. It is the collateral to be preferred above all others, and the safest means of investing money.

George Washington:
Strongly I am impressed with the beneficial effects which our country would receive if every good citizen of the United States owned his own home!

William E. Harmon, noted realty operator:
Land increases more rapidly in value at the centers and about the circumferences of cities.

John Ruskin:
The substantial wealth of man consists in the earth he cultivates, with its pleasant or serviceable animals and plants and in the rightly produced work of his own hands.

Dr. Samuel Johnson:
To be happy at home is the ultimate result of all ambition, the end to which every enterprise and labor tends and of which every desire prompts the prosecution.

Calvin Coolidge:
The ownership of a home, the feeling of independence that comes with the possession of a bit of the earth are among the most powerful incentives to high civic interest and usefulness.

B. C. Forbes, business analyst:

Our stock of everything useful, which cannot be increased, becomes more and more valuable because there are more and more people to bid for it. The best example is real estate.

Franklin D. Roosevelt:

Real estate cannot be lost or stolen, nor can it be carried away. Purchased with common sense, paid for in full, and managed with reasonable care, it is about the safest investment in the world.

Russell Sage:

Real estate is an imperishable asset, ever increasing in value. It is the most solid security that human ingenuity has devised. It is the basis of all security, and about the only indestructable security.

Theodore Roosevelt:

Every person who invests in well selected real estate in a growing section of a prosperous community adopts the surest and safest method of becoming independent, for real estate is the basis of wealth.

Jesse H. Jones, former federal government financier:

I have always liked real estate—farm land, pasture land, timber land and city property. I have had experience with all of them. I guess I just naturally like "the good earth," the foundation of all our wealth.

Glenn Frank, noted educator:

The ownership of an urban home, or a farm, unharrassed by fear of loss either through economic pressure or political policy, is one of the most stabilizing factors we can have in American civilization.

Grover Cleveland:

No investment on earth is so safe, so sure, so certain to enrich its owner as undeveloped realty. I always advise my friends to place their savings in realty near some growing city. There is no such savings bank anywhere.

Andrew Carnegie:

Ninety per cent of all millionaires become so through owning real estate. More money has been made in real estate than in all industrial investments combined. The wise young man or wage earner invests his money in real estate.

Beaconsfield:

I have always felt that the best security of civilization is the dwelling, and upon properly appointed and becoming dwellings depends more than anything else the improvement of mankind. Such dwellings are the nursery of all domestic virtues.

Francis H. Sisson:

Only as we move out of the more speculative stages of our tremendous industrial expansion and transportation developments will we begin to appreciate the value of real estate and its securities for the safe and profitable employment of money.

Billy Sunday, Evangelist:

The renter who sings "Home Sweet Home" is kidding himself and serenading the landlord. Rent money once handed over is gone forever but the money you put into a house is still yours. It changes its form—it becomes property instead of gold and simply passes from your right pocket to your left.

Warren G. Harding:

Believing that nothing can do more toward the development of the highest attributes of good citizenship than the ownership by every family of its own home, I am always glad to endorse effective efforts to encourage home ownership. Nothing better could happen to the United States than a very notable increase in the ownership of homes.

Dean Jonathan Swift (1667–1745):

> I've often wished that I had a clear
> For life, six hundred pounds a year:
> A handsome house to lodge a friend,
> A river at my garden's end:
> A terraced walk and half a rood
> Of land set out to plant a wood!

Thomas Robinson Ward, banker:

No matter where you live—in city, village or farm—hang on to your real estate. It's a good investment and worth all that was paid. Real estate at today's prices is the best investment of which I know. Good real estate at the right prices—is sure to be a thrifty investment. People who own real estate should make every effort to keep it. It's worth every dollar it cost.

Henry George.

So far as we can see with any certainty, the quality of value has longer and more constantly attached to the ownership of land than to any other valuable thing. Everywhere, in all time, among all peoples, the possession of land is the base of aristocracy, the foundation of great fortunes, the source of power. Those who own the land must be the masters of rest. Land can exist without labor but labor cannot exist without land.

Roger W. Babson:

Real estate is about the last thing to rise in price during a period of general prosperity, and it also is about the last thing to decline during a period of depression. Therefore, real estate is always worthy of consideration as an investment.

A modest, up-to-date home, well-chosen as to locality...offers one of the most attractive hedges against inflation, as a useful store of value, and a real necessity.

Buy productive real estate—sell unproductive holdings. Don't gamble in real estate—buy for use only. Moreover, except for a home or business, pay cash. Avoid unnecessary mortgages. The right kind of real estate will benefit from inflation. Real estate is real, it can't run away. It is the only investment our forefathers had. It is fundamental.

Bruce Barton:

The other day I visited the suburb where I used to live. There was a vacant lot opposite my house which could have been bought then for five thousand dollars. A month ago a man bought it for twenty-eight thousand, and two weeks later sold it for sixty thousand. I take off my hat to him. He saw it was a gold mine. But I looked at it every morning for four years, and it didn't look to me like anything more than a vacant lot.

Henry Ward Beecher:

There is a distinct joy in owning a piece of land unlike that which you have in money, in houses, in books, in pictures, or anything else which men have devised. Personal property brings you into society with men. But land is a part of God's estate in the globe; and when a parcel of ground is deeded to you, and you walk over it, and call it your own, it seems as if you had come into partnership with the original proprietor of the earth.

Edgar Guest:

> To own a home and all that's in it,
> Here is a man's dream for every minute
> To own a home enriched with beauty
> Here is the joy that lightens duty.
> World over, man goes out to labor,
> To own a home and play the neighbor!

Adam Smith, economist:

Land is a fund of a more stable and permanent nature; and the rent of public lands, accordingly, has been the principal source of the public revenue of many a great nation that was much advanced beyond the shepherd state.

The purchase and improvement of uncultivated land is the most profitable employment of the smallest as well as greatest capitals, and the road to all the fortune which can be acquired in that country "America."

Walt Mason, poet philosopher:

I'd rent no place of brick or stone; for an old caboose I can call my own is better far, though it's cheap and small, than a fine hotel or a rented hall. I want to sit on my dinky porch and pull away at a 5-cent torch, mark the growth of the sparrowgrass, or pull the weeds from the garden sass. I want to tinker round at dawn, and nail a board where I see one's gone, or tie a string to the pumpkin vine and know that everything there is mine. . . . To have a home and be out of debt, well that is truly the best scheme yet.

Will Durant (in an editorial entitled "Modern Marriage") :

If I could live my life again I would marry early—before twenty years. . . I would have an individual home, no matter where I had to move to get it. I would sacrifice everything. . . to give my bride a spot all her own. As for happiness, I would look for it not in any lasting physical allurement but in our partnership in helping our home and our children to grow. For a home must grow, too, with the care and love of years until it becomes a part of life—an old friend to whom we willingly return!

Gladstone, quoted by Puelicher:

There are so many elements of respectability that come to him who finds permanent shelter for his loved ones. It is a force for law, since a home owner desires protection by law. He acquires respect for the property of others. He wants good, sound government and desires to become an advocate of law and order. Ownership makes him vigilant. I think it was Gladstone who said: "Property always sleeps with one eye open."—John H. Puelicher, president of the American Bankers' Association.

Abraham Lincoln:

Property is the fruit of labor; property is desirable; it is a positive good in the world. That some should be rich shows that others may become rich, and hence is just encouragement to industry and enterprise.

Let not him who is houseless pull down the house of another, but let him work diligently and build one for himself, thus by example assuring that his own shall be safe from violence when built.

Col. H. Oswald:

An acre of ground can't run away; it can't burn up or down; it can't be stolen and hidden away out of sight; it represents the most solid, substantial and permanent investment possible. Most of the great historic fortunes are based on land. Never did fairy god-mother with limitless power pluck diamonds and gold out of the thin air, bestow on her prime favorite such riches as have followed early investments in real estate in a good, productive country. Investors, with our present rate of increase of population, how long will there remain any good, cheap lands in this country? Our lands are sure to advance in price very rapidly.

The wise man is he who puts every spare dollar into good, cheap, land. Land does not explode; farms are not carried away by panic· trusts cannot get a corner on the earth. And yet it is the source of all wealth.

Senator W. E. Brock:

Statisticians advise us to buy stock, but I advise you to buy real estate. When you buy real estate you can go to bed at night perfectly comfortable, for you know it will be there tomorrow. Investments in stocks and bonds, depending as they do largely on management, may be good today and lost tomorrow A minority stock holder has very little say so as to how his own dollar is used. In buying real estate, however, you are the sole owner and manager. You have a freedom of possession which other investments do not give. No one can freeze you out. No one can run you off. It is yours. I made a real estate deal sixteen years ago against a banker's advice, and sold the property in five years for over $100,000 profit, plus 6 per cent income. If I had put this profit back in stock, I would have lost practically all of it when the crash came.

Herbert Hoover:

The present large proportion of families that own their homes is both the foundation of a sound economic and social system and a guarantee that our society will continue to develop rationally as changing conditions demand. A family that owns its own home takes a pride in it, maintains it better, gets more pleasure out of it, and has a more wholesome, healthful, and happy atmosphere in which to bring up children. The home owner has a constructive aim in life. He works harder outside his home; he spends his leisure more profitably, and he and his family live a finer life and enjoy more of the comforts and cultivating influences of our modern civilization. A husband and wife who own their own home are more apt to save. They have an interest in the advancement of a social system that permits the individual to store up the fruits of his labor. As direct taxpayers they take a more active part in local government. Above all, the love of home is one of the finest instincts and the greatest of inspirations of our people.

Arthur Brisbane:

When a man owns his own home he is somebody! Until he does own his house he is only somebody else's tenant, a useful, cash-producing personage, but a different being from the man that owns his own home. Civilization, as we know it, began when the man owned his own house, lived in it, stayed in one place, developed it, and fought for his right to keep all others out of it. Own your own home, watch it grow in value, get your share of that much discussed "unearned increment," which means the increased value of land caused by rising population. Living away from the center of the city in a house with light on all sides gives a one hundred per cent better chance to your children. It means changing your outlook upon life; it means making you one of those that actually own part of the United States. It means independence. Buy your house, get it paid for as quickly as you can, above all buy what you know you can pay for, and have the satisfaction of seeing what you own grow in value, and the infinitely greater satisfaction of leaving your wife and children, when you must leave them, with a roof over their heads that they actually own.

Benjamin Franklin:

There are croakers in every country; always, boding its ruin. Such a one lived in Philadelphia; a person of note, an elderly man with a wise look and a very grave manner of speaking; his name was Samuel Mickle. This gentleman, a stranger to me, stopped one day at my door and asked me if I was the young man who had lately opened a new printing house. Being answered in the affirmative, he said he was sorry for me, because it was an expensive undertaking, and the expense would be lost; for Philadelphia was a sinking place, the people already half bankrupt or near being so; all appearances to the contrary, such as new buildings and the rise of rents, being to his certain knowledge fallacious, for they were, in fact, among the things that would soon ruin us. And he gave me such a detail of misfortunes now existing, or that were soon to exist, that he left me half melancholy. Had I known this before I engaged in business, probably I never should have done it. This man continued to live in this decaying place, and to disclaim in the same strain, refusing for many years to buy a house there, because all was going to destruction, and at last I had the pleasure of seeing him give five times as much for one as he might have bought it for when he first began croaking.

FORTY-ONE

What the Future Holds in
Store for Real Estate

During the past twenty-five years America has witnessed greater advances in the fields of science, medicine, chemistry, machinery, transportation, education, economics, and the development of real estate than have happened in all previous ages combined.

Impact of modern technology

Men live longer and are healthier, buildings are bigger and better, men whizz along the ground and fly through the air with amazing speed and comfort, and technological advances have bestowed tremendous benefits. Jet air travel at hundreds of miles per hour is the most common means of travel and supersonic travel for the ordinary citizen is only a few years away.

Mankind has seen the coming of oil lamps, gas lights, electric illumination, and mysterious rays of a dozen kinds. The scythe was followed by the reaper and the combination binder, powered with great tractors cutting swaths many feet wide and dumping off sacked grain every few feet. The amazing telephone and telegraph were soon surpassed and outmoded by radio which hurls a message around the entire world in a fraction of second. Television pictures are being flashed around the world via satellites that whirl over thousands of miles in space. Crude lumbering horseless carriages were succeeded by motorcars, to be followed by sleek sports cars traveling 100 miles an hour. Wagons were succeeded by trailer trucks. Air freight has come into wide prominence with deliveries being made coast to coast in a matter of hours. Orchids can be picked in Hawaii in the morning to be delivered by noon in the major continental cities. Nickelodeon shows with painfully fluttering pictures were transformed, in only a few years, into picture palaces. Today, the marvel of color TV is in many American homes.

In the field of building enterprise the changes which have taken place are no less startling and unique. With the coming of the elevator mankind was able to steadily raise the height of buildings from four stories, which were as high as the average man would climb, up to eighty-five stories, 1,045 feet, the height of the towering Empire State Building in New York.

With the advent of facilities for smelting steel, and creating structural units of it, builders became able to fashion structures of any size and magnitude. Smooth polished plate glass took the place of wavy distorted small panes which for so long let in the sunlight. Crude adobe bricks were replaced by beautiful brick from huge presses, fashioned in many patterns, with devious shades of colors and textures. Common woods scarcely seasoned, were replaced by a host of beautiful woods from worldwide forests, richly textured and splendid to see.

It is only three generations since the first tin American bathtub made its appearance and caused heated discussions as to both its utilitarian and sanitary values. Tin, zinc, steel, porcelain and plastics came in quick succession to make bathrooms and kitchens veritable palaces compared to those in use only a generation ago!

About 1879 the wizard Edison invented his first incandescent lamp, which was to replace oil lamps which had but a little while before displaced the tallow candle. Tremendous progress has since been made in the field of illumination, to the benefit of everyone.

Look back over the past twenty-five years and realize that material progress in that short time outstrips all previous records in every field. The pioneers lived their lives in the raw, sheltered in rude log cabins, enjoying no comforts of life as now known. Today the poorest laborer in

America enjoys vastly more physical comforts of existence than did European monarchs of a century ago.

These contributions to progress all had their definite effects on real estate, its use and value. They have been indelibly associated with the progress of building and land utilization in all of its manifold phases. Refinements in all types of occupancy have been made possible. It has become possible to build great apartments and hotels capable of housing hundreds, even thousands, of persons, permitting them to live lives of luxury compared to those of home owners of a few decades ago. Small shop buildings have blossomed out into great mercantile palaces. Offices, which formerly occupied the upper stories of small structures, are now built tier upon tier until they rise to more than four score stories in height.

What of the future? Can we look forward to continued advancement in real estate and building activity? What technological advances are in sight and how will they affect the use and value of real estate in the years to come?

There are many self-evident facts which appear from time to time, which indicate somewhat what the trend will be. Lessons are learned from former mistakes. It seems impossible to quench the eager bubbling of inventive genius which seeks to bestow new miracles upon a waiting universe. Glimmerings of what the future has in store are reflected by inventions and trends which appear from time to time.

Modern construction techniques and materials

Many interesting changes are in sight in building construction. With air conditioning now available, a number of important structures have been erected in different parts of the country which are without windows of any kind. All lighting is artificial and air conditioning provides adequate ventilation. Not only office buildings but numerous factories and stores are constructed with these principles in mind.

Buildings are now being constructed of bricks made of glass. These are somewhat stronger than clay bricks and freely admit light while keeping prying eyes from seeing what goes on within. Such glass bricks have a high degree of heat resistance and are widely used for decorative and ornamental purposes. They are particularly useful in buildings where air conditioning is being installed. Glass bricks of a wide variety of designs, are also utilized in residential construction for bathrooms, hallways, blank walls looking out upon undesirable vistas and many other places. A vast increase in their use can be expected in the next few years.

Glass surfacings, replacing tile, for use in bathrooms, kitchens, hallways, and store fronts are coming into extensive use. Their cost compares favorably with tile and plastics employed in similar ways. They are made so heavy that their tensile strength offsets danger of breakage.

Plastics of new and pleasing colors and textures are appearing in many forms and are already being utilized in building construction where their use is certain to increase on a vast scale in future years. Hardware trims of all kinds are made of plastic materials. Plastics have come into wide use as substitutes for tile settings around kitchen sinks and for the complete revamping of bathrooms. Some plastics are said to be as durable as iron, will not easily scratch, come in an assortment of colors and textures, and are relatively cheap to make. Ambitious manufacturers are now producing complete sets of furniture from plastic materials, and such things as kitchen cabinets and even house doors and trim may later be provided.

There is no operation which is quite so slow, wasteful and out of tune with a finely balanced industrial era as the age-old methods of constructing small houses. During the postwar years considerable experimenting with prefabricated houses was engaged in; but to a large extent, the public has turned away from prefabricated houses. The American public is unwilling to accept the sameness inherent in the prefabs; most people prefer houses designed just for them, and are quite willing to pay the price.

Changes have taken place in construction methods reducing the costs. Many materials now may be placed economically in large sheets with minimum labor. Construction costs have been reduced by mass production methods, not geared to many houses of the same design but by the expedient of having crews of workers specializing in certain skills. For instance, one crew lays foundations while another puts up sheetrock or plaster. Clever sub-contracting has been the boon to the modern builder, and our people are now better housed in dwellings having individual style and a singular architectural appeal as contrasted with the humdrum appearance of identical houses placed row on row.

Building construction is certain to see new materials introduced in the coming years. There is no reason why wood has to be used extensively in houses. There are millions of tons of straw going to waste annually which under proper chemical treament and huge pressing machines could be converted into wall boards. These, properly insulated and waterproofed, would make excellent materials for both exterior and interior walls of small houses. Such wallboard would be light, easily machined and inexpensive. A wide array of materials such as corn husks, refuse from the sugar cane fields, even common weeds, might be so used. Sawdust is no longer burned or buried but is pressed into materials now employed in building operations. Technicians in the next few years are certain to revolutionize the production of building materials, and the plastic manufacturers will supply the bright and cheerful touches needed for trimming these new factory-made dwellings of the future.

A home without television is almost unthinkable these days; many have several sets, with a color set besides. For many years after the introduction of television, it was feared that there would be a demise of the movies. This has not proved to be the case. We have more and better movies and movie houses than ever before. People have found that they must get away from the house for ouside entertainment. Television has promoted a more artistic film industry, and the competition has been good for both media.

Television programming will probably get better. There is much agitation for a system of television programs for which the customer will pay through coin-operated sets to offset the dullness brought about by overly zealous advertising now so much a part of the television program received free in the home.

What will the airplane do to the future of real estate? No one doubts but that the automobile has done more to affect real estate in the past fifty years than any other single factor. It has widened the boundaries of cities tremendously and brought into use countless areas which under old time conditions were too far distant to be of much use for residential purposes. The automobile has had much to do with the creation of outlying business districts and the building of residential districts on the fringes of cities. The farmer who was isolated on his farm thirty miles from town on a mud road a generation ago is now just thirty or forty minutes from the best movie in town!

The airplane probably will never come into such wide and general use as the automobile, yet people are now using planes regularly in their business and pleasure. This means a tremendous continued increase in the use of real estate utilized for landing fields. Airplanes, especially jets, need wide spaces on which to take off and land. These must be near towns and cities where land is expensive. The cost involved in the purchase of land and the preparation of it to a completion stage will continue to involve the expenditures of vast amounts of money in the next few years.

The airplane, too, has brought closer to urban centers many attractive "hidden valley" retreats, snuggled down twenty-five, fifty or a hundred miles from the borders of a town or city. Here nature lovers have built their homes, "far from the madding crowd," and are commuting in airplanes and helicopters in many instances. This will continue to bring into utilization many tracts of land heretofore considered too far distant to use.

Air travel has done much for the tourist business all over the nation. Los Angeles is three hours or less from Chicago, and about five from New York. It is only a two hour jaunt from New York to Miami. The airplane will continue to speed up transportation, and will have its very definite effect on real estate in the years to come.

The government has authorized the construction of the experimental model of the SST, a super aircraft that will transport four or five hundred persons at speeds of up to 2000 miles per hour. Such aircraft will have a profound effect on transportation!

It is predicted by experts that air travel which now costs as low as four cents a mile may be priced several years hence at about one cent a mile. If so, a two hour flight across America would cost about $30! One will think nothing of making the transcontinental hop every week or so, to relax in a mountain retreat in California or to enjoy the lakeside home in Florida.

Heating systems, too, have undergone great changes. Coal has virtually gone out of use in many communities; and gas or electricity is widely used for heating purposes. Large power projects which produce abundant electrical current cheaply and economically are being promoted. The widespread use of atomic energy for generating electricity seems just around the corner.

Greater use will be made of unlimited supplies of electricity, and vast new industries will rise up to manufacture the equipment needed for its use, just as the electric light, electric stove and radio industries have thrived in recent years. The creation of new mechanical devices and their installation in new buildings, whether of a business or residential character, spells obsolescence for all older buildings not possessing the new equipment. This means that all structures must be overhauled from time to time and new apparatus installed if the older buildings are to be kept up to date and to their full earning capacity.

American cities are being throttled with vehicular congestion. The popularity of the automobile is extending every year and more people are rolling about on wheels than ever before. There is a car to about every three persons in the United States and in California there is a car for every two persons. Streets are jammed with traffic, accidents abound on every hand. Authorities continue to clamor for new high speed highways, devoid of cross traffic lanes extending out from the centers of big urban communities to their suburbs. The next generation or two will see more vast sums spent for real estate for the opening of such superhighways and the creation of new values along such avenues of traffic.

There will be double decking of city streets and borings beneath them for subways while man still seeks to find ways for getting there faster. There may be monorail rapid transit systems to the suburbs with cars suspended from one rail or hidden in cuplike channels on single concrete pillars in the middle of wide thoroughfares. Vast bridges, like the Golden Gate in San Francisco, will appear in many sections of the country, spanning hitherto impassable spaces.

Atomic sources of power will create vast reservoirs of power now hidden from the eyes of man. With cheap unlimited suplies of power, myriads of machines to do his work, and automation, mankind may be in a position of simply having to push buttons and wait quietly until many of his needs are satisfied.

The threat of monumental taxes due to increasing public debts faces real estate in the years to come. The world is changing steadily politically, socially, and economically. What was decried as radical a few years ago is now the law of the land as represented by many statutes controlling the ways and doings of man. The social consequences which have grown out of two world wars will have their lasting effects on the way in which mankind lives, and in no field will they make more changes than in the use of real estate.

For better or for worse, mankind is coming increasingly under government control. This means that local and regional planning bureaus are going to legislate just what one can and cannot do in the way of improving real estate. Perhaps it will mean better city planning and the creation of new and more beautiful communities.

And, in the meantime, men will go on buying real estate, erecting buildings and living their lives, just as they have lived them for ages, but under new standards and with new yardsticks of value. And, doubtless, many of them will continue to make money out of their operations.

Appendix

Statement of Escrow

(Here are typical escrow statements as rendered by an escrow department of a title insurance company. One is the statement given to the grantor, or seller, and the other goes to the grantee, or buyer.)

STATEMENT FOR GRANTOR

July 22, 19x2
John Doe (Grantor) (Seller) ....
Peter Smith (Grantee) (Buyer) ....
Sale Price $20,150.00
Down Payment .... $ 500.00
Balance of 1st mtg. assumed by grantee.
   (The Blank Trust Co.) 9,200.00
2nd mtg. to grantor 4,200.00
Value of unearned fire ins. premium—Royal Ins. Co.
   Policy No. 5260 for 3 yr. 14,000 Premium $84.00—
   expires June 1, 19x3. Date recorded deed July 22,
   19x2 to June 1, 19x3 ....   20.90
Taxes and assessments last ½ 19x1 ....   124.60
Refund to grantee of pro-rata part 19x2 taxes and assess-
   ments on 19x1 basis. Jan. 1, 19x2 to July 22, 19x2 ..   139.09
Refund to grantee of interest on 1st mtg. from date of last
   payment to date recording deed June 15, 19x2 to
   July 22, 19x2. 6% $9,200.00 ....   56.71
Commission in full to The Cleveland Co. 837.50
New certificate of title 35.00
Half escrow fee 12.50
Preparing deed 3.00
Recording of 2nd mtg. 1.65
Revenue stamps on deed 11.00
Balance due John Doe 5,049.85
                                                  _____   _____
                                                  $20,170.90 $20,170.90

STATEMENT FOR GRANTEE

July 22, 19x2
Peter Smith (Grantee) ....
John Doe (Grantor) ....
Purchase Price $20,150.00
Down Payment .... $ 500.00
Balance 1st mtg. assumed held by The Blank Trust Co. .   9,200.00
2nd mtg. to grantor 4,200.00
Deposit in escrow 6,250.00
Value of unearned fire insurance premiums on Royal Ins.
   Co. Policy 5260—3 year policy—Premium $84.00—
   date recording deeds July 22, 19x2 to June 1, 19x3 ..   20.90
Refund of pro-rata part 19x3 taxes and assessments—date
   recording deed on 19x2 basis Jan. 1, 19x2 to July 22,
   19x2 ....   139.09
Refund of interest on 1st mtg. from date last payment
   June 15, 19x2 to July 22, 19x3 ....   56.71
Half escrow fee 12.50
Recording of deed 1.00
Preparing 2nd mtg. and note 3.00
Balance due Peter Smith 158.40
                                                  _____   _____
                                                  $20,345.80 $20,345.80

Syndicate Agreement

(This is an interesting type of syndicate agreement used by a group of investors who have taken over a ninety-nine year lease. It can be easily adapted to a sale in fee simple.)

This Agreement entered into as of Oct., 19——, by and between the undersigned, witnesseth:

WHEREAS, Richard Roe has deeded to The Union Trust Company the following described property:

(Give careful legal description of premises here.)

AND WHEREAS, The Jones and Smith Company has agreed to enter into a ninety-nine (99) year lease on said premises, which lease shall run to a corporation to be hereafter formed by the undersigned, which corporation shall be known as The State Realty Company, and,

WHEREAS, The undersigned are desirous of becoming stockholders in said Company and have contributed the sums set opposite their names in payment for stock in said company, to-wit:

John Doe	$25,000.
Wm. L. Smith	$25,000.
John R. Brown	$25,000.
Geo. M. Kerr	$25,000.
Charles C. Keys	$25,000.

And Whereas, it is the intention of the undersigned as stockholders of said Company to cause the Company to construct a building upon the premises leased to it by Richard Roe, which building shall have a value of not less than Two-Hundred-Fifty Thousand Dollars ($250,000), and,

WHEREAS, it may become necessary from time to time for the undersigned as stockholders of said Company to advance money to said Company for the purpose of completing construction, paying taxes and assessments, insurance, water rents, repairs and other items including rent provided under the lease, for the purpose of carrying on this property and operating the same, and for the purpose of meeting the obligations of the Company from time to time as they accrue, now therefor,

IN CONSIDERATION, of the mutual promises herein contained, each of the undersigned agrees with each of the others as follows:

That the capital stock of The State Realty Company, now owned or hereafter acquired by him shall be charged with the following obligations of the undersigned:

1. Each of the undersigned agrees to pay into the Treasury of The State Realty Company, as a loan to said Company, his proportionate share in accordance with the terms of this agreement, of all payments required to meet the installments of rent under the lease from Richard

Roe to The State Realty Company as the same becomes due, and the various charges for insurance, taxes, building construction, and other expenses necessary to maintain and keep said lease in full force and effect. Each of the undersigned further agrees to deposit his proportionate share of any securities which may be necessary to meet the obligations of said lease.

2. John Doe and William Smith shall act as Agents of The State Realty Company for the purpose of operating the leased property, and in the management of the premises, the collection of rents therefrom, the making of repairs, the paying of taxes and insurance thereon, the paying of all other expenses in connection with the management and operation of the property and further in connection with the consummation of all details concerning the purchase, the lease or sublease and sale of all or any part of the property. Said managers shall have authority to rent the buildings on the property for whatever consideration they think reasonable, and shall have the right to make any repairs and incur any expenses in connection with the management of the property or the operation thereof, which in their judgment may be necessary. All expenses incurred by the managers including taxes, insurance, interest and principal payments upon any loans obtained by the Company, rentals or other obligations under the lease shall be paid from the income derived from said property and the operation thereof, so long as any funds from such source are available, and in case such funds are insufficient, they shall notify the undersigned stockholders of the proportion due from each and the undersigned stockholders agree forthwith to forward sufficient funds to meet the deficiency.

Said managers shall have authority to borrow money for the purpose of carrying on and managing the property, pledging as security for such loan the property, but in no case shall they be entitled to pledge the personal credit of the stockholders of the Company. The Managers shall receive as compensation for their services ten per cent (10%) of whatever profit is derived from the property when, if and as said property is disposed of, either by sale or lease at a profit, such compensation to be deducted from the sale price of the property after all expenses have been paid and the full purchase price, plus pro-rata expenses, if any, paid by the stockholders, has been returned to them.

3. Each of the undersigned agrees to abide by the decisions of the majority in interest of the undersigned on all questions of assessments against the undersigned for the purpose of meeting the installments of rent under said lease and the various charges for insurance, taxes, building construction and other expenses necessary to maintain and keep said lease in full force and effect and for the purpose of operating the property, and with reference to security to be deposited in order to met the obligations of said lease. The will of the majority in interest of the undersigned may be expressed either in writing, signed by a majority in interest or by vote at a meeting of which each of the undersigned

shall have at least one day's notice, or shall have waived in writing no-tice of such a meeting. At such meeting any of the undersigned may be represented by proxy.

4. Each of the undersigned agree that in case he fails to make such payments or assessment, and or to deposit such securities referred to above, within thirty (30) days after demand made upon him for such payment or for such deposit on security by said agents, the other un-dersigned may cure such default contributing equally thereto and being subrogated to the interest of the undersigned in default.

5. The undersigned shall have a first and paramount lien upon all of the capital stock of The State Realty Company held by the under-signed for the liabilities and engagements of each of the undersigned hereunder and such liens shall extend to all dividends declared on such shares. After thirty (30) days default by any of the undersigned here-under, as hereinbefore provided, the agents at the option of the un-designed not in default, may either (1) enforce by suit or other proceedings the obligations imposed upon the undersigned in default, together with interest at eight per cent (8%) per annum for the time of such default or (2) on ten (10) days' notice by mail or publication, may sell the shares of the undersigned so in default at public or private sale with the right on the part of the agents or any of the undersigned to become purchasers thereof and after paying all expenses incident to such sale, the net proceeds thereof shall be applied in or towards satisfying all such defaults, and the residue, if any, paid to the under-signed in default or to his executors, administrators and assigns

6. Certificates for all such shares of stock held by the undersigned shall contain a notice to the effect that they are held subject to the terms of his Agreement and such certificates shall be deposited with ...., as Trustee, indorsed in blank, and each of the undersigned hereby constitutes such Trustees, from time to time, to act as his true and lawful attorney, irrevocable to transfer the certificates of stock represented thereby, owned by him, on the books of The State Realty Company for the purpose of making any sale or transfer provided for hereunder.

7. In case any of the undersigned, for any reason, desires to sell or dispose in any manner of any or of all of said stock otherwise than by will or gift, he shall first offer it to the other undersigned, their exec-utors, administrators or assigns at the price at which he is willing to sell said stock. Such offer shall be in writing and filed with the man-agers, who shall forthwith give written notice of such offer to all of the undersigned and shall call a meeting to consider such offer. Each of the undersigned, his executors, administrators and assigns shall be entitled to participate in the purchase of such stock in proportion to his stockholdings in said Company, and the purchase right of any of the undersigned not desiring to participate in the purchase of such stock shall be apportioned among the undersigned in proportion to their

interests or in such proportion as they may agree. In case the undersigned or any of them do not accept such offer in writing within fifteen (15) days after the same is filed with the managers, the undersigned desiring to sell may dispose of such stock to any person whomsoever at not less than the price named in said offer filed with the managers, subject, however, to the terms of this agreement by which the assignee shall be bound, but he shall not sell to other than the undersigned at a lower price without first offering it at such lower price to the undersigned by a new written offer filed as aforesaid. In the event of the disposal of all or any part of the capital stock of The State Realty Company by any of the undersigned to any person, other than the remaining undersigned, then the undersigned so disposing of such stock shall remain liable as surety for the performance by the transferee of the obligations hereof.

8. In the absence of any action by the undersigned fixing the amount of assessments as specified in section 3 hereof, the managers of The State Realty Company in the management of the leased premises shall have power to make calls for assessments for amounts needed to pay rentals, taxes, ordinary repairs, insurance, operating expenses and other expenses not to exceed six (6) months in advance. All assessments so collected shall be deposited in the name of The State Realty Company. The Managers may with the written consent of the majority in interest of the undersigned, commence suit in their own names for the collection of any assessments made by them as aforesaid; but no assessments for unusual repairs or construction of buildings and no call for deposit of securities shall be made except by authority of the majority in interest hereunder or by the order of an executive committee hereafter to be appointed by the undersigned.

9. The majority in interest of the undersigned for the purpose of this Agreement shall be determined by the number of shares of the capital stock owned by each in The State Realty Company. Likewise the proposed obligation of each of the undersigned shall be determined by the amount of such stock held by each of the undersigned.

10. This Agreement shall be binding upon and inure to the benefits of the executors and administrators of each of the undersigned and to any person to whom the rights of any of the undersigned, and the stock held by any of the undersigned are transferred in accordance with the terms hereof, but nothing in this Agreement shall constitute the managers partners with each other or of any of the stockholders partners with the syndicate managers or with each other.

The proportion by which each of the undersigned holds his interest is as follows:

John Doe ....One-fifth.
Wm. L. Smith ....One-fifth.
John R. Brown ....One-fifth.
Geo. M. Kerr ....One-fifth.
Charles C. Keys ....One-fifth.

IN WITNESS WHEREOF the undersigned have hereunto affixed their signatures as of the day and year first above written.

(Signed) JOHN DOE

(Signed) WM. L. SMITH

(Signed) JOHN R. BROWN

(Signed) GEO. M. KERR

(Signed) CHARLES C. KEYS

Units of Measurement of Length

A *meter* (m.) is a unit of length equivalent to the distance between the defining lines on the international prototype meter at the International Bureau of Weights and Measures when this standard is at the temperature of melting ice (0° C.)

A *yard* (yd.) is a unit of length equivalent to $\frac{3600}{3937}$ of a meter.

1 kilometer (km.) = 1,000 meters.

1 hectometer (hm.) = 100 meters.

1 decameter (dcm.) = 10 meters.

1 decimeter (dm.) = 0.1 meter.

1 centimeter (cm.) = 0.01 meter.

1 millimeter (mm.) = 0.001 meter = 0.1 centimeter.

1 micron (μ) = 0.000,001 meter = 0.001 millimeter

1 millimicron (mμ) = 0.000,000,001 meter = 0.001 micron

1 foot (ft.) = $\frac{1}{3}$ yard = $\frac{1200}{3937}$ meter.

1 inch (in.) = $\frac{1}{36}$ yard = $\frac{1}{12}$ foot = $\frac{100}{3937}$ meter.

1 link (li.) = 0.22 yard = 7.92 inches.

1 rod (rd.) = 5½ yards = 16½ feet.

1 chain (ch.) = 22 yards = 100 links = 66 feet = 4 rods

1 furlong (fur.) = 220 yards = 40 rods = 10 chains.

1 statute mile (mi.) = 1,760 yards = 5,280 feet = 320 rods

1 hand = 4 inches.

1 point = $\frac{1}{72}$ inch.

1 mil = 0.001 inch.

1 fathom = 6 feet.

1 span = 9 inches = ⅛ fathom.

1 nautical mile ⎫
1 sea mile ⎬ United States = 6,080.20 feet = 1.151,553 statute miles = 1,853.249 meters.
1 geographical mile ⎭

Courtesy United Stat. Bureau of Standards.

Land Contract

THIS AGREEMENT, Made at ....this.......day
of............A. D. 19...., by and between..... ....of the
..........of......................County of.. .. ..and State
of......, PARTY OF THE FIRST PART, AND......... ....
of..................., PARTY OF THE SECOND PART,

WITNESSETH: That the said party of the first part hath this day
agreed to sell unto the party of the second part,...... ....
heirs, executors, administrators or assigns, the following described tract
or lot of land, situated in the............of......................
County of ....and State of........:

(Description of Property)

together with all the hereditaments and appurtenances thereof, but
subject to all legal highways.

And the said party of the second part doth hereby agree to pay to
the said party of the first part,..................heirs, executors,
administrators or assigns, for the land aforesaid, the sum of..........
.......................Dollars, ($....................,) being the
value of said premises, payable as follows:
....Dollars, ($.................,)
cash in hand, receipt whereof is hereby acknowledged, and the balance
of..............

IT IS EXPRESSLY AGREED by and between the parties to this agreement,
that if any one of said installments, or the interest accrued thereon, shall
not be paid when due, then all of said installments remaining unpaid
shall at once become due and payable, at the option of the first party.

The party of the second part further agrees to keep the building now
on said land, or which may hereafter be erected thereon, insured for
not less than $.........., in a solvent insurance company approved by
the party of the first part, for the benefit of the party of the first part
as..........interest may appear, and to place and keep the policy of
such insurance with the party of the first part, and to pay all taxes and
assessments of every description whatsoever that may be levied or
assessed upon said land or any part thereof, from and after the date of
these presents.

In case default shall be made by the party of the second part,......
..........heirs, executors, administrators or assigns, in any of the
conditions above stipulated to be performed by... ...., it shall

and will be lawful for the party of the first part, if......so elect, to treat this contract as thenceforth void, and to re-enter upon said premises at any time after such default, without serving on the party of the second part, or any person holding under..........a notice to quit said land; and in case this contract shall be so treated as thenceforth void, the party of the second part, or those claiming under.........., shall thenceforth, be deemed a mere tenant at will under said party of the first part, and be liable to be proceeded against without notice to quit, under the provisions of the law regulating proceedings in cases of forcible detainer; and the part of the first part, in such case, shall be at liberty to sell the land and premises to any person whatsoever, without being liable in law or in equity to the party of the second part or any person claiming under............for any damages in consequence of such sale or to return any payments made on acocunt of or under this contract, and the payments that shall have been made may be retained by the party of the first part as stipulated damages for the non-performance of this contract on the part of the party of the second part.

Now, if the party of the second part,..............heirs, executors, administrators or assigns, shall well and truly pay the full purchase money aforesaid, with interest, taxes, assessments and insurance, at the time and in the manner above stipulated, then, on the full receipt thereof, and not otherwise, the said party of the first part,............ heirs, executors, administrators or assigns, shall well and truly make and deliver, or cause to be made and delivered, to said party of the second part and on surrender of.........duplicate contract, a good and sufficient Warranty Deed, and Certificate, of Title showing good title to the land aforesaid, subject to any mechanic's lien or incumbrance caused by the acts of the second party, and subject to the conditions, restrictions and stipulations herein named; otherwise free from any and all incumbrances save taxes and assessments due and to become due, which said second party assumes.

And I,........................of said....................in consideration of the making of the payments by the second party as herein provided for, and of one dollar to me paid, the receipt whereof is hereby acknowledged, consent to the terms of the foregoing contract and bind myself to unite in the aforesaid deed and therein release all my right and expectancy of dower in the premises above described to said second party,..................heirs or assigns,

IN WITNESS WHEREOF,....................hereunto set....hand ...., this.........day of..........in the year of our Lord one thousand nine hundred and..................
Signed and acknowledged in the presence of
....
....

. . . .
. . . .
. . . .
. . . .

THE STATE OF. . . . .   BEFORE ME, a. . . . .

                     ss.

. . . . .County,

                                       in and for said County,
                                       personally appeared the
                                       above named. . . . .

. . . .

who acknowledged that they did sign the foregoing instrument, and
that the same is their free act and deed.

                              . . . .

                                 . . . .

Multiplication Table

1	2	3	4	5	6	7	8	9	10	11	12
2	4	6	8	10	12	14	16	18	20	22	24
3	6	9	12	15	18	21	24	27	30	33	36
4	8	12	16	20	24	28	32	36	40	44	48
5	10	15	20	25	30	35	40	45	50	55	60
6	12	18	24	30	36	42	48	54	60	66	72
7	14	21	28	35	42	49	56	63	70	77	84
8	16	24	32	40	48	56	64	72	80	88	96
9	18	27	36	45	54	63	72	81	90	99	108
10	20	30	40	50	60	70	80	90	100	110	120
11	22	33	44	55	66	77	88	99	110	121	132
12	24	36	48	60	72	84	96	108	120	132	144

Quick Interest Calculator

MULTIPLY THE PRINCIPAL BY AS MANY ONE HUNDREDTHS AS THERE ARE
DAYS, AND THEN DIVIDE AS FOLLOWS:

Per Cent	4	5	6	7	8	9	10	12
Divide by ...	90	72	60	52	45	40	36	30

EXAMPLE:

Problem: Find interest on $100 for 90 days at 5%.
Solution: $100 × .90 = $90.00 divided by 72 = $1.25

Conversion of Weights and Measures

Lineal feet	× .00019	= miles.
Lineal yards	× .0006	= miles.
Square inches	× .007	= square feet.
Square feet	× .111	= square yds.
Square yards	× .0002067	= acres
Acres	× .4840	= square yds.
Cubic inches	× .00058	= cubic feet.
Cubic feet	× .03704	= cubic yards.
Circular inches	× .00546	= square feet.
Cylindrical inches	× .0004546	= cubic feet.
Cylindrical feet	× .02909	= cubic yards.
Links	× .22	= yards.
Links	× .66	= feet.
Feet	× 1.5	= links.
Width in chains	× .8	= acres p. mile.
183.346 circular inches		= 1 square ft.
2200 cylindrical inches		= 1 cubic foot.
Cubic feet	× 7.48	= U. S. gallons.
Cubic inches	× .004329	= U. S. gallons.
Cylindrical feet	× 5.874	= U. S. gallons.
Cylindrical inches	× .0034	= U. S. gallons.
U. S. gallons	× .13367	= cubic feet.
U. S. gallons	× 231	= cubic inches.
Cubic feet	× .8036	= U. S. bushel.
Cubic inches	× .000465	= U. S. bushel.
U. S. bushels	× .0461	= cubic yards.
U. S. bushels	× 2150.42	= cubic feet.
U. S. bushels	× 1.2446	= cubic inches.
Cylin. ft. of water	× 6	= U. S. gallons.
Lbs. avoirdupois	× .009	= cwt. (112).
Lbs. avoirdupois	× .00045	= tons (2240).
Cubic ft. of water	× 62.5	= lbs. avoir.
Cubic in. of water	× .03617	= lbs. avoir.
Cylin. ft. of water	× 49.1	= lbs. avoir.
Cylin. in. of water	× .02842	= lbs. avoir.
13.43 U. S. gallons of water		= 1 cwt.
268.6 U. S. gallons of water		= 1 ton.

Metric, or French, Lineal Measure

	Meters	U. S. In.	Ft.	Yards	Miles
Millimeter* =	.001 =	.03937 =	.00328		
Centimeter† =	.01 =	.3937 =	.03280		
Decimeter =	.1 =	3.937 =	.32807 =	.10936 =	
Meter =	1. =	39.3685 =	3.2807 =	1.0936	
Decameter =	10.	=	32.807 =	10.936	
Hectometer =	100.	=	328.07 =	109.36 =	.0621347
Kilometer =	1000.	=	3280.7 =	1093.6 =	.6213466
Myriameter =	10000.	=	= 32807. =	10936. =	6.213466

* Nearly the 1/25 part of an inch. † Full ⅜ inch.

Weights and Measures

Troy Weight

24 grains = 1 pwt.
20 pwt. = 1 ounce.
12 ounces = 1 pound.
Used for weighing gold, silver
    and jewels.

Apothecaries' Weight

20 grains = 1 scruple.
3 scruples = 1 dram.
8 drams = 1 ounce.
12 ounces = 1 pound.

Avoirdupois Weight

27 11-32 grains = I dram.
16 drams = 1 ounce.
16 ounces = 1 pound.
25 pounds = 1 quarter.
4 quarters = 1 cwt.
2,000 lbs. = 1 short ton.
2,240 lbs. = 1 long ton.

Dry Measure

2 pints = 1 quart.
8 quarts = 1 peck.
4 pecks = 1 bushel.
36 bushels = 1 chaldron.

Liquid Measure

4 gills = 1 pint.
2 pints = 1 quart.
4 quarts = 1 gallon.
31½ gallons = 1 barrel.
2 barrels = 1 hogshead.

Long Measure

12 inches = 1 foot.
3 feet = 1 yard.
5½ yards = 1 rod.
40 rods = 1 furlong.
8 furlongs = 1 stat. mile.
3 miles = 1 league.

Mariners' Measure

6 feet = 1 fathom
20 fathoms = 1 cable length.
7½ cable lengths = 1 mile.
5,280 feet = 1 stat. mile.
6,085 feet = 1 naut. mile.

Surveyors' Measure

7.92 inches = 1 link.
25 links = 1 rod.
4 rods = 1 chain.
10 square chains or 160 square
    rods = 1 acre.
640 acres = 1 sq. mile.
36 sq. miles (6 miles square)
    1 township.

Cubic Measure

1728 cubic in. = 1 cu. ft.
27 cubic ft. = 1 cubic yd.
128 cu. ft. = 1 cord (wood).
40 cu. ft. = 1 ton (ship'g).
2,150 cu. in. = 1 standard bushel.
231 cu. in. = 1 standard gallon.
1 cu. ft. = about four-fifths of a bu,

Contents of Fields and Lots

220 feet by 198   feet of land equals   1 acre.
440 feet by 99   feet of land equals   1 acre.
110 feet by 396   feet of land equals   1 acre.
 60 feet by 726   feet of land equals   1 acre.
120 feet by 363   feet of land equals   1 acre.
240 feet by 181½   feet of land equals   1 acre.
200 feet by 108⁹⁄₁₀ feet of land equals ½ acre.
100 feet by 145²⁄₁₀ feet of land equals ⅓ acre.

There are 12 city lots, 25 × 100 feet, in an acre with the street cut
through; 17 $\frac{424}{1000}$ city lots, 25 × 100 feet, in an acre without the street
cut through.

Metric Equivalents

Linear Measure

1 centimeter = 0.3937 in.
1 in. = 2.54 centimeters.
1 decimeter = 3.937 in. = 0.328 feet.
  1 ft. = 3.048 decimeters.
1 meter = 39.37 in. = 1.0936 yards.
  1 yard = 0.9144 meter.
1 dekameter = 1.9884 rods.
1 rod = 0.5029 dekameter.
1 kilometer = 0.62137 mile.
1 mile = 1.6093 kilometers.

Square Measure

1 sq. centimeter = 0.1550 sq. in.
  1 sq. inch = 6.452 square centimeters.
1 sq. decimeter = 0.1076 sq. ft.
  1 sq. ft. = 9.2903 square decimeters.
1 sq. meter = 1.196 sq. yd.
1 sq. yd. = 08361 sq. meter.
1 are. = 3.954 sq. rods.
1 sq. rod = 0.2529 are.
1 hektar = 2.47 acres.
1 acre = 0.4047 hektar.
1 sq. kilometer = 0.386 sq. m.
  1 sq. mile = 2.59 square kilometer.

Measure of Volume

1 cu. centimeter = 0.061 cu. in.
  1 cu. inch = 16.39 cu. centimeters.
1 cu. decimeter = 0.0353 cu. ft.
  1 cu. foot = 28.317 cu. decimeters.
1 cu. m'r = 1.308 cu. yd.
1 ster = 0.2759 cd.

1 cu. yd. = 0.7646 cu. meter.
1 cord = 3.624 sters.
1 liter = 0.908 qt. dry.
         1.0567 qt. liq.
1 qt. dry = 1.101 liters.
1 qt. liq. = 0.9463 liter.
1 dekaliter = 2.6417 gal.
              .135 pecks.
1 gal. = 0.3785 dekaliter.
1 peck = 0.881 dekaliter.
1 hektoliter = 2.8375 bush.
1 bu. = 0.3524 hektoliter.

Weights

1 gram = 0.03527 ounce.
1 ounce = 28.35 grams.
1 kilogram = 2.2046 lbs.
1 lb. = 0.4536 kilogram.
1 metric ton = 1.1023 English ton.
  1 English ton = 0.9072 metric ton.

Approximate Metric Equivalents

1 decimeter = 4 inches.
1 liter = 1.06 qt. liquid.
         0.9 qt. dry.
1 meter = 1.1 yards.
1 kelometer = ⅝ of mile.
1 hektoliter = 2⅘ bu.
1 hektar = 2½ acres.
1 kilogram = 2 1-5 lbs.
1 ster. or cu. meter = ¼ of a cord.
  1 metric ton = 2200 lbs.

Miscellaneous Units of Measure

Sheets, Reams

12 units or articles............1 dozen
24 sheets paper................1 quire
20 quires.....................1 ream
2 reams.....................1 bundle
5 bundles....................1 bale
Printer's token.............250 sheets

Palm, Span, Cubit

3 inches......................1 palm
9 inches.................1 Bible span
18 inches.....................1 cubit
28.8 inches...............1 Bible cubit
2½ feet.............1 military pace
6 feet.....................1 fathom

Degrees

60 seconds.................1 minute
60 minutes.................1 degree
30 degrees..................1 sign
90 degrees.............1 quadrant
360 degrees.................1 circle
60 miles...................1 degree

Comparison of U. S. and Foreign Lineal Measures

U.S. Inches

United States and Britain........	Foot	12.
Amsterdam	"	11.144
Antwerp	Fuss	11.275
Austria	"	12.445
Belgium	Elle	39.371
Brazil	Cubit	25.98
Bremen	Fuss	11.38
Brunswick	" or Schuh	11.23
China	Chick (Commerce)	14.1
Denmark	Fod	12.357
Egypt	Derah	25.49
Florence	Braccio	22.98
Greece	Cubit	18
India	"	18
Japan	Shaku	11.93
Mexico	Pie	11.28
Norway	Fod	12.353
Persia	Arish	38.27
Portugal	Foot	13.33
Prussia	Fuss	12.357
Rome	Pie (Commerce)	11.592
Russia	Foot	12.00
Sardinia	Oucia	1.686
Sicily	Palmo	9.53
Spain	Pie	10.968
Switzerland (B'e)	Fuss	11.81
" (Geneva)	"	23.028
Turkey	Pic (Great)	27.9

Lots Per Acre

This table shows the number of lots that can be obtained per acre, using the following dimensions as average-sized lots. Allowance has been made for the lots in front on a 50-foot street, with cross streets every 800 feet for the smaller lots and increasing proportionately up to 2,000 feet for the largest.

Size of Lots	Number of Lots per Acre	Size of Lots	Number of Lots per Acre
40 × 100	8.23	60 × 200	3.10
40 × 120	7.07	70 × 175	3.00
40 × 150	5.80	70 × 200	2.67
45 × 125	6.11	80 × 200	2.35
45 × 150	5.25	80 × 240	1.99
50 × 150	4.74	100 × 250	1.54
50 × 175	4.14	100 × 300	1.31
60 × 175	3.48		

Units of Length

Units		Inches	Links	Feet	Yards	Rods	Chains	Miles
1 inch	=	1	0.126 263	0.083 333 3	0.027 777 8	0.005 050 51	0.001 262 63	0.000 015 782 8
1 link	=	7.92	1	0.66	0.22	0.04	0.01	0.000 125
1 foot	=	12	1.515 152	1	0.333 333	0.060 606 1	0.015 151 5	0.000 189 393 9
1 yard	=	36	4.545 45	3	1	0.181 818	0.045 454 5	0.000 568 182
1 rod	=	198	25	16.5	5.5	1	0.25	0.003 125
1 chain	=	792	100	66	22	4	1	0.0125
1 mile	=	63 360	8000	5280	1760	320	80	1
1 centimeter	=	0.3937	0.049 709 60	0.032 808 33	0.010 936 111	0.001 988 384	0.000 497 096 0	0.000 006 213 699
1 meter	=	39.37	4.970 960	3.280 833	1.093 611 1	0.198 838 4	0.049 709 60	0.000 006 621 369 9

Units of Area

Units		Square Inches	Square Feet	Square Yards	Square Rods	Acres	Square Miles
1 square inch	=	1	0.006 944 44	0.000 771 605	0.000 025 507 6	0.000 000 159 423	0.000 000 000 249 1
1 square link	=	62.7264	0.4356	0.0484	0.0016	0.000 01	0.000 000 000 015 625
1 square foot	=	144	1	0.111 111 1	0.003 673 09	0.000 022 956 8	0.000 000 000 035 870 1
1 square yard	=	1296	9	1	0.033 057 85	0.000 206 612	0.000 000 000 322 831
1 square rod	=	39 204	272.25	30.25	1	0.006 25	0.000 000 009 765 625
1 square chain	=	627 264	4356	484	16	0.1	0.000 156 25
1 acre	=	6 272 640	43 560	4840	160	1	0.001 562 5
1 square mile	=	4 014 489 600	27 878 400	3 097 600	102 400	640	1
1 square centimeter	=	0.154 999 7	0.001 076 387	0.000 119 598 5	0.000 003 953 67	0.000 000 024 710 4	0.000 000 000 038 610 06
1 square meter	=	1549.9969	10.763 87	1.195 985	0.039 536 7	0.000 247 104	0.000 000 386 100 6
1 hectare	=	15 499 969	107 638.7	11 959.85	395.367	2.271 04	0.003 861 006

Courtesy U. S. Bureau of Standards.

THE STANLEY McMICHAEL ORGANIZATION

6335 YUCCA, AT IVAR • HOLLYWOOD 28, CALIFORNIA

OFFER TO PURCHASE

Los Angeles, California _____, 19____

RECEIVED FROM _____
(Purchaser)

_____ DOLLARS ($ _____)
(Make check payable to the Stanley McMichael Organization)

to apply on the purchase of certain real estate, together with appurtenances thereto, known as

_____ in the city of _____

and more particularly known as No. _____

Los Angeles County, Calif., having a frontage of _____ feet and a depth of _____ feet, more or less, this day agreed to be

purchased at a price of _____ DOLLARS ($ _____)

Balance, in addition to above mentioned earnest money, to be paid as follows:

upon delivery of a properly executed grant or warranty deed, together with a policy of title insurance furnished by a responsible title company and to be paid for by the seller, showing the seller to have good and merchantable title to the property, clear and free of encumbrances, except conditions, restrictions, reservations, easements, and rights of way, of record, and such other exceptions as are noted herein. All interest on mortgages; rentals; insurance premiums; water, gas and electric charges; taxes and assessments, whether general or special, and all other charges of whatsoever nature shall be prorated as of date of transfer of title. The purchaser accepts the herein described property in its existing condition, having inspected it and being satisfied as to representations made concerning it. The purchaser agrees that in the event said purchaser fails to deposit the balance of said purchase price within the time limit set for such payment or complete purchase as herein provided, the amounts paid hereon shall be retained, one half by the seller of the property, and one half by the agent herein, in consideration of accepting this agreement. It is mutually agreed between purchaser and seller that this agency contract shall become an integral part of the escrow proceedings in which the transfer of this property is consummated and that all agreements herein contained shall be binding on both parties, even if such are not specifically recorded or mentioned in escrow proceedings set up by the escrow agent named here.

Within_____days of the final acceptance of this offer all papers and considerations necessary for the closing of this transaction, as stated herein, shall be placed in escrow with the agency indicated below. Time is of the essence of this contract; but the time for any act required to be done may be extended not longer than thirty days by the undersigned agent. When this offer is accepted by the seller and approved by the Stanley McMichael Organization, it shall constitute a contract for the purchase and sale of said property upon these terms; if not accepted and approved, the afore mentioned deposit shall be returned to the purchaser without any liability upon the part of the Stanley McMichael Organization to either party.

THE STANLEY McMICHAEL ORGANIZATION, Agent

By _____ Salesman

APPROVED_____

California Real Estate Broker's License No._____

_____

_____ **(PURCHASER)**

(Date)   (Address)   (Tel. No.)

ESCROW AGENT IS TO BE:

THE UNDERSIGNED ACCEPTS THE ABOVE OFFER, agrees to make conveyance, recognizes the Stanley McMichael Organization as the agent in this transaction and agrees to pay it the regular Los Angeles Realty Board rate of commission on the total purchase price or consideration, when transfer of title takes place or one half of the deposit in the event the same is forfeited by the purchaser

OTHER CONDITIONS AND REMARKS.

_____

_____ **(SELLER)**

(Date)   (Address)   (Tel. No.)

(Continued on back hereof)

353

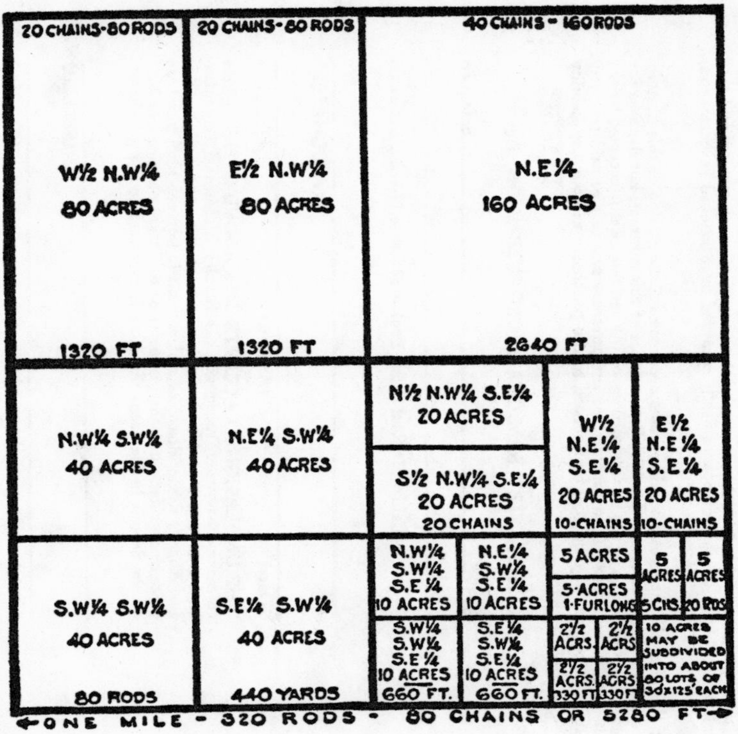

20 CHAINS - 80 RODS	20 CHAINS - 80 RODS	40 CHAINS = 160 RODS
W½ N.W¼ 80 ACRES	E½ N.W¼ 80 ACRES	N.E¼ 160 ACRES
1320 FT	1320 FT	2640 FT

N.W¼ S.W¼ 40 ACRES | N.E¼ S.W¼ 40 ACRES

N½ N.W¼ S.E¼ 20 ACRES
S½ N.W¼ S.E¼ 20 ACRES
20 CHAINS

W½ N.E¼ S.E¼ 20 ACRES 10-CHAINS | E½ N.E¼ S.E¼ 20 ACRES 10-CHAINS

S.W¼ S.W¼ 40 ACRES | S.E¼ S.W¼ 40 ACRES

N.W¼ S.W¼ S.E¼ 10 ACRES | N.E¼ S.W¼ S.E¼ 10 ACRES | 5 ACRES 5-ACRES 1-FURLONG | 5 ACRES 5 CHS | 5 ACRES 20 RODS

S.W¼ S.W¼ S.E¼ 10 ACRES 660 FT. | S.E¼ S.W¼ S.E¼ 10 ACRES 660 FT. | 2½ ACRS 330 FT | 2½ ACRS 330 FT | 10 ACRES MAY BE SUBDIVIDED INTO ABOUT 60 LOTS OF 50x125 EACH

80 RODS | 440 YARDS

←ONE MILE = 320 RODS = 80 CHAINS OR 5280 FT→

Area and Distances of a Full Section of Land.
(1 square mile or 640 Acres.)

SURVEYORS' MEASUREMENTS

7.92 inches =	1 link	10 sq. chains or 160 sq. rods =	1 A.
25 links =	1 rod	640 acres =	1 sq mile
4 rods =	1 chain	36 sq. mi. (6 mi. sq.) =	1 township

Inches	Feet	Yards	Rods	Furlongs	Miles
12	1	....	....	....	....
36	3	1	....	....	....
198	16½	5½	1	....	....
7,920	660	220	40	1	....
63,360	5,280	1,760	320	8	1

TYPES OF ODD SHAPED LOTS

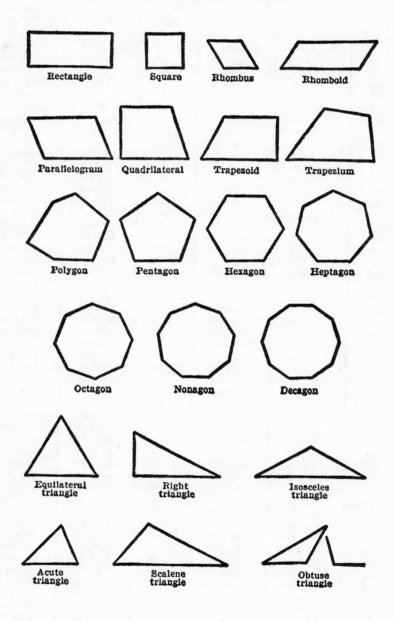

Rectangle   Square   Rhombus   Rhomboid

Parallelogram   Quadrilateral   Trapezoid   Trapezium

Polygon   Pentagon   Hexagon   Heptagon

Octagon   Nonagon   Decagon

Equilateral triangle   Right triangle   Isosceles triangle

Acute triangle   Scalene triangle   Obtuse triangle

Value Per Square Foot of Land with Corresponding Value for a Lot 25 × 100; Also, Corresponding Value for an Acre

(To find the value per foot front, multiply the value per square foot of land in the first column by 100.)

Value per Sq. Ft. of Land	Value of a Lot 25 × 100	Value of an Acre	Value per Sq. Ft. of Land	Value of a Lot 25 × 100	Value of an Acre
$.01	$ 25.00	$ 435.60	$ .51	$1,275.00	$22,215.60
.02	50.00	871.20	.52	1,300.00	22,651.20
.03	75.00	1,306.80	.53	1,325.00	23,086.80
.04	100.00	1,742.40	.54	1,350.00	23,522.40
.05	125.00	2,178.00	.55	1,375.00	23,958.00
.06	150.00	2,613.60	.56	1,400.00	24,393.60
.07	175.00	3,049.20	.57	1,425.00	24,829.20
.08	200.00	3,484.80	.58	1,450.00	25,264.80
.09	225.00	3,920.40	.59	1,475.00	25,700.40
.10	250.00	4,356.00	.60	1,500.00	26,136.00
.11	275.00	4,791.60	.61	1,525.00	26,571.60
.12	300.00	5,227.20	.62	1,550.00	27,007.20
.13	325.00	5,662.80	.63	1,575.00	27,442.80
.14	350.00	6,098.40	.64	1,600.00	27,878.40
.15	375.00	6,534.00	.65	1,625.00	28,314.00
.16	400.00	6,969.60	.66	1,650.00	28,749.60
.17	425.00	7,405.20	.67	1,675.00	29,185.20
.18	450.00	7,840.80	.68	1,700.00	29,620.80
.19	475.00	8,276.40	.69	1,725.00	30,056.40
.20	500.00	8,712.00	.70	1,750.00	30,492.00
.21	525.00	9,147.60	.71	1,775.00	30,927.60
.22	550.00	9,583.20	.72	1,800.00	31,363.20
.23	575.00	10,018.80	.73	1,825.00	31,798.80
.24	600.00	10,454.40	.74	1,850.00	32,234.40
.25	625.00	10,890.00	.75	1,875.00	32,670.00
.26	650.00	11,325.60	.76	1,900.00	33,105.60
.27	675.00	11,761.20	.77	1,925.00	33,541.20
.28	700.00	12,196.80	.78	1,950.00	33,976.80
.29	725.00	12,632.40	.79	1,975.00	34,412.40
.30	750.00	13,068.00	.80	2,000.00	34,848.00
.31	775.00	13,503.00	.81	2,025.00	35,283.60
.32	800.00	13,939.20	.82	2,050.00	35,719.20
.33	825.00	14,374.80	.83	2,075.00	36,154.80
.34	850.00	14,810.40	.84	2,100.00	36,590.40
.35	875.00	15,246.00	.85	2,125.00	37,026.00
.36	900.00	15,681.60	.86	2,150.00	37,461.60
.37	925.00	16,117.20	.87	2,175.00	37,897.20
.38	950.00	16,552.80	.88	2,200.00	38,332.80
.39	975.00	16,988.40	.89	2,225.00	38,768.40
.40	1,000.00	17,424.00	.90	2,250.00	39,204.00
.41	1,025.00	17,859.60	.91	2,275.00	39,639.60
.42	1,050.00	18,295.20	.92	2,300.00	40,075.20
.43	1,075.00	18,730.80	.93	2,325.00	40,510.80
.44	1,100.00	19,166.40	.94	2,350.00	40,946.40
.45	1,125.00	19,602.00	.95	2,375.00	41,382.00
.46	1,150.00	20,037.60	.96	2,400.00	41,817.60
.47	1,175.00	20,473.20	.97	2,425.00	42,253.20
.48	1,200.00	20,908.80	.98	2,450.00	42,688.80
.49	1,225.00	21,344.40	.99	2,475.00	43,124.40
.50	1,250.00	21,780.00	1.00	2,500.00	43,560.00

Monthly Loan Payment Table

(This table shows the monthly payment required to pay off a $100 loan in various periods and at various interest rates. To find the monthly payment required for loans of larger denomination, multiply the above payments by the number of hundreds in the loan. Thus, the monthly payment on a $1,250 loan for 3 years at 6% would be 12.5 × $3.04.)

Monthly Payments

Loan Period (Months)	5%	6%	7%	8%	9%	10%	11%	12%	13%	14%	15%	16%	17%	18%	19%	20%
12	$8.56	$8.61	$8.65	$8.70	$8.75	$8.79	$8.84	$8.88	$8.93	$8.98	$9.03	$9.07	$9.12	$9.17	$9.22	$9.26
13	7.92	7.96	8.01	8.06	8.10	8.15	8.19	8.24	8.29	8.33	8.38	8.43	8.48	8.52	8.57	8.62
24	4.39	4.43	4.48	4.52	4.57	4.61	4.66	4.71	4.76	4.80	4.85	4.89	4.94	4.99	5.04	5.09
25	4.22	4.27	4.31	4.36	4.40	4.45	4.49	4.54	4.59	4.63	4.68	4.73	4.78	4.83	4.87	4.92
36	3.00	3.04	3.09	3.13	3.18	3.23	3.27	3.32	3.37	3.42	3.47	3.51	3.57	3.62	3.67	3.71
37	2.92	2.97	3.01	3.06	3.11	3.15	3.20	3.25	3.30	3.34	3.39	3.44	3.49	3.54	3.59	3.64
48	2.30	2.35	2.39	2.44	2.49	2.54	2.58	2.63	2.68	2.73	2.78	2.83	2.89	2.94	2.99	3.04
49	2.26	2.31	2.35	2.40	2.45	2.49	2.54	2.59	2.64	2.69	2.74	2.79	2.84	2.90	2.95	3.00
60	1.89	1.93	1.98	2.03	2.08	2.12	2.17	2.22	2.28	2.33	2.38	2.43	2.49	2.54	2.59	2.65
61	1.86	1.91	1.95	2.00	2.05	2.10	2.15	2.20	2.25	2.30	2.35	2.40	2.46	2.51	2.57	2.62
72	1.61	1.66	1.70	1.75	1.80	1.85	1.90	1.96	2.01	2.06	2.11	2.17	2.22	2.28	2.34	2.39
84	1.41	1.46	1.51	1.56	1.61	1.66	1.71	1.77	1.82	1.87	1.93	1.99	2.04	2.10	2.16	2.22
96	1.27	1.31	1.36	1.41	1.47	1.52	1.57	1.63	1.68	1.74	1.79	1.85	1.91	1.97	2.03	2.09
108	1.15	1.20	1.25	1.30	1.35	1.41	1.46	1.52	1.58	1.63	1.69	1.75	1.81	1.88	1.94	2.00
120	1.06	1.11	1.16	1.21	1.27	1.32	1.38	1.43	1.49	1.55	1.61	1.67	1.74	1.80	1.87	1.93
132	.99	1.04	1.09	1.14	1.20	1.25	1.31	1.37	1.43	1.49	1.55	1.61	1.68	1.74	1.81	1.88
139	.95	1.00	1.05	1.11	1.16	1.22	1.28	1.33	1.40	1.46	1.52	1.58	1.65	1.72	1.78	1.85
144	.92	.98	1.03	1.08	1.14	1.20	1.25	1.31	1.37	1.44	1.50	1.57	1.63	1.70	1.77	1.85

Interest Calculations

Rule.—Multiply the principal by as many one-hundredths as there are days, and then divide as follows:

Per Cent	4	5	6	7	8	9	10	12
Divide by	90	72	60	52	45	40	36	30

Examples.—Interest on $100, for 90 days at 5 per cent: 100 × .90 = 90.0, divided by 72 = 1.25 (one dollar and 25 cents); on $1, for 30 days at 6 per cent: 1 × .30 = .3, divided by 60 = .005 (5 mills).

Table.—Showing the number of days from any date in one month to the same date in any other month.

From	Jan.	Feb.	March	April	May	June	July	Aug.	Sept.	Oct.	Nov.	Dec.
January	365	31	59	90	120	151	181	212	243	273	304	334
February	334	365	28	59	89	120	150	181	212	242	273	303
March	306	337	365	31	61	92	122	153	184	214	245	275
April	275	306	334	365	30	61	91	122	153	183	214	244
May	245	276	304	335	365	31	61	92	123	153	184	214
June	214	245	274	304	334	365	30	61	92	122	153	183
July	184	215	243	273	304	335	365	31	62	92	123	153
August	153	184	212	243	273	304	334	365	31	61	92	122
September ...	122	153	181	212	242	273	303	334	365	30	61	91
October	92	123	151	182	212	243	273	304	335	365	31	6,
November ...	61	92	120	151	181	212	242	273	304	334	365	30
December	31	62	90	121	151	182	212	243	274	304	335	365

Example.—How many days from May 5 to October 5? Look for May at left and October at the top; in the angle is 153. In leap year, add one day if February is included.

358

Table of Geometrical Progression

1	1	15	16384	29	268435456	43	4398046511104
2	2	16	32768	30	536870912	44	8796093022208
3	4	17	65536	31	1073741824	45	17592186044416
4	8	18	131072	32	2147483648	46	35184372088832
5	16	19	262144	33	4294967296	47	70368744177664
6	32	20	524288	34	8589934592	48	140737488355328
7	64	21	1048576	35	17179869184	49	281474976710656
8	128	22	2097152	36	34359738368	50	562949953421312
9	256	23	4194304	37	68719476736	51	1125899906842624
10	512	24	8388608	38	137438953472	52	2251799813685248
11	1024	25	16777216	39	274877906944	53	4503599627370496
12	2048	26	33554432	40	549755813888	54	9007199254740992
13	4096	27	67108864	41	1099511627776	55	18014398509481984
14	8192	28	134217728	42	2199023255552	56	36028797018963968

Illustrations—The 13th power of 2 M 8192, and the 8th root of 256 M 2.

Roman and Arabic Numerals

I 1	VI 6	XI 11	XVI 16
II 2	VII 7	XII 12	XVII 17
III 3	VIII 8	XIII 13	XVIII 18
IV 4	IX 9	XIV 14	XIX 19
V 5	X 10	XV 15	XX 20

XXX 30	LXXX or XXC ...80	CCC 300	DCCC ...800
XL 40	XC ...90	CCCC ...400	CM 900
L 50	C 100	D 500	M or
LX 60	CC 200	DC 600	CIↃ 1,000
LXX 70		DCC 700	MM 2,000

Note.—A dash over a numeral multiplies the value by 1,000; thus, $\overline{X}$ = 10,000; $\overline{L}$ = 50,000; $\overline{C}$ = 100,000; $\overline{D}$ = 500,000; $\overline{M}$ = 1,000,000; $\overline{\text{CLIX}}$ = 159,000; $\overline{\text{DLIX}}$ = 559,000.

Other rules in using Roman numerals are: (1) repeating a letter repeats its value, as, XX = 20, CCC = 300; (2) a letter placed after one of greater value adds thereto, as, VI = 6, DC = 600; (3) a letter placed before one of greater value subtracts therefrom, as IV = 4

Arabic numerals are those now commonly in use, namely, 0, 1, 2, 3, 4, 5, 6, 7, 8, 9, etc.

Table Showing Number of Days in any One Month to the Same Date in Any Other Month

From—To	Jan.	Feb.	March	April	May	June	July	Aug.	Sept.	Oct.	Nov.	Dec.	To—From
January	365	31	59	90	120	151	181	212	243	273	304	334	..... January
February	334	365	28	59	89	120	150	181	212	242	273	303	..... February
March	306	337	365	31	61	92	122	153	184	214	245	275	.... March
April	275	306	334	365	30	61	91	122	153	183	214	244	.... April
May	245	276	304	335	365	31	61	92	123	153	184	214	.... May
June	214	245	273	304	334	365	30	61	92	122	153	183	.... June
July	184	215	243	274	304	335	365	31	62	92	123	153	.... July
August	153	184	212	243	273	304	334	365	31	61	92	122	...... August
September	122	153	181	212	242	273	303	334	365	30	61	91	..... September
October	92	123	151	182	212	243	273	304	335	365	31	61	..... October
November	61	92	120	151	181	212	242	273	304	334	365	30	..... November
December	31	62	90	121	151	182	212	243	274	304	335	365	..... December

Example: How many days from May 5th to October 5th?   153 days.

Solution: Locate May in the end column and October at the top of the table.

The point of intersection of the two columns shows the number of days.

360

Conversion of Land Prices

PRICE PER SQUARE FOOT EXPRESSED IN VALUE PER ACRE [1]

Cts. per Sq. Ft.	Value per Acre	Cts. per Sq. Ft.	Value per Acre	Cts. per Sq. Ft.	Value per Acre
1 =	$ 435.60	35 =	$15,246.00	69 =	$30,056.40
2 =	871.20	36 =	15,681.60	70 =	30,492.00
3 =	1,306.80	37 =	16,117.20	71 =	30,927.60
4 =	1,742.40	38 =	16,552.80	72 =	31,363.20
5 =	2,178.00	39 =	16,988.40	73 =	31,798.80
6 =	2,613.60	40 =	17,424.00	74 =	32,234.40
7 =	3,049.20	41 =	17,869.60	75 =	32,670.00
8 =	3,484.80	42 =	18,295.20	76 =	33,105.60
9 =	3,920.40	43 =	18,730.80	77 =	33,541.20
10 =	4,356.00	44 =	19,166.40	78 =	33,976.80
11 =	4,791.60	45 =	19,602.00	79 =	34,412.40
12 =	5,227.20	46 =	20,037.60	80 =	34,848.00
13 =	5,662.80	47 =	20,473.20	81 =	35,283.60
14 =	6,098.40	48 =	20,908.80	82 =	35,719.20
15 =	6,534.00	49 =	21,344.40	83 =	36,154.80
16 =	6,969.60	50 =	21,780.00	84 =	36,590.40
17 =	7,405.20	51 =	22,215.60	85 =	37,026.00
18 =	7,840.80	52 =	22,651.20	86 =	37,461.60
19 =	8,276.40	53 =	23,086.80	87 =	37,897.20
20 =	8,712.00	54 =	23,522.40	88 =	38,332.80
21 =	9,147.60	55 =	23,958.00	89 =	38,768.40
22 =	9,583.20	56 =	24,393.60	90 =	39,204.00
23 =	10,018.80	57 =	24,829.20	91 =	39,639.60
24 =	10,454.40	58 =	25,264.80	92 =	40,075.20
25 =	10,890.00	59 =	25,700.40	93 =	40,510.80
26 =	11,325.60	60 =	26,136.00	94 =	40,946.40
27 =	11,761.20	61 =	26,571.60	95 =	41,382.00
28 =	12,196.80	62 =	27,007.20	96 =	41,817.60
29 =	12,632.40	63 =	27,442.80	97 =	42,253.20
30 =	13,068.00	64 =	27,878.40	98 =	42,688.80
31 =	13,503.60	65 =	28,314.00	99 =	43,124.40
32 =	13,939.20	66 =	28,749.60	100 =	43,560.00
33 =	14,374.80	67 =	29,185.20		
34 =	14,810.40	68 =	29,620.80		

PRICE IN DOLLARS PER ACRE EXPRESSED IN CENTS PER SQUARE FOOT

Dollars per Acre	Cts. per Sq. Ft.	Dollars per Acre	Cts. per Sq. Ft.	Dollars per Acre	Cts. per Sq. Ft.
1,000 =	2.296	16,000 =	36.732	31,000 =	71.167
2,000 =	4.592	17,000 =	39.029	32,000 =	73.462
3,000 =	6.888	18,000 =	41.323	33,000 =	75.758
4,000 =	9.183	19,000 =	43.620	34,000 =	78.054
5,000 =	11.480	20,000 =	45.914	35,000 =	80.350
6,000 =	13.775	21,000 =	48.210	36,000 =	82.646
7,000 =	16.070	22,000 =	50.506	37,000 =	84.942
8,000 =	18.367	23,000 =	52.803	38,000 =	87.237
9,000 =	20.663	24,000 =	55.098	39,000 =	89.552
10,000 =	22.960	25,000 =	57.393	40,000 =	91.828
11,000 =	25.254	26,000 =	59.689	41,000 =	94.124
12,000 =	27.550	27,000 =	61.985	42,000 =	96.419
13,000 =	29.846	28,000 =	64.280	43,000 =	98.715
14,000 =	32.141	29,000 =	66.575		
15,000 =	34.437	30,000 =	68.871		

[1] From *McMichael's Appraising Manual.*

Table for Collecting Rents

Rent per Year	Rent per Month	Rent per Day (30 days)	Rent per Day (31 days)	Rent per Year	Rent per Month	Rent per Day (30 days)	Day Rent per (31 days)
$ 1	$ .09	.....	.....	1,025	85.42	2.847	2.756
2	.17	.....	.....	1,050	87.50	2.917	2.823
3	.25	.....	.....	1,075	89.59	2.986	2.890
4	.34	.....	.....	1,100	91.67	3.056	2.958
5	.42	.....	.....	1,125	93.75	3.125	3.025
6	.50	.....	.....	1,150	95.84	3.195	3.092
7	.59	.....	.....	1,175	97.92	3.264	3.159
8	.67	.....	.....	1,200	100	3.334	3.226
9	.75	.....	.....	1,225	102.09	3.403	3.293
10	.84	.028	.027	1,250	104.17	3.472	3.36
20	1.67	.056	.054	1,275	106.25	3.541	3.428
25	2.09	.070	.068	1,300	108.34	3.611	3.495
30	2.50	.084	.081	1,325	110.42	3.681	3.562
40	3.34	.111	.108	1,350	112.50	3.75	3.629
50	4.17	.139	.134	1,375	114.59	3.82	3.697
60	5.00	.166	.161	1,400	116.67	3.889	3.764
70	5.84	.195	.189	1,425	118.75	3.958	3.831
75	6.25	.208	.202	1,450	120.84	4.028	3.898
80	6.67	.222	.215	1,475	122.92	4.098	3.965
90	7.50	.25	.242	1,500	125	4.167	4.033
100	8.34	.278	.269	1,525	127.09	4.236	4.10
125	10.42	.347	.336	1,550	129.17	4.306	4.167
150	12.50	.417	.403	1,575	131.25	4.375	4.234
175	14.59	.486	.470	1,600	133.34	4.445	4.301
200	16.67	.556	.538	1,625	135.42	4.514	4.369
225	18.75	.625	.605	1,650	137.50	4.584	4.436
250	20.84	.695	.672	1,675	139.59	4.653	4.503
275	22.92	.764	.740	1,700	141.67	4.723	4.570
300	25.00	.834	.807	1,725	143.75	4.792	4.638
325	27.09	.903	.874	1,750	145.84	4.861	4.705
350	29.17	.972	.941	1,775	147.92	4.931	4.772
375	31.25	1.042	1.009	1,800	150	5	4.84
400	33.34	1.112	1.076	1,825	152.00	5.07	4.906
425	35.42	1.181	1.143	1,850	154.17	5.139	4.973
450	37.50	1.25	1.21	1,875	156.25	5.209	5.04
475	39.59	1.32	1.277	1,900	158.34	5.278	5.108
500	41.67	1.389	1.344	1,925	160.42	5.347	5.175
525	43.75	1.458	1.412	1,950	162.50	5.417	5.242
550	45.84	1.528	1.479	1,975	164.59	5.487	5.31
575	47.92	1.598	1.546	2,000	166.67	5.56	5.377
600	50	1.667	1.613	3,000	250	8.334	8.065
625	52.09	1.737	1.68	4,000	333.34	11.111	10.753
650	54.17	1.806	1.748	5,000	416.57	13.889	13.441
675	56.25	1.875	1.815	6,000	500	16.667	16.13
700	58.34	1.945	1.882	7,000	583.34	19.445	18.818
725	60.42	2.01	1.950	8,000	666.67	22.223	21.506
750	62.50	2.084	2.017	9,000	750	25	24.194
775	64.59	2.153	2.084	10,000	833.34	27.778	26.882
800	66.67	2.223	2.151	11,000	916.67	30.556	29.57
825	68.75	2.292	2.218	12,000	1,000	33.34	32.259
850	70.84	2.361	2.286	13,000	1,083.34	36.111	34.947
875	72.92	2.431	2.352	14,000	1,166.67	38.889	37.635
900	75	2.50	2.420	15,000	1,250	41.667	40.323
925	77.09	2.57	2.487	16,000	1,333.34	44.445	43.011
950	79.17	2.639	2.554	17,000	1,416.67	47.223	45.699
975	81.25	2.708	2.621	18,000	1,500	50	48.388
1,000	83.34	2.778	2.689	19,000	1,583.34	52.778	51.076

To Value Deep Lots

The table below, known as the Cleveland Standard, in which is adopted a number of existing methods, may be used to determine the percentage of value in lots of varying depth. Assuming the land to be worth $100 per foot front, 100 feet deep, it may be seen that a lot 200 feet in depth is worth $122 per foot front for that depth. Any value and depth may be secured.

PERCENTAGE OF UNIT VALUE FOR LOTS FROM 1 TO 700 FEET DEEP
100 feet depth—100%

Depth									
1 ft.	3.10%	50	72.50	100	100.00	150	115.00	200	122.00
1	3.10%	1	73.25	1	100.41	1	115.19	1	122.10
2	6.10	2	74.00	2	100.85	2	115.38	2	122.20
3	9.00	3	74.75	3	101.27	3	115.57	3	122.30
4	11.75	4	75.50	4	101.70	4	115.76	4	122.40
5	14.35	5	76.20	5	102.08	5	115.95	5	122.50
6	16.75	6	76.90	6	102.48	6	116.12	210	122.95
7	19.05	7	77.55	7	102.88	7	116.29	15	123.38
8	21.20	8	78.20	8	103.25	8	116.46	20	123.80
9	23.20	9	78.85	9	103.62	9	116.62	30	124.60
10	25.00	60	79.50	110	104.00	160	116.80	240	125.35
1	26.70	1	80.11	1	104.36	1	116.96	50	126.05
2	28.36	2	80.77	2	104.72	2	117.13	60	126.75
3	29.99	3	81.38	3	105.08	3	117.30	70	127.40
4	31.61	4	82.00	4	105.43	4	117.47	80	128.05
5	33.22	5	82.61	5	105.78	5	117.64	90	128.65
6	34.92	6	83.21	6	106.13	6	117.79	300	129.25
7	36.41	7	83.82	7	106.47	7	117.94	10	129.80
8	37.97	8	84.42	8	106.81	8	118.09	20	130.35
9	39.50	9	85.01	9	107.15	9	118.24	30	130.90
20	41.00	70	85.60	120	107.50	170	118.40	340	131.40
1	42.50	1	86.15	1	107.80	1	118.54	50	131.90
2	43.96	2	86.70	2	108.11	2	118.70	60	132.40
3	45.30	3	87.24	3	108.41	3	118.85	70	132.85
4	46.61	4	87.78	4	108.75	4	119.00	80	133.30
5	47.90	5	88.30	5	109.05	5	119.14	90	133.75
6	49.17	6	88.82	6	109.35	6	119.28	400	134.20
7	50.40	7	89.35	7	109.65	7	119.41	10	134.60
8	51.61	8	89.87	8	109.93	8	119.54	20	135.00
9	52.81	9	90.39	9	110.21	9	119.67	30	135.40
30	54.00	80	90.90	130	110.50	180	119.80	440	135.80
1	55.05	1	91.39	1	110.76	1	119.92	50	136.15
2	56.10	2	91.89	2	111.02	2	120.05	60	136.50
3	57.15	3	92.38	3	111.28	3	120.18	70	136.85
4	58.20	4	92.86	4	111.55	4	120.31	80	137.20
5	59.20	5	93.33	5	111.80	5	120.43	90	137.55
6	60.30	6	93.80	6	112.05	6	120.55	500	137.85
7	61.25	7	94.27	7	112.28	7	120.66	10	138.15
8	62.20	8	94.73	8	112.52	8	120.77	20	138.45
9	63.10	9	95.17	9	112.76	9	120.88	30	138.75
40	64.00	90	95.60	140	113.00	190	121.00	540	139.05
1	64.95	1	96.04	1	113.20	1	121.10	50	139.30
2	65.90	2	96.50	2	113.43	2	121.21	60	139.55
3	66.75	3	96.95	3	113.64	3	121.32	70	139.80
4	67.60	4	97.40	4	113.85	4	121.43	80	140.05
5	68.45	5	97.85	5	114.05	5	121.53	600	140.55
6	69.30	6	98.30	6	114.25	6	121.62	20	140.95
7	70.10	7	98.74	7	114.45	7	121.71	40	141.35
8	70.90	8	99.17	8	114.64	8	121.80	60	141.75
9	71.70	9	99.58	9	114.82	9	121.90	80	142.05
50	72.50	100	100.00	150	115.00	200	122.00	700	142.35

Method of Reducing Square Feet to Acres

Rule.—Multiply the number of square feet by .000023, or multiply by 23 and point off six places.

Example.—How many acres in 130,680 square feet?

$$130,680$$
$$.000023$$

$$392040$$
$$261360$$

$$3.005640$$

Proof:—43,560) 130,680 (3
        130,680

The reason why dividing by 43,560 is the same as multiplying by .000023 is that dividing by a number is the same as multiplying by its reciprocal:

$$1 \div 43,560 = .000023 \text{ (the reciprocal of 43,560)}.$$

Table for Proration of Taxes

Months				
1	.1666		4	.6666
2	.3333		5	.8333
3	.50		6	1.000

Days				
1	.0055		16	.0888
2	.0111		17	.0944
3	.0166		18	.0999
4	.0222		19	.1055
5	.0277		20	.1111
6	.0333		21	.1166
7	.0388		22	.1221
8	.0444		23	.1277
9	.05		24	.1333
10	.0555		25	.1389
11	.0611		26	.1444
12	.0666		27	.15
13	.0722		28	.1555
14	.0777		29	.1611
15	.0833		30	.1666

The above is for computing the prorata of taxes for six months. For example, you are prorating taxes as of October 22, so there is to be charged against the seller three months and 22 days. Refer to the table, and you find three months .50 and 22 days .1221, making a total of .6221, the amount to be charged against the seller, per $1.00 of taxes.

Computing Square Feet

Sq. Ft.	Acres	Cents per Sq. Ft.	Dollars per Acre
1,742,400	40	1	435.60
1,306,800	30	2	871.20
871,200	20	3	1,306.80
435,600	10	4	1,742.40
392,040	9	5	2,178
348,480	8	6	2,613.60
304,920	7	7	3,049.20
261,360	6	8	3,484.80
217,800	5	9	3,920.40
174,240	4	10	4,356
130,680	3	12	5,227.20
87,120	2	14	6,098.40
43,560	1	16	6,969.60
39,204	0.9	18	7,840.80
34,848	0.8	20	8,712
30,492	0.7	25	10,890
26,136	0.6	30	13,068
21,780	0.5	35	15,246
17,424	0.4	40	17,424
13,068	0.3	45	19,602
8,712	0.2	50	21,780
4,356	0.1	55	23,958
3,920.4	0.09	60	26,136
3,484.8	0.08	65	28,314
3,049.2	0.07	70	30,492
2,613.6	0.06	75	32,670
2,178	0.05	80	34,848
1,742.4	0.04	85	37,026
1,306.8	0.03	90	39,204
871.2	0.02	95	41,382
435.6	0.01	100	43,560

Inches Reduced to Fractions of a Foot

1 inch equals... 0.08⅓ foot
2 inches equal.. 0.16⅔ foot
3 inches equal.. 0.25 foot
4 inches equal................................. .... 0.33⅓ foot
5 inches equal............................. .... 0.41⅔ foot
6 inches equal.. 0.5 foot
7 inches equal.. 0.58⅓ foot
8 inches equal.. 0.66⅔ foot
9 inches equal.. 0.75 foot
10 inches equal... 0.83⅓ foot
11 inches equal...... .... 0.91⅔ foot
12 inches equal... 1.0 foot

Land Measure

The following table will assist in making an accurate estimate of the amount of land in different fields:

10 rods by 16 rods.............1 acre	40 yds. by 121 yds............1 acre
8 rods by 20 rods.............1 acre	220 feet by 198 feet...........1 acre
5 rods by 32 rods.... ....1 acre	110 feet by 396 feet...........1 acre
4 rods by 40 rods.............1 acre	60 feet by 726 feet...........1 acre
5 yds. by 968 yds.............1 acre	120 feet by 363 feet...........1 acre
10 yds. by 484 yds.............1 acre	300 feet by 145.2 feet ....1 acre
20 yds. by 242 yds.............1 acre	400 feet by 108.9 feet ....1 acre

Metric, or French, Square Measure

	Sq. Meters	U. S. Sq. In.	Sq. Feet	Sq. Yards	Acres
Sq. Centim. =	.0001 =	.155			
Sq. Decim. =	.01 =	15.5 =	.10763 =	.01196	
Centare =	1. =	1549.88 =	10.763 =	1.196 =	.00025
Are =	10. =	154988. =	1076.3 =	119.6 =	.0247
Hectare =	100.		107630. =	11959. =	2.47
Sq. Kilometer =	.38607 Sq. Miles.			=	247.
Sq. Myriameter =	38.607 " "			=	24708.

Rental Percentages for Retail Stores[*]
Based on Gross Sales

Type of Business	Per Cent	Type of Business	Per Cent
Appliances	3-4	Furniture	4-6
Auto:		Fur stores	5-6
Accessories	2-4	Hardware	4-5
Agencies, new cars	1½-3	Hosiery	7-10
Bakeries	4-6	Jewelry	8-10
Barbers	7-10	Liquor	4-5
Beauty parlors	7-10	Millinery	7-10
Book stores	5-10	Office supplies	5-6
Candy and confectionery	8-10	Paint and wallpaper	4-6
Cigar stores (tobacco shops)	6-8	Pharmacies	6-10
Clothing stores:		Photographic supplies	8-10
Children's	6-8	Shoe stores	5-7
Family	4-7	Sporting goods	5-7
Men's	5-7	Stationery	5-10
Women's	4-6	Supermarkets	1
Drug stores	4-6	Variety stores	5-6
Florists	8-10		

[*] Check with current rentals charged locally. Any table of this character can be considered approximate only.

Form Approved
Budget Bureau No. 63-R1087

FHA MORTGAGEE NO.	DEPARTMENT OF HOUSING AND URBAN DEVELOPMENT FEDERAL HOUSING ADMINISTRATION	FHA CASE NO.

STATEMENT OF APPRAISED VALUE FOR
A MORTGAGE TO BE INSURED UNDER
THE NATIONAL HOUSING ACT

☐ SEC. 203(b) ☐ SEC.

PROPERTY ADDRESS

MORTGAGEE

ESTIMATED FHA VALUE	MONTHLY ESTIMATES
(☐ Replacement Cost Sec.213 or 220)	Fire Ins. . . . . . $
Value (Excl.Cl.Costs) . . $	Taxes . . . . $
Closing Costs . . . . $	Main. & Repairs $
FHA VALUE. . . . . $	Heat & Utilities $

STATEMENT ISSUED BY (Authorized Agent)   DATE

196

DEFINITION OF APPRAISED VALUE

The Federal Housing Commissioner has valued the above identified property for mortgage insurance purposes in the amount shown.

FHA's estimate of "Value" or "Replacement Cost" (Section 213 or 220) does not fix a sales price; does not indicate FHA approval of a purchaser of the property; nor does it indicate the amount of an insured mortgage that would be approved.

"Value" is an estimated total price of a property, excluding payments for closing costs and prepaid expenses such as taxes and insurance. Value assumes the property is held in fee simple without special assessments.

"Replacement Cost" is an estimate of the current cost to reproduce the property including land, labor, site survey and marketing expense but excluding payments for prepaid expenses such as taxes and insurance and closing costs.

"FHA VALUE" is the sum of the estimate for "value" or "replacement cost" and the FHA estimate of closing costs, such as survey,

title evidence, recording fees, etc. Under those sections of the National Housing Act (such as 213 or 220) where the maximum mortgage amount must be based on estimated replacement cost, the "FHA Value" shall be deemed to mean "replacement cost" for mortgage insurance purposes.

The law requires that FHA mortgagors receive a statement of "appraised value" prior to the sale of the property. If the sales contract has been signed before the mortgagor receives such a statement, the contract must contain, or must be amended to include, the following language:

"It is..agreed that,...the purchaser shall not be obligated to complete the purchase...or to incur any penalty...unless the seller has delivered to the purchaser a written statement... setting forth...the value of the property for mortgage insurance purposes not less than $. The purchaser shall have the privilege...of proceeding with...this contract without regard to the amount of the...valuation."

ADVICE TO HOME BUYERS

ADVANCE PAYMENTS—Make extra payments when able. You pay less interest and have your home paid for sooner. Notify the lender in writing at least 30 days before the regular payment date on which you intend to make an advance payment.

DELINQUENT PAYMENTS—Monthly payments are due the first day of each month and should be made on or before that date. The lender may make a late charge up to 2 cents for each dollar of any payment more than 15 days late. If you fail for 30 days to make a payment, or to perform any other agreement in the mortgage, your lender may fore-

CLOSING COSTS - In the heading is FHA's estimate of anticipated closing costs, such as fees for preparation of mortgage instruments, attorneys' fees, title insurance, origination fees and documentary stamp taxes. The estimate does not include charges for such prepayable items as taxes, fire insurance.

BUILDER'S WARRANTY.—When FHA approves a home before construction, the builder is required to warrant that the house conforms to FHA approved plans. This warranty is for 1 year following the date on which title is conveyed to the original buyer or the date on which the house was first occupied, whichever occurs first.

* Courtesy of the Federal Housing Administration.

FHA Form 2800

close. You could lose your home, damage your credit, and prevent your obtaining further mortgage loans. If extraordinary circumstances prevent your making payments on time, see your lender at once. If you are temporarily unable to make your payments because of illness, loss of job, etc., your lender may be able to help you. Ask your lender to explain FHA's forbearance policy. YOUR CREDIT IS AN IMPORTANT ASSET; DON'T LOSE IT THROUGH NEGLECT.

ADJUSTED PREMIUM CHARGE---If you make extra payments in any year of more than 15% of the original mortgage amount, you may have to pay an adjusted premium charge. This charge is 1% of the original mortgage. FHA is authorized to charge a premium of not less than ¼ of 1% nor more than 1% per year, but has set the premium at ½ of 1% assuming it will be paid over the whole mortgage term. When a mortgage is paid off in advance, the premiums collected do not cover FHA cost and an adjusted premium is charged to offset the loss. If this charge were not made, the premium would have to be higher. An adjusted premium is not made if a new FHA mortgage is placed on the property, or if the FHA insurance is in force for 10 years or longer.

TAXES, ASSESSMENTS, AND INSURANCE---Send your lender bills for taxes, special assessments, or fire insurance that come to you. The fire insurance the lender requires you to carry usually covers only the balance of the loan. Check this with your lender. You may wish to take out additional insurance so that if the house is damaged your loss will be covered as well as the lender's. If your home is damaged by fire, windstorm, or other cause, write your lender at once. Taxes for the coming year can't be known until the bills are received. If they exceed the amount accumulated from your payments, you will be asked to pay the difference. If they are less, the difference will be credited to your account. The same is true of fire insurance. Some States allow homestead or veteran's tax exemptions. Apply for any exemption to which you may be entitled. When it is approved, notify your lender.

If during the warranty period you notice defects for which you believe the builder is responsible, ask him in writing to correct them. If he fails to do so, notify the FHA insuring office in writing. Mention the FHA case number shown in the heading. If inspection shows the builder to be at fault, the FHA will try to persuade him to make correction. If he does not, you may seek legal relief under the builder's warranty. Most builders take pride in their work and will make justifiable corrections. They cannot be expected to correct damage caused by ordinary wear and tear or by poor maintenance. Keeping the house in good condition is the owner's responsibility.

OPERATING EXPENSES---In the heading are FHA estimates of monthly costs of taxes, heat and utilities, fire insurance, maintenance and repairs. The estimated figures will probably have to be adjusted when you receive the actual bills. BEAR IN MIND THAT IN MOST COMMUNITIES TAXES AND OTHER OPERATING COSTS ARE INCREASING. The estimates should give some idea of what you can expect the costs to be at the beginning. In some areas FHA's estimate of taxes may also include local charges such as sewer charges, garbage collection fees, water rates, etc.

IF YOU SELL---If you sell while the mortgage exists, the buyer may finance several ways. Understand how these arrangements may affect you. Consult your lender.

1. You may sell for all cash and pay off your mortgage. This ends your liability.
2. The buyer can assume the mortgage and pay the difference between the unpaid balance and the selling price in cash. If the FHA and the lender are willing to accept the buyer as a mortgagor, you can be released from further liability. This requires the specific approval of the lender and the FHA. (EITHER OF THE ABOVE TWO METHODS IS PREFERABLE TO METHOD NUMBER 3.)
3. The buyer can pay the difference in cash and purchase subject to the unpaid mortgage balance. FHA or lender approval is not necessary BUT YOU REMAIN LIABLE FOR THE DEBT. IF THE BUYER DEFAULTS, IT COULD RESULT IN A DEFICIENCY JUDGMENT AND IMPAIR YOUR CREDIT STANDING.

THE COST OF BORROWING

When you borrow to buy a home, you pay interest and other charges which add to your cost. A larger downpayment will result in a smaller loan. Borrow as little as you need and repay in the shortest time. If you borrow $10,000 at 5-3/4%, the monthly payment to principal and interest is $11.90 less for a 30-year loan than it would be for a 20-year loan; but in 30 years you pay $4,152.28, or 62% more interest than in 20 years.

The tables show the monthly payments, interest and mortgage insurance for some typical loans at 5-3/4%. Taxes and fire insurance are not shown in the tables, although they are included in your monthly payments.

MONTHLY PAYMENTS, PRINCIPAL & INTEREST, MORT. INS. PREMIUM, TOTAL INTEREST & MORT. INS. PREMIUMS PAID @ 5¾%

Term	$10,000-LOAN				$15,000-LOAN				$20,000-LOAN			
	Prin. & Int. Mo. Poyt.	Total Int.	Mtg. Ins. Premium Mo. Poyt.	Total	Prin. & Int. Mo. Poyt.	Total Int.	Mtg. Ins. Premium Mo. Poyt.	Total	Prin. & Int. Mo. Poyt.	Total Int.	Mtg. Ins. Premium Mo. Poyt.	Total
20 Yrs.	$70.30	$ 6,830.93	$4.12	$594.12	$105.45	$10,246.49	$6.17	$ 891.24	$140.60	$13,661.71	$8.23	$1,187.88
25 "	63.00	8,840.37	4.13	768.84	94.50	13,260.76	6.20	1,153.20	126.00	17,681.02	8.26	1,537.32
30 "	58.40	10,983.21	4.14	955.56	87.60	16,474.63	6.21	1,432.92	116.80	21,966.11	8.28	1,909.92

SEND TO MORTGAGEE FOR DELIVERY TO HOME BUYER

FHA FORM NO. 2800 - 6 Rev. 8/66

DEPARTMENT OF HOUSING AND URBAN DEVELOPMENT
FEDERAL HOUSING ADMINISTRATION

Form Approved
Budget Bureau No. 63-R1087

FHA UNDERWRITING REPORT

1. FHA MORTGAGEE NO.

CASE NO.

WARNING: All persons by signing this report certify that they have no interest present or future, in the property, application or mortgage.

4. PROPERTY ADDRESS

3.

MORTGAGE TO BE INSURED UNDER

☐ SEC.203(b) ☐ SEC.

5. MORTGAGEE

6. ESTIMATED FHA VALUE

(☐ Replacement Cost Sec.213 or 220)

Value (Excl. Cl. Costs) .. $

Closing Costs .... $

FHA VALUE .... $

7. MONTHLY ESTIMATES

Fire Ins. ..... $
Taxes .... $
Main. & Repairs $
Heat & Utilities $

8. APPROVED FOR COMMITMENT

9. COMMITMENT DATE

196

10. COMMITMENT TERMS MAX.MORT.AMT. $ _____ NO.MOS. _____ MAX.INTEREST 5¾%

11. ☐ EXISTING ☐ PROPOSED

12. EXISTING HOUSE   Name of Occupant (Owner if unoccupied)

Phone   Key Encl. ☐ or at (Address)

Mon. & Yr. Completed   ☐ Never Occup. ☐ Vacant Occupied By ☐ Owner ☐ Tenant At $ Per Mon. ☐ Furn. ☐ Unfurn.

13. PROPOSED UNDER CONST.   Builder's Name & Address

Model Ident.

Plans: ☐ First Subm. ☐ Prob. Repeat Cases ☐ Yes ☐ No   ☐ Prev. Proc. as FHA Case No.

14. DESCRIPTION

		Stories	Bedrooms	☐ Store Rm.	Mineral Rights Reserved	Type of Heating
☐ Detached	☐ Wood siding	☐ Split level	Liv. room	☐ Util. Rm.	☐ No ☐ Yes (Explain)	
☐ Semi-det.	☐ Wood shingle		Din. room			☐ Cent.Air Cond.
☐ Row	☐ Asb. shingle	___ % Basement	Kitchen	☐ Garage	Utilities Public Comm.Individual	Type of Paving
	☐ Fiber board	☐ Slab on ground	No. Rms.	☐ Carport	Water ☐ ☐ ☐	
☐ Frame	☐ Brick or stone	☐ Crawl space	Baths	☐ No. care	Gas ☐ ☐ ☐	☐ Curb & Gutter
☐ Masonry	☐ Succo or c.blk	___ % Non-resid.	½ Baths	☐ Built-in	Elect. ☐ ☐ ☐	☐ Sidewalk
Factory Fabricated	☐ Comb. types	___ Living Units		☐ Attached Sanit.	Sept. Cess. tank pool ☐ ☐	☐ Storm Sewer
☐ Yes ☐ No				☐ Detached Sewer		

15. SPEC.ASSESS. Prepayable $ _____ Non-Prepay. $ _____ Int. ___ %

Ann.Pay. $ _____ Unpd.Bal. $ _____ Rem. Term ___ Yrs.

16. LOT DIMENSIONS   Ft. ×   Ft. =   Sq. Ft.

17. GENERAL LOCATION:

18. ANN.R.EST.TAXES $ 19. ANN.FIRE INS. $

20. SALE PRICE $

21. REMOVABLE EQUIP.IN VALUE: ☐ Range or counter cook unit & oven   ☐ Refrig. ☐ Dishw.

☐ Auto.washer ☐ Dryer ☐ Window/wall oir cond. ☐ Garb.disp. ☐ Vent fan ☐ Other

24. CAPIT. INCOME
Mon. Rent $ _____ – Excess Exp. $ _____ =
$ _____ × Rent Multiplier of _____
= CAPIT INCOME .... $

22. COST DATA   23. REPL. COST   Review

2800-3 for ☐ Integ.
☐ 2014-d
Calcu. Area Bldg. Sq. Ft. _____
Cost @ $ _____ Per Sq. Ft. = $ _____

27. BLDG. DESC./VARS.   –   +

Fdns. .... $
Frpl. .... $
Ext. Wall .... $
Shtg. .... $
Sub. Fl. .... $
Fin. Fl. .... $
Rfg. .... $
Int. Wall .... $
Plg. .... $
Htg. .... $
Insul. .... $

Equip. .... $
Tot. variations .... $
Net variations .... $
Basic cost. .... $
Main Bldg. .... $
Gar./Car Port .... $
Porches/Terr. .... $
Walks/Drives. .... $
Ldsp./Pltg./Fin.Gr. .... $
Other on-site imp. .... $
On-site Imp.unadj. .... $
Gen.overh'd.& profit _____ % + 100% ×
Loc. _____ % + Wkmp. _____ % = Comb. ____ %
On-site imp.adj. .... $
Arch.services .... $
EST.REPL. COST IMP. .... $

Repl. Cost Impr. .... $
Mkt.Price Eq. Site. ...... $
Miscl.Allow.Costs .... $
Mktg.Exp. .... $
REPL.COST. .... $

28. NEIGHBORHOOD DATA
Fut.Dev.Under ☐ Present ☐ Antic.use is _____
Land Uses
_____ % Blt-up _____ % Own. _____ % Ten. _____ % Vac.
Change in: ☐ Use ☐ Occupancy is
☐ Taking Place ☐ Antic.
Age Typ. Bldg. _____ To _____
Owner Occ.Appeal
Mo.Rent Typ.Prop. $ _____ To _____
Price Typ.Prop. ... $ _____ To _____
Inc.Range .... $ _____ + _____ To _____
Typ.Occup. ....
Dem.Comp.Prop. ....
Dem.Amm.Prop. .....
Dem.Rent.Prop....

29. BASIC CASE

38.

COMPARABLE HOUSES	(A)									
	(B)									
	(C)									
	Sq. Ft. Area	Sto-ries	Rms.	Bd Rms	Bath	Const.	Gar.	Age/cond.	Price	Date
(A)										
(B)										
(C)										

39. (A) Remarks   (C) Reject Reasons
(B) Specific Conditions   (D) Neigh. Charac.

25. MARKET PRICE .... $
26. VALUE
Value (Excl.Cl.Costs) $
+ Closing Costs ...... $
= FHA VALUE .... $

30. SITE	**31. PHY.SEC.**
Land uses...	Visual Appeal
Phy./Soc.Att.	Livability...
Com.Centers	Nat.Light/Ven.
Transport...	Struc.Qual. ..
Util.& Serv...	Resist.to Elem.
Taxes/Assess	Mech.Equip.
Marketability	Conformity
Location	Property

32. BUILDING CONDITION

33. REM.ECON.LIFE... _____ Yrs.

34. COST REPAIRS/IMPROVEMENTS
Prop. $ _____ Req. $

35. COOLING/HEATING COST
Mon. Cost Heat .... $
Mon. Cost Cool .... $

36. FI/DT NO.

37. SUB FILE NO.

(E) Land Excl. From Val.
(F) Items Excl. From Repl. Cost

41. INSPECTIONs ☐ Proposed Construction
☐ Approve Arch. Exam. Date ☐ Repair Date ☐ Review
☐ Reject
☐ Commit.Staff Val. ☐ Other ☐ Mortgagee's Certificate
☐ Reject Review Date

40. LOW COST
☐ MPS

Review
$ _____
$ _____

☐ S – + =
Date Insp.

CONDOMINIUM DEED *

THE STATE OF TEXAS |

COUNTY OF McLENNAN | KNOW ALL MEN BY THESE PRESENTS:

     THAT LAKE AIR LINES, INC., a Texas corporation, with its principal office and

place of business in the City of Waco, McLennan County, Texas, acting herein by and through

its duly authorized officers, hereinafter called "Grantor," for and in consideration of the sum

of TEN and No/100 ($10.00) DOLLARS, and other good and valuable consideration, paid

and the receipt and sufficiency of which consideration is hereby confessed and acknowledged,

has GRANTED, BARGAINED, SOLD, and CONVEYED and by these presents does GRANT,

BARGAIN, SELL and CONVEY unto

of McLennan County, Texas, hereinafter called "Grantee," all of the following described

real property situated in the County of McLennan, Texas, to wit:

     (a)   APARTMENT No.   , and the space encompassed by the boundaries
          thereof, located at the   Floor of Building "A",

     (b)   AN UNDIVIDED   % ownership interest in and to the Common Areas
          and Facilities of the Condominium Project known as Lake Air Tower,

     as more fully described in the Declaration of Condominium Regime, dated
the 26th day of January, 1967, executed by LAKE AIR LINES, INC., as
Developer, and recorded in Vol. 1, page 1, Condominium Records of Mc-
Lennan County, Texas, hereinafter called the "Declaration," to which
Declaration and all of its terms and provisions reference is here made for
all purposes and which is incorporated herein as though it were set forth
in full, subject, however, to the following: (a) the provisions of the Condominium Act of the State of Texas, as now existing or hereafter amended,
hereby incorporated herein and made a part hereof; (b) the easements,
restrictions, covenants and conditions otherwise appearing of record and
affecting the project land or this Family Unit or any part hereof.

     This deed is executed by Grantor and accepted by Grantee subject to and burdened

with all of the terms and provisions, easements, rights, divisions, covenants, restrictions,

conditions and limitations, of every kind or character, set forth and imposed in the said

Declaration and Bylaws of the Condominium Project, and all amendments thereto hereafter

lawfully made (which said Declaration and Bylaws are hereby incorporated herein as though

set forth in full), all of which shall be binding upon Grantee, his heirs, executors,

* Courtesy Lake Air Lines, Inc., Waco, Tex.

administrators, devisees, successors and assigns, and which shall be deemed to be covenants running with the land.

In addition, by acceptance of this conveyance and as part of the consideration therefor, Grantee, his heirs, executors, administrators, devisees, successors and assigns, does covenant and agree, and shall be obligated and bound:

(a) To abide by and comply with each and all of the provisions of said Declaration and By-Laws, and the government and administration of said Condominium Project in accordance with the provisions thereof;

(b) To observe and comply with all lawful decisions and resolutions at any time made by the Council of Owners of said Condominium Project;

(c) To promptly pay, as the same shall become due and payable, the pro-rata share and part, assessable against the above described family unit, of all costs, charges and expenses, for the administration, upkeep, maintenance, and repair of the Common Areas and Facilities of said Condominium Project, as well as the pro-rata share and part, assessable against the above described family unit, of all other valid charges and assessments at any time made or levied by the said Council of Owners in accordance with the provisions of said Declaration and By-Laws, and to secure the payment of all of which pro-rata part and share of costs, expenses, charges and assessments, Grantor does hereby expressly except and reserve unto Grantor, its successors and assigns, a prior and continuing vendor's lien, additionally secured by the power of sale provided in said Declaration, against the hereinabove described and herein conveyed property and premises, which lien, however, shall be secondary and inferior to (a) all taxes and special assessments levied by the government and taxing authorities and to (b) the vendor's lien and deed of trust hereinafter reserved to secure _____ in the payment of the first lien indebtedness described below;

(d) To generally fulfill and discharge all the obligations, duties and responsibilities as Owner of a family unit in the above named Condominium Project.

That as part of the consideration for this conveyance, the amount of $_____ is evidenced by Grantee's promissory note of even date herewith, payable to the order of _____ in such amount, and bearing interest at the rate set out in said note, with interest upon all unpaid principal and interest after maturity at the rate of ten per cent (10%) per annum. Said note is payable in monthly installments of $_____ with the first such monthly installment being due and payable on or before the 1st day of _____, 19___, and with a like monthly installment due and payable on the 1st day of each successive month thereafter until paid. Said note contains provisions for attorney's fees and acceleration of maturity in the event of contingencies therein stated. In addition to the vendor's lien and superior title hereinafter retained as security for the payment of said note, the payment of said note is additionally and further

secured by that certain Deed of Trust of even date herewith made by Grantee herein to

_____, Trustee, covering the hereinabove described

premises.

A vendor's lien and superior title are hereby expressly retained in favor of Grantor,

and transferred to _____, upon and in and to

the property herein described, until the promissory note hereinabove described is paid in full

according to its face and tenor, effect and reading, whereupon this Deed shall become absolute.

If "Grantee" is more than one person, it shall be construed as "Grantees" and all

singular pronouns shall include the plural and the masculine gender shall include the feminine

and neuter.

TO HAVE AND TO HOLD the above described premises together with all and singular

the rights and appurtenances thereunto in any wise belonging unto the said Grantee, his heirs,

administrators, executors, and assigns forever, and Grantor does hereby bind itself, its

successors and assigns, to warrant and forever defend, all and singular, the said premises

unto the said Grantee, his heirs and assigns, against every person whomsoever lawfully

claiming or to claim the same or any part thereof, except as to the said Declaration, vendor's

lien and superior title, Deed of Trust, and other matters to which this Deed is expressly

made subject.

EXECUTED this _____ day of _____, 19____.

LAKE AIR LINES, INC., Grantor

ATTEST: By_____
                                                                            President

_____
                              Secretary

THE STATE OF TEXAS   I
COUNTY OF McLENNAN   I

BEFORE ME, the undersigned, a Notary Public in and for the State and County aforesaid, on this day personally appeared _____, President of LAKE AIR LINES, INC., a corporation, known to me to be the person and officer whose name is subscribed to the foregoing instrument, and acknowledged to me that he executed the same as the act and deed of said corporation for the purposes and consideration therein expressed and in the capacity therein stated.

GIVEN UNDER MY HAND AND SEAL OF OFFICE this _____ day of _____, 19____.

_____
Notary Public in and for McLennan County, Texas

DECLARATION OF CONDOMINIUM REGIME

LAKE AIR TOWER APARTMENTS *

THE STATE OF TEXAS |

                                   KNOW ALL MEN BY THESE PRESENTS:

THE COUNTY OF McLENNAN |

ARTICLE ONE. - RECITALS

A. LAKE AIR LINES, INC., a corporation, organized under the laws of the State of Texas, and which principal office and place of business is in the City of Waco, McLennan County, Texas, herein called "Developer," owns all of the following described land located in McLennan County, Texas, being Lot 1, Block A, of the North Tower Addition, City of Waco, more particularly described on Plat attached hereto as Exhibit "A," to which reference is made for all purposes, hereinafter called the "land."

B. Developer has constructed upon said land a condominium project consisting of a ten-story building which contains sixty-five (65) individual apartment-type family units, a basement, lobby, elevators, corridors, and other common areas, together with parking spaces, paving, walks, fences, walls, and other improvements, structures, facilities, and appurtenances. This condominium project is designated and shall be known as "LAKE AIR TOWER."

By this Declaration the Developer intends to establish a plan under the Provisions of the Condominium Act of The State of Texas for the individual ownership of the area of space contained in each of the "family units" in said project, and the co-ownership by individuals and separate owners thereof, as tenants in common, of all of the remaining land and improvements, all as more fully hereinafter set forth and described:

NOW THEREFORE, said Developer hereby declares that all of the said land and improvements constructed thereon, or to be constructed thereon, are held and shall be held, conveyed, hypothecated, encumbered, leased, rented, used, occupied and improved subject to the following divisions, covenants, restrictions, limitations, conditions, rights, privileges, obligations, liabilities, and uses, all of which said divisions, covenants, restrictions, limitations, conditions, rights, privileges, obligations, liabilities and uses shall run with the land and shall be binding on said Developer, its successors and assigns, and all subsequent owners, possessors or users of all or any part of said land and project, property and improvements, together with their respective grantees, successors, heirs, executors, administrators, devisees or assigns.

* Courtesy Lake Airlines, Inc., Waco, Texas.

Index

375